Jews in Old China
Expanded Edition

Jews in Old China
Expanded Edition
STUDIES BY CHINESE SCHOLARS

Translated, compiled and edited by

SIDNEY SHAPIRO

HIPPOCRENE BOOKS
NEW YORK

Expanded Edition, 2001
Copyright © 1984 by Sidney Shapiro.
Paperback edition, 1988.

For information, address: Hippocrene Books, Inc.,
171 Madison Avenue, New York, NY 10016.

Printed in the United States of America.

ISBN 0-7818-0833-2

Cataloging-in-Publication Data available from the Library of Congress

Printed in the United States of America.

Contents

(Illustrations follow page 106.)

Acknowledgments

Much of the Chinese material referred to in this volume is either out of print or, though new, published in such limited editions as to be virtually unavailable. I am therefore indebted to several Chinese scholars:

Zhang Zhishan helped me obtain a copy of *A Survey of Historical Material Regarding Contacts Between China and the West* by his father Zhang Xinglang, and provided me with biographical data.

Weng Tu-chien presented me with his monograph "A Study of *Wotuo*," and commented further on this contentious issue.

Chen Zhichao inscribed a copy to me of his father's *The Academic Theses of Chen Yuan*, which he edited and which contains the famous "A Study of the Israelite Religion in Kaifeng."

Pan Naimu, editor of *Jews in Ancient China—A Historical Survey*, written by her father Pan Guangdan, supplied me with a copy of the page proofs even before the book came off the press, and gave me the exclusive right to translate it into English for inclusion in this volume.

Gao Wangzhi, Li Jixian and Zhu Jiang, at my request, wrote their articles specifically for this volume. Chen Changqi gave me his unpublished article "Some Questions Regarding the History of the Kaifeng Jews" to facilitate my use of pertinent sections. Wu Zelin permitted me to adapt his preface to Pan Guangdan's book as a seperate item.

I also was not only able to obtain Wang Yisha's unpublished treatise, but had the opportunity to discuss the Kaifeng Jews with him for several hours.

In addition, Xia Nai, Director of the Institute of Archaeology, Academia Sinica, in response to my queries devoted considerable time to dispelling the Prevost theory of the "Han dynasty inscriptions." Zhuang Weiji, specialist in the history of Fujian, has been keeping me informed of his efforts to find early Jewish tombstones in the vicinity of the ancient seaport of Quanzhou. Gao Wangzhi, of the Academic Council of World Religions, has provided unstinting guidance and assistance . . .

Preface to Expanded Edition

The publication of *Jews in Old China: Studies by Chinese Scholars* in 1984 aroused considerable interest among general readers in the West, in addition to attracting specialists in the fields of religion, archaeology, and history. This was due perhaps not only to the quality of the material, but to the fact that for the first time, it became possible to hear what the Chinese scholars themselves had to say about the history of the Jews in China prior to the 20th century. The book attained a respectable hardcover circulation in America, supplemented by a paper edition in 1988. It was translated into Hebrew and published in Tel Aviv in 1987.

Within China the number of scholars researching the Jews in Chinese history grew rapidly. Dozens of articles have appeared in print in the last decade and a half. From these, exercising the prerogative of translator and editor, I have selected three which I find particularly intriguing, and present them in Part Two of this edition. Each introduces much new evidence and a few new concepts.

In "Jews in Yuan Dynasty China," Liu Yingsheng describes the life of the Jews as a rather privileged ethnic minority under the rule of the Mongols, themselves an alien non-Han nationality. He tells, too, of their relations with other ethnic minorities, and of the development of the synagogues.

Gong Fangzhen's treatise is entitled "Jewish Merchants on the Silk Road." He tells of Jewish traders, known as Radanites, who traveled by land and by sea from Europe, the Middle East and North Africa with merchandise destined for China during the Tang and Song dynasties. Gong claims those coming overland delivered most of their goods to other merchants in what was then the Jewish kingdom of Khazaria (along the lower reaches of the Volga River), who then relayed the shipments to the Chinese capital.

Yin Gang paints a broad canvas in his treatise "The Jews of Kaifeng: Their Origins, Routes, and Assimilation." He relates the history of the Jews in what became their largest and longest-lasting community in China, covering a period of four dynasties—Jin, Yuan, Ming and Qing. A few of his conclusions may stir up controversy, but the quality of his research is beyond reproach.

We have corrected errors discovered in the first edition, and have revised the Index to include entries from the three new articles presented here. I thank friends and scholars on several continents for their criticisms and support, and hope they will continue to give us the benefit of their comments.

Sidney Shapiro

The Year 2000
Beijing, China

Prologue

In recent years visitors from the West have dropped in on me and said: "You've been living in China for over thirty years and your name is Shapiro, so of course you know all about the Chinese Jews. What is the story?"

The fact was I knew very little. As much out of embarrassment as curiosity, I began looking into the matter, starting with the origins of the Jewish migrants. I found a time-frame which ran as follows:

HISTORICAL BACKGROUND

930 B.C.   Kingdom of Israel split into Israel, in the north, and Judah, in the south. Ten of the 12 tribes in Israel, 2 in Judah.

722 B.C.   Assyria destroys Israel and takes the ten tribes into captivity. These are scattered and gradually vanish.

586 B.C.   Babylon crushes Judah, destroys the Temple and takes nearly the entire population of the two tribes into captivity. Known as the Babylonian Exile.

About 50 years later.   Persia, having defeated Babylonia, permits the Jews to return to Palestine.

By the middle of the 5th century B.C.   Jerusalem restored and the Temple rebuilt.

5th to 4th centuries B.C.   Persians shift some Jews into Persia and the Media on the southern shore of the Caspian Sea.

Mid-4th century BC.   Greeks, under Alexander of Macedon, conquer Palestine.

164 B.C.   Maccabees recapture Jerusalem and the Temple.

143 B.C.   Judah re-established under the Hasmonean dynasty.

63 B.C.   Conquered by the Romans and named Judea.

70 A.D.   After a series of national revolts, again conquered by the Romans. The Second Temple destroyed.

135 A.D. Defeat by the Romans of the Bar Cochba revolt. Jews expelled from Jerusalem.

It was at this point that the large-scale Diaspora, or dispersal, began. Over the next five hundred years, thousands of Jews migrated into Persia and Arabia. Part of these continued north into Afghanistan, Balkh, Samarkand and Bokhara, in Central Asia, all on the old Silk Road. Some, probably around the 7th century, moved overland from there into northwest China, also known as Chinese Turkestan, where they settled, though not in large number. A few advanced further into north China.

Another part of the Jews in Persia and Arabia migrated south into India, settling mainly in southwest ports along the Arabian Sea. Some of these became merchants and travelled to China on Arab, Persian or Chinese vessels during Tang and Song (7th to 13th centuries), and settled in seaports on China's southeast coast.

Jews then still living in Persia may have sailed directly on ships via the Red Sea and the Persian Gulf.

More Jews arrived in China during the Yuan dynasty (13th and 14th centuries) when numbers of Middle Easterners and Southern Europeans returned with the conquering Mongol armies.

By then, cities known or believed to have hosted Jewish communities included Luoyang, Sian, Kaifeng, Dunhuang, Hangzhou, Ningbo, Yangzhou, Canton, Quanzhou, Beijing, Nanjing and Ningxia.

In the 19th century, Iraqi Jews, mostly from Baghdad, flocked to the booming port of Shanghai.

The 1905 and 1917 revolutions in Russia brought an influx of Jewish refugees, who settled mainly in the northeast (then called Manchuria) and in the seaport of Tientsin (Tianjin). Many dealt in furs.

Finally, several thousand German and Austrian Jews, fleeing Nazi persecution during the late 1930's, settled temporarily in Shanghai, while awaiting visas to other countries.

Today, almost all are gone—the early settlers have gradually been absorbed into the vast one billion Chinese population, the others returning to their native lands or moving on to countries in other parts of the world. Some historical relics remain, and a few people who know they are of Jewish descent.

This, then, is a rough outline of the history of the Chinese Jews.

But although they have vanished as a race and religion in China, interest in them has continued to grow. Since the 17th century "discovery" of them by the West, we have had hundreds of studies, books and articles by Christian missionaries, Jewish scholars, and Western Sinologists.

Virtually nothing, however, has been seen abroad of the views of the Chinese themselves. This is because, for one thing, Chinese research on the Jews did not begin until the eve of the 20th century. For another, treatises by Chinese historians were not published widely in China until very recently. They are little known in the West and have not so far, to the best of my knowledge, been published in translation.

These works are fascinating and of major importance. For they not only comment on existing theories by Western Sinologists, but offer the findings and views of Chinese historians from the vantage point of a thorough understanding of China's language, history and culture, so often limited in some Western scholars.

Rushing in "where angels fear to tread," I have translated into English the treatises of China's leading experts on the Chinese Jews, and edited and compiled them, with my own observations and cross references, into a single volume. Our main emphasis is on those Jews who arrived in China prior to the 17th century and their descendants. Although I have had some aid from Chinese colleagues, it is entirely possible that, because of my limited abilities, error has crept in. I beg the reader's indulgence and request his, or her, criticism.

A few of the articles append bibliographies, and I have added my own, plus a general Index. Direct quotations are indented. The remaining text consists of condensations of passages from the authors, and my own comment. The only exception is the article on the Bianjing (Kaifeng) economy during Song, which is almost entirely a condensed translation. My few remarks on this piece are in parentheses.

Before going into the contents of our book, a brief introduction to the Sinologue writings our authors discuss may be helpful.

WESTERN AWARENESS OF THE CHINESE JEWS

The earliest report noted in the Western world of the presence of Jews in China came via Arab traveller Aboul Zeyd al Hassan, also known as Abu Zaid, who wrote in the 9th century of an alleged massacre in a south China seaport, possibly Canton, of "120,000 Muslims, Jews, Christians and Parsees" by the rebel Huang Chao.

Venetian Marco Polo in the 13th century told of his meetings with Jews in Khanbalik (Beijing) in the court of Kublai Khan. Andrew of Perugia, Catholic "Bishop" of Quanzhou in Fujian, complained in a letter dated 1300 to his superior in Rome that he was unable to convert any Jews. Jean di Marignolli, Roman Catholic, claims he debated with them in Khanbalik on religious matters in 1342. Arab Ibn Batuta wrote in 1346 of a Jewish community in Hangzhou.

These attracted only desultory attention. But the news in Europe in the 17th century of the discovery of an existing Jewish community in the city of Kaifeng, and the findings there of Jesuit missionaries, created a sensation. Not only were there living Jews in Kaifeng, but they had records carved in stone containing detailed accounts of their origins, their history and their beliefs. Since European Catholics were contending that the Talmudists had deliberately tampered with sections of the Old Testament, the Jesuits hoped to find "original materials" in the Kaifeng Scriptures, believed to have been produced before the compilation of the Talmud.

In the centuries which followed, this inspired a surprising amount of research and speculation by Western Sinologists, ranging from the excellent to the absurd, and creating a host of theories as to when the Jews reached China, where they came from, the routes they travelled, where they settled, how they lived.

Complicating matters was the fact that the stone records—three inscriptions in Chinese commemorating rebuildings of the Kaifeng synagogue, and dated 1489, 1512 and 1663, respectively—offered three different dates for the time of the arrival of the Jews in China. Namely, again respectively, the Song dynasty (960–1279), the Han dynasty (206 B.C. to 220 A.D.), and the Zhou dynasty (1056 B.C. to 256 B.C.)

WESTERN DATING OF THE JEWISH ARRIVAL IN CHINA

Manasseh ben Israel, Chief Rabbi of Amsterdam in the 17th century, thought the Chinese Jews were part of the Ten Lost Tribes of Israel, which would place their coming in Zhou times.

Vinogradov, a 19th-century prelate of the Greek Orthodox Church in Russia, at first alleged the Jews reached China before the time of Moses, then also opted for the Zhou dynasty. He was supported by French Jesuit Gaubil, French Roman Catholic Sionnet, plus Sinologists Finn, Bainbridge and Perlmann.

Perlmann and several others based their contention on the prophesy in *Isaiah* 49:12 that the Jews would be returning from "Sinim." Since "Sinim" meant China, they said, and since Isaiah lived in the 8th, or possibly in the 6th, century B.C., both within the period of Zhou (11th to 3rd centuries B.C.), it proved that the Jews were already there.

Sionnet alleged he found references in Zhou dynasty folklore to the Tree of Knowledge, the Rainbow After the Deluge, Seven Years of Famine . . . clear evidence of Jewish influences. He claimed also a mention of Jehovah in the writings of Lao Zi (Laotze), the 6th century B.C. philosopher, and said this could only have been learned from Israelites in China.

Many more foreign historians maintained the Jews fled to China during Han (3rd century B.C. to 3rd century A.D.). These include Brotier, Murr, Mishovsky, Noyé, Ausubel, Ezra, Lacouperie, Tobar,

Cordier, Prévost, Wilhelm and MacGillivray. Most considered the destruction of Jerusalem by the Romans the pivotal cause.

Prévost offered the only tangible evidence—three fragments of a stone inscription discovered in Luoyang, the capital of China in Han. He claimed they were written in Palmyrian Hebrew, and dated them around the 2nd century A.D.

Tang (618 to 907) as an arrival time has many protagonists among Western historians. They point to the account of Abu Zaid of the slaughter of foreigners, including Jews, in Canton, reports of 9th and 10th century Jewish travellers, the Semitic features of tomb figures unearthed in Tang dynasty graves, Hebrew writings of Tang date found in Xinjiang, formerly Chinese Turkestan . . .

As to when precisely within Tang, opinions vary. Hall says 7th century, Shyrock favors the 9th, White and Williams say the method of calendar calculation used by the Kaifeng Jews shows it had to be the 10th. Goodrich believes they may have left Persia at that time, but did not enter China until later.

Chavannes asserts we have no reliable material for any entry period other than Northern Song. Lowenthal insists it was not until the 12th century that large numbers of Jews took up permanent residence in China. He points to Yuan dynasty (13th and 14th century) laws and regulations which refer to Jews, in various transliterations of the word, but agrees with Pelliot that *Wotuo* is not one of them.

WESTERN ESTIMATES OF WHEN THE JEWS LEFT THEIR HOMELAND

There are broad areas of disagreement among foreign scholars on this, as well. Estimated departure dates range from before Moses (prior to 1300 B.C.), to between the exodus from Egypt and the Assyrian conquest (1300 to 700 B.C.), to between the Babylonian exile and the Roman conquest (586 B.C. to 70 A.D.), to between the start of the Diaspora and the completion of the Talmud (70 to 600 A.D.).

Supporters of the second time-frame include adherents of the theory that the Chinese Jews are descendants of the Lost Tribes. Earliest to express this view was Manasseh ben Israel who wrote that the Ten Tribes migrated to Central Asia, but were driven out by the Tartars. Some drifted to the Americas, he said, where they became the American Indians, others ended up in China.

Sionnet, Forster, Bainbridge and Perlmann agree that the Ten Lost Tribes were the first Jews to enter China, and add that this happened during the Zhou dynasty. Their argument runs thus: Ten of the twelve tribes lived in Israel, two in Judah. When Israel was defeated by Assyria in 722 B.C., its people were led into captivity and gradually scattered. The Chinese Jews knew themselves only as "Israelites," and were unfamiliar with the term "Jew," which was derived from "Judah." Therefore, they are descendants of the Ten Lost Tribes of Israel.

Godbey calls the Ten Lost Tribes story a myth. Finn says that since the Kaifeng Jews in their commemorative tablets hail Ezra as the "Second Law Giver," they had knowledge of the building of the Second Temple in Jerusalem in the 5th century B.C. They also possessed the *Book of Esther*, written between the 4th and 3rd centuries B.C., and a few verses from *Daniel*, probably created in the 2nd century B.C. To Finn this means the Jews had to arrive in China after that time, but probably before the advent of Christ, since they apparently had no knowledge of him.

Godbey does not state when exactly he believes the Jews left their homeland, but he does indicate a preference for a time prior to the successful revolt of the Maccabees in 164 B.C. He contends that since Chinese Jews did not observe the Feast of the Lights, or Hanukkah, which celebrates the victory, their departure had to have preceded it.

Main supporters of a migration date between the Roman conquest in 70 A.D. and the completion of the Talmud in 600 A.D. are Finn and Gozani, a Catholic Jesuit. Finn thought the presence of rabbis and the observance of rabbinical customs in Kaifeng showed a Talmudic influence. Gozani insisted that their "Talmudic" Bible proved they must have left their homeland while the Talmud was being compiled. (It was during this period that rabbis and synagogues replaced the Temples and priests.)

WESTERN OPINIONS OF THE ROUTES THEY FOLLOWED

Between a departure from Palestine and an arrival somewhere in China there was a time lag to be considered. Here, too, the Sinologists voice the usual disagreement. Forster, an adherent of the Lost Tribes theory, believes these tribes split into two bodies: the first travelling north and integrating with the Khazars to become the Tartars; the second moving through Media and Persia into China. He points to peoples along the old routes to China by land and by sea, such as the Durani in Afghanistan and Jews in the Bombay area of India today, both of whom call themselves "Ben-i-Israel." Forster contends this clearly shows the direction in which the Lost Tribes travelled en route to China. Perlmann generally concurs, but believes most of this second contingent settled and remained in Afghanistan.

Godbey says the Chinese Jews came from Persia, because their synagogue resembled the *mikdash* type found in the Persian areas. Brotier and Adler both claim to have been told by Kaifeng Jews that their religion had been influenced by Persian Jewry. Several foreign visitors to Kaifeng noted the presence of Persian words in notations to the Hebrew Scriptures. Many think they travelled overland, though a sea route is also considered as a possible addition.

Adherents of a migration from India include Chavannes, who considers the Persian travel allegation unreliable, and Goodrich, who is convinced that the Kaifeng Jews, at any rate, arrived with cotton goods from Cochin, India. Both felt they came by sea during Tang and Song.

WESTERN RESEARCH ON KAIFENG

The main objects of study by the Sinologists investigating Chinese Jews concern Kaifeng, which once contained the largest and longest-lasting Jewish community in China. It was visited by foreigners during Ming and Qing, when they could observe Chinese Jews who still prayed in their synagogue, retained some of their ancient customs, and possessed Hebrew scripture and records of their history inscribed in stone. Their reports aroused interest in Europe, England and America, and many foreign scholars wrote books and articles. Of course, they did not limit their analyses to Kaifeng, but embraced Jews in all of China. Inevitably, they argued over the interpretation of facts.

For example, the name by which the Jews were described in Chinese documents and records—*Yicileye* (Israelites), *Zhuhu, Zhuhe, Zhuwu* (all phonetic renderings of "Jew"), *Wotuo* (denied by some to mean Jew at all) . . . What was the derivation of these terms? Which of them were accepted by the Jews? How long did they remain in use?

What was life like in Kaifeng? And in other cities in which the Jews lived? What were their relations with the Han Chinese? With the ethnic races? Did any of them attain prominence? In what capacity? Why have they vanished in China as a race and a religion? What remains of them today?

All of the foregoing have been discussed at length by Western Sinologists, and their writings constitute a valuable contribution to an understanding of the Chinese Jews. Now let us take a look at how Chinese scholars view these expositions, and what additions they have to offer, for these constitute the contents of our book.

THE STUDIES BY CHINESE HISTORIANS

First, a few words about how I collected my materials. My search was greatly facilitated by the very recent availability of the Chen Yuan and Pan Guangdan works. I was also able to discover three other articles which touched upon the Chinese Jews, by Hong Jun, Zhang Xinglang and Weng Dujian. But all five essays were written decades ago, and left many questions unanswered. Had there been any new research by Chinese scholars, any new findings, in the years which followed?

If there were, they certainly eluded me. My inquiries among scholars in Beijing, where I live, proved fruitless. It seemed to me the only thing to do was to go to those places which scholars like Chen Yuan and Pan Guangdan listed as once having hosted Jewish communities, and try to persuade the local historians to undertake the necessary research. And surely I could arouse the interest of at least some of the scholars in Beijing.

Travelling by plane, bus, and train, in the autumn of 1982 I visited Fuzhou, Quanzhou, Xiamen (Amoy), Guangzhou (Canton), Hangzhou, Yangzhou, Shanghai, Ningbo, Zhengzhou, Kaifeng and Yinchuan, where I met with noted historians, archeologists, and sociologists. They were very helpful, and provided valuable leads. Several promised to write special articles for me. All agreed that the new government policy of actively encouraging academic studies had created a favorable environment for research. Those whose field was foreign religions said they were already probing into the development in China of such creeds as Islam, Nestorianism and Manicheism, but had not previously considered Judaism. They were glad I had called the subject to their attention, and said it was a "blank spot" which they would attempt to fill. In Beijing, too, I had a number of enthusiastic responses, and soon was able to include some remarkable new findings regarding Chinese Jews.

I decided to introduce my accumulated materials more or less in the order in which they had been written. By showing which aspects of the saga of the Chinese Jews attracted the attention of Chinese historians, and when, I could demonstrate their lines of reasoning, their styles and personalities, as well as presenting the fruits of their studies.

And so we start our book with Hong Jun, at the very end of the 19th century. He was the first Chinese scholar to mention Jews in any formal study. In his famous work, *Annotations to the Chinese Translation of the Yuan Annals,* he maintains that the word *Wotuo,* as used in 13th-century documents, meant Jews, provoking a controversy which rages to this day. Was this the first written reference to Jews in Chinese history?

Next comes Zhang Xinglang, noted for his 1930 treatise *A Survey of Material Regarding Contacts Between China and the West.* It includes a chapter about the Jews, in which Zhang concurs that the *Wotuo* were Jews. But he disagrees with those who says that "Sinim" in *Isaiah* meant China, and explains why. One might say that this, in essence, is a question of dating the first reference to China in Jewish history.

We follow with Weng Dujian, an authority on Mongolian history. His article "A Study of *Wotuo*," published in 1941 in the *Yenching Journal of Chinese Studies,* I have moved a bit forward out of place in my chronological presentation because it is a direct refutation of the views of Hong and Zhang regarding the identity of the *Wotuo.*

Chen Yuan, our next scholar, is considered by many the Grand Old Man of the history of Chinese Judaism. A specialist on foreign religions in China, he was the first to comprehensively examine the role of the Jews in Chinese history. His analyses were set forth in a series of magazine articles published in Shanghai in the early twenties. Allan Edward Ross translated most of them for a Master's thesis in 1970 at the University of Southern California, with interesting comment appended. Since the articles were later revised and published in a single treatise entitled "A Study of the Israelite Religion in Kaifeng" in 1980, I have translated the new edition, and added a few thoughts of my own. Chen Yuan's work has been the point of departure for almost every Chinese scholar who subsequently researched the history of the Jews in China.

Pan Guangdan wrote about the Jews at even greater length. His many articles were compiled as lecture notes in 1953. But although they appeared in much truncated form as a magazine article in 1981, they were not published in full as a book until 1983, sixteen years after his death. Wide-ranging, the book, entitled *Jews In China—A Historical Survey,* runs from the Jews' earliest origins, to their journeys to China, to when and where they settled, and analyzes the opinions of foreign and Chinese scholars on these and other related matters. It includes, of course, the views of the author and contains an extensive bibliography.

We offer next an article which makes no direct mention of China's Israelites, but tells rather of Kaifeng centuries ago, when it had the largest Jewish community in China. Why had Jews concentrated in this city, then known as Bianjing? What was the attraction? An article entitled "Glimpses of the Urban Economy of Bianjing, Capital of the Northern Song Dynasty," by two Shanghai economists, gives a detailed and colorful picture of Kaifeng when the first large contingent of Jews settled there. I insert it as a useful background for our review of Chinese Judaism.

All of the articles which follow, except for a brief backward glance at an obscure anti-Semitic sneer, were written in the last year or so, most of them specifically for inclusion in this book.

Gao Wangzhi, of China's Academy of Social Sciences, is an authority on world religions. His essay, "Concerning Chinese Jews," presents original views on the first permanent Jewish settlements in China, on the Kaifeng community, on the *Wotuo* controversy, on why the Chinese Jews were assimilated—a question which intrigues several of our scholars.

Li Jixian, also a member of the Chinese Academy of Social Sciences, is a historian whose speciality is the Ming (1368–1644) and the Qing (1644–1911) dynasties. At my request he concentrated his research on a single point. A 1489 tablet, in Chinese, commemorating a rebuilding of the Kaifeng synagogue, includes mention of An Cheng, Jewish physician, and states that some sixty years before he had been rewarded by the emperor for meritorious service. Chinese-American historian Fang Chao-ying, in an article entitled "Notes on the Chinese Jews of Kaifeng," published in America in 1965, alleges that the statement was a hoax, an elaborate cover-up for the nefarious conduct of another Jew called An San; that An Cheng, in fact, never existed. Fang quoted the imperial history to substantiate his claim. I asked Li Jixian to examine the Ming *Records* and reply. In a striking example of historical detection, in "An San and An Cheng" he has marshalled his facts and countered with a devastating rebuttal.

Young historian Chen Changqi boldly undertakes to prove what no scholar, Chinese or foreign, has yet been able to establish—an exact date for the arrival of the Jews in Kaifeng and the name of the ruling emperor. His arguments, contained in an article entitled "Buddhist Monk or Jewish Rabbi?" are most ingenious.

Historian and archeologist Zhu Jiang, in an unusual study of the Muslims in his native city of Yangzhou, has found traces among them of a former Jewish population. His chief evidences include blue hats and Muslim family genealogies—a creative approach, not only to studying the history of the Yangzhou Jews, but also to confirming the presence in former times of Jews in other cities as well.

Persons unfamiliar with Chinese history cannot readily believe, in view of the sad record in the Western world, that the Jews in China were never persecuted for racial or religious reasons. Actually, it has been Chinese tradition to welcome foreign religions and cultures, and to utilize what is best in them. In 67 A.D., Han emperor Ming Di financed the building and upkeep of one of the first Buddhist temples in China, the White Horse Monastery, outside Luoyang. Today, the government of the People's Republic of China is still providing funds for the maintenance of temples, mosques, churches, nunneries, seminaries, and the like, of a large number of faiths and creeds.

Jews and Judaism flourished in this environment. When they finally went into a decline it was because of factors other than racial or religious oppression. A number of articles bear this out.

This does not mean that every single one of the hundreds of millions of Chinese was completely free of anti-Semitism. While the vast majority never even heard of Jews, a tiny handful of Chinese Christians, infected by the European disease, preached it in their churches during the twenties, thirties and forties. Some confusion, too, existed among persons who had read *The Merchant of Venice,* in English, or in Chinese translation. One or two friends, on learning that I was Jewish, said they had heard the Jews were smarter than other peoples and quickly amassed riches. My response was to laughingly reply: "I only wish it were true!" In general, anti-Semitism was extremely limited in scope in China, and had no appreciable effect. Today, the Chinese Constitution guarantees freedom of religion.

I was hard put to find documentary evidence of Chinese anti-Semitism. All I could dig up was an article by a Chinese priest, Xu Songhe, written in 1943, in which he rejoices over what he fondly believes to be the imminent disappearance of the "Israelite Religion" from the face of the earth. I quote from Father Xu primarily to set the stage for our next writer, Wu Zelin, whose article is thoughtful and scholarly.

Professor Wu, who is well into his eighties, is a social anthropologist and an authority on Chinese ethnic history. Although he wrote this article not for me but as a preface to the book by Pan Guandan, his old friend, he has been kind enough to let me use it. His essay notes the treatment to which the Jews were subjected in the West, and the effect this has had on their way of life and their attitude toward their religion. His analysis of such racial and religious persecution is rare among Chinese scholars. He contrasts this with the life the Jews led in China and explains the reason for their ultimate integration.

We conclude our review with a unique survey of the Kaifeng Jews over the past hundred years, and especially of their descendants, including specific figures and information. The scholar is Wang Yisha, Curator of the Kaifeng Museum.

Readers should find valuable the bibliographies attached to the treatises by Pan Guangdan and Gao Wangzhi. In addition we have compiled our own Bibliography, a Chronological Table of Chinese Dynasties, and an Index.

Jews in Old China
Part One

Hong Jun

A SURVEY OF THE VARIOUS RELIGIOUS SECTS DURING THE YUAN DYNASTY, 1897

The first Chinese historian to address the subject of Jews in ancient China was Hong Jun (Hung Chun), born in 1839. A man of remarkable intellect, he passed the Imperial Examinations with the highest marks (Zhuang Yuan) at the age of thirty. In 1888 he was appointed China's envoy to Germany, and was simultaneously accredited to Russia, Austria and the Netherlands. Recalled in 1890 to assume the post of Secretary of State for the War Ministry, he died in 1893.

Hong Jun was acquainted with Western culture and religion from his travels abroad. Although impressed, he was hardly overawed. "When visiting a church in a Western country," he relates, "I was told by my companion that church propriety forbade the wearing of hats inside. I laughed and replied that Jesus was also an Asian, with black hair and eyes just like mine. If he knew an Asian had come, he would hurry to welcome me and not fuss about European etiquette. What harm would it do if I didn't remove my hat?"

His main interest was Chinese history. He was an expert on the Yuan dynasty (1279–1368), when China was ruled by the Mongols. Yuan records, statutes and regulations were written in Mongolian and translated into Han Chinese. Many of the renditions were faulty, and Hong's definitive work *Yuan Shi Yi Wen Zheng Bu (Annotations to the Chinese Translation of the Yuan Annals)*, published in 1897 after his death, cleared up some of the errors.

In the *Annotations* Hong Jun includes a section 29 entitled "Yuan Shi Ge Jiao Ming Kao" ("A Survey of the Various Religious Sects During the Yuan Dynasty"), in which he alleges that the term *Wotuo*, appearing in certain Yuan regulations, could only mean Jew, and states his reasons.

3

If correct, this would be the earliest reference to Jews so far found in any Chinese written record.

First, Hong Jun quotes the "Regulations":

> *Jing Shi Da Dian (Administrative Code),* Chapter 29 *Ma Zheng Bian* ("Regulations Regarding Horses"): The Fourth year of the Zong Tong period (1263). The Premier directs the governors of the regions of Dongping, Daming and Henan to buy seven stout strong horses from every family of all Hui Hui tong shi (Arabic and Persian interpreters), *Wotuo,* Zeng (Buddhist monks), Dao (Taoist priests) *Dashiman* (Muslim mullahs), *Yelikewen* (Christian pastors), and *Weiwuer* (Uygur Manichean clergy), and pay 100 ounces of silver for each, whether draft animal or saddle horse.
>
> . . . The 26th year of the Zhi Yuan period (1279). The War Ministry acknowledges an order from the Royal Chamberlain to purchase as many horses as possible from local functionaries, Buddhist monks, Taoist priests, Christian pastors, and *Wotuo,* be they military persons or civilians. All Buddhist monks, Taoist priests, Christian pastors, Muslim mullahs, and *Wotuo* are directed to deliver all horses four years of age and above to the government, whether saddle horses, draft animals or ponies, and they will receive immediate payment.

We are fortunate in the recent (December, 1981) publication by Shanghai Translations Press of the *Zong Jiao Cidian (A Dictionary of Religions).* It explains some of the terms mentioned above.

Dashiman, says the *Dictionary,* is from the Persian *Danishmand,* meaning a learned man.

> During the Yuan Dynasty it was a common term in China for Muslims. It appeared in official documents—along with Buddhist monks, Taoist priests and Christian pastors—to indicate clergy in the Islamic religious order . . .

Yelikewen the *Dictionary* describes as a religion which entered China during Yuan.

> Transliterated from the Mongolian meaning the blessed, it was used to designate Christian priests and pastors. Believers were fairly numerous during Yuan. Marco Polo (1254–1324) saw Christian churches in Beijing, Hangzhou, Xian, Gansu, Ningxia, Zhenjiang (Yangzhou), and Quanzhou. Both the Franciscans and the Nestorians sent missionaries. But these religious orders vanished from the Central Plain after Yuan.

Since this is a term we will meet again, we interject the definition of Central Plain (Zhong Yuan) set forth in the *Xiandai Hanyu Cidian (A*

Modern Dictionary of Han Chinese) published by the Commercial Press, Beijing, in 1973:

> The southern reaches of the Yellow River, including most of Henan, the western section of Shandong, and the southern parts of Hebei and Shanxi.

It was Chen Yuan who explained who the *Weiwuer* were. In his "Hui Hui Jiao Ru Zhong Guo Shi Lue" ("A Brief History of the Entry of the Muslim Religion Into China"), which is contained in *Chen Yuan Xueshu Lunwen Ji (The Academic Theses of Chen Yuan),* he tells us that the *Weiwuer* (Uygur) during the Yuan Dynasty were believers in Manichaeism. Originating in Persia, the religion came to China in the sixth and seventh centuries through Central Asia into what is now Xinjiang, home of the Uygurs. As used in the "Regulations Regarding Horses," the term appears to refer to religious leaders rather than Manicheans generally.

Having defined our terms, we can now return to Hong Jun. He offers his analysis:

> The term *Wotuo* appearing in the *Administrative Code* means Jewish religionists. According to the original sound (in Hebrew) it should be rendered as *Yute (Yehuda) . . . Rudeya* (Judea) is the word for their homeland (after the Roman conquest in 63 B.C.). *Ru-de* (Jude) is the same as *Yute.* Listing *Wotuo* with Buddhist monks, Taoist priests, Muslim mullahs, and Christian pastors shows beyond any doubt that they were all members of religions. Similarly, the origin of the term *Wotuo* and the context in which it appears prove unquestionably that it means Jews.

Other scholars, whom we shall meet later on, differ. Zhang Xinglang supports Hong. Weng Dujian (Tu-chien) disagrees. Chen Yuan is not sure. The subject is of importance in dating the first reference to Jews in a Chinese document.

Hong Jun had some knowledge of Jewish history, but comments on it only briefly:

> After the fall of the Jewish kingdom its people dispersed in all directions. Many of the merchants in Europe today are Jews. They are numerous also in Persia and Bokhara.

Although he himself had never been to Kaifeng, he notes the confusion then prevailing about the Jews among the local populace:

> Chinese who don't know, mistake them for Muslims. Their noses are also high and hooked. Many of them are cattle butchers.

About their religion he observes: "Kaifeng has Jewish memorial tablets." These are the monuments erected to celebrate the rebuilding of the synagogue on several occasions from the 15th to the 17th centuries. We will see them described in detail in subsequent chapters. They set forth, in Chinese, the history of the community and its religious beliefs, which gradually were reconciled with Confucian concepts. As a result, Hong Jun had the impression that the religious principles of the Kaifeng Jews were "vague and obscure."

But other aspects he treats more favorably:

> Of the three Western religions, Judaism is the most ancient, and from it Catholicism and Islam are derived. The Ten Commandments are said to have been given to Moses, father of the Jewish religion, by God on Mount Sinai. The belief in one God, the practice of resting one day in seven, are Jewish traditions. Their writing is horizontal, from right to left, like Turkic. Western worshippers must learn Hebrew, since the Jewish Bible was written in the language of their homeland.

And that is all we have from Hong Jun on Chinese Jews—not very much, but it stimulated an interest in other Chinese historians.

Zhang Xinglang

CONTACTS BETWEEN ANCIENT CHINA AND THE JEWS, 1930

Zhang Xinglang (1888–1951) no doubt inherited his interest in China's Jews from his distinguished father, Zhang Xiangwen, a historian and geographer who visited Kaifeng, along with Xinglang's sister, Xinghua, in 1910. Although the father's article, contained in his collected works *Nanyuan Conggao (Collected Writings About the South)* presented nothing new, it corroborated earlier reports of the existence of the memorial tablets and the disintegrated condition of the Jewish community.

As a young man, Zhang Xinglang studied in Europe and America. He took post-graduate courses at Harvard and received his Master's Degree at the University of Berlin. After returning to China he became Dean of the Department of Advanced Chinese Studies at Amoy University, and, later, Head of the Department of History at Fu Jen University, in Beijing.

His monumental *Zhong Xi Jiaotong Shiliao Huibian (A Survey of Historical Material Regarding Contacts Between China and the West)* was first published in Beijing in 1930. It was re-issued in 1978 in Beijing by Zhonghua Shuju.

Our interest centers on Section Five, entitled "Gudai Zhongguo Yu Youtai Jiao Bian" ("Contacts Between Ancient China and the Jews"), particularly the first two chapters: "Foreign Documents" and "Chinese Documents." Chapter Three "Kaifeng Jews in the Ming and Qing Dynasties" is mainly a brief listing of some of the foreign comments on the Kaifeng community, more fully treated in other parts of this volume. Chapter Four reproduces the texts of the three stone inscriptions, covered here in the section on Chen Yuan.

The following are the pertinent extracts from Chapters One and Two.

ONE. FOREIGN DOCUMENTS

Although there are no Chinese records prior to Yuan of contacts with the Jews, in the Hebrew Old Testament, Book of Isaiah (49:12) it says: "Look, they are coming from afar, from the north and from the west, and from the land of Sinim."

Many Western archeologists thought that Sinim was a transliteration of China, the word used by later Greco-Roman writers, and that China was derived from Ch'in.

Sinim could not have been a transliteration of China. Isaiah, who talked of Sinim, lived in the 8th century B.C. The Ch'in, or Qin, dynasty, from which the word China is derived, did not come into being until five hundred years later. In any event, Sinim is now believed by biblical scholars to be Aswam in southern Egypt.

That the name Ch'in reached Judah on the Mediterranean coast at the far western end of Asia was offered as proof that there was contact between the two places in very ancient times.

The earliest the name Ch'in could have reached Judah was in 255 B.C. when the Ch'in dynasty was established. But it is more likely to have happened after 63 B.C. when Judah was conquered by Rome, which already had some commercial traffic with China.

In Syria members of the Druse tribe say their ancestors came from China, Zhang notes, and if they do good deeds during their lifetime, their souls will return to China when they die. (Cyril Graham in the *Journal* of the Royal Geographic Society, No. 2, Vol. XXV pp. 262–63.)

Toward the end of Tang (618–905) Arab traveller Abu Zaid Hassan notes that during Huang Chao's attack on Khanfu (Canton) many Muslims, Jews, Christians and Mazdaists (Persian Zoroastrians) were killed. At that time people of various races from Western Asia came to China, since sea trade was brisk.

In Yuan (13th and 14th centuries), Zhang continues, from Western Europe came travellers like Marco Polo, Giovanni di Monte Corvino (first Roman Catholic archbishop of Khanbalik, later Beijing, 1307), Jean di Marignolli, and Ibn Batuta (from North Africa). All said there were Jews in China. In *The Travels of Marco Polo*, Book II, Chapter Five, it says:

After the Great Khan (Kublai) had defeated Nayan (a Tartar chieftain), the Saracens (Muslims), idolaters (Buddhists), Jews, and many others who do not believe in God (Christ), made mock of the cross which Nayan had borne on his banner. They jeered at the Christians and said: "Nayan was a Christian who worshipped the cross, but what help did the cross of your God render him!"

And in Chapter Six:

> Kublai remained in Khanbalik until March, the season of our Easter. He sent for all Christians and directed them to bring the Gospels. After treating the book to repeated applications of incense with great ceremony, he kissed it devoutly and ordered his barons and lords there present to do the same. This usage he regularly observes on the principal feast days of the Christians, such as Easter and Christmas. And he does likewise at the principal feasts of the Saracens, Jews and idolaters.'
>
> Being asked why he did so, he replied: "There are four prophets who are worshipped and to whom all the world does reverence. The Christians say that their God was Jesus Christ, the Saracens Mohamet, the Jews Moses, and the idolaters Sakyamuni Burkhan (Buddha) who was the first to be represented as God in the form of an idol. I do reverence to all four, so that I may be sure of doing it to him who is greatest in Heaven and truest, and to him I pray for aid . . ."

Monte Corvino also alludes to Jews. Marignolli, in his *Recollections of Travel in the East,* alleges he debated with them in Khanbalik. Ibn Batuta recalls a Jewish community in Hangzhou . . .

TWO. CHINESE DOCUMENTS

In Western writings there is quite early reference to contacts between China and the Jews. But in Chinese history, no mention is made of them until Yuan (13th and 14th centuries). At that time there were two terms for Jews in China, says Zhang.

> One was *Zhuhu.* According to the Archimandrite Palladius, Superior of the (Russian) Greek Orthodox Mission in Peking (late 19th century), *Zhuhu* is derived from *Djuhud,* the Arabic (and New Persian) word for Jew. In Yuan times *Zhuhu* was the appellation given to the Jews by the Muslims (many of whom were Persian-speaking Arabs).
>
> The other term for Jews which appeared during the Yuan Dynasty was *Wotuo.* The Greeks called them *Ioudaios* or *Ioudaia* (Judeans). The Roman term was *Judaeus.* In Modern German . . . the Jews are called *Jude. Wotuo* is derived from the European

pronunciation. When the Mongols invaded southern Europe, Russia and Poland, and their legions penetrated Germany, Hungary and Austria, they captured many Jews and brought them back to China, where the terms *Jude* and *Ioudaia* were soon transposed into *Wotuo.*

As evidence, says Zhang, we present passages from Yuan Dynasty documents regarding the *Zhuhu* and *Wotuo.*

ZHUHU

Second month of the Tian Li period, second year (1331). All Buddhist monks, Taoists priests, Christian pastors, *Zhuhu,* and Muslim mullahs who engage in commerce will pay the usual taxes. *Yuan Shi Wen Zong Ben Ji, Zhuan 33 (History of the Yuan Dynasty Regarding Emperor Wenzong, Book 33).*

Fifth month of the 14th year of the Zhi Zheng period (1354). Skilled archers of Ningxia, and wealthy Muslims and *Zhuhu* from all over shall report to the capital for military service. *Yuan Shi Shun Di Ben Ji, Zhuan 43 (History of the Yuan Dynasty Regarding Emperor Shundi, Book 43).*

The word "wealthy" suggests that the authorities were conscripting, at this point, people able to pay handsomely for exemptions, rather than actual soldier material.

WOTUO

Here Zhang repeats Hong Jun's quotations from the Yuan Dynasty "Regulations Regarding Horses," and Hong's contention that the *Wotuo* mentioned therein must be Jews, since all the others listed with them are members of religions. He also quotes a number of other Yuan writings which refer to *Wotuo.* He concludes this chapter with a refutation of Pelliot's allegation that the term did not mean Jews, but commercial organizations of the Muslims.

Rudolph Lowenthal in his *The Jews in China* on page 130 quotes the Frenchman Pelliot as saying *Wotuo* is a transliteration of the Mongolian *ortoq,* and that it probably is a term for various Muslim commercial organizations. Pelliot goes on to say that Mongols did not engage in commerce, but entrusted their money to the Muslims to invest for them. In spite of Pelliot's contention, the foregoing "Regulations" prove that the *Wotuo* were not a commercial organization. For example, in Chapter 29 of the *Jing Shi Dadian (Administrative Code)*, a section in the "Regulations Regarding Horses" lists the *Wotuo* with the Muslim interpreters, Buddhist monks, Taoist priests, Muslim mullahs, Christian pastors, Uygur Manichean priests, and other religious orders. Plainly, they were referred to as members of a religion.

In Mongolian the R sound is very long and drawn-out, and is always transliterated in Chinese. For example, Prince Orda in the *History of the Yuan Dynasty* is transposed in Han Chinese as *Woerda*, with *er* representing R. Mongolian for Christian is *Erkem*, or *Arkaim*, which the *History* renders as *Yelikewen*, with *li* representing R. Urghendj in the *History* becomes *Yulongjuchi*, with *long* for R.

There are many such examples. *Ortoq* in Chinese would have to be *Woertuo* or *Wolituo*. The R sound could not be omitted. Pelliot's contention, therefore, is not credible.

Weng Tu-Chien (Weng Dujian)

A STUDY OF *WOTUO*, 1941

Weng Tu-chien, born in 1906, is one of China's foremost authorities on ethnic Chinese. He is presently Advisor to the Institute of Nationalities Studies of the Chinese Academy of Social Sciences.

He does not agree with the contention of Hong Jun and Zhang Xing-lang that *Wotuo* means Jews. In a conversation with me at his home in Beijing in August, 1982, he discussed first the types of persons listed in the *Ma Zheng Bian* ("Regulations Regarding Horses") of the *Jing Shi Da Dian (Administrative Code)* of the Yuan Dynasty. It is these "Regulations" which Hong and Zhang quote to support their allegation.

Professor Weng stressed that those listed were not ordinary people, but persons of prestige and economic standing within their various categories. *Hui Hui tong shi,* for example, were men who were fluent in Persian and Arabic, and could have been members of any race other than Han or Mongol. They held important positions in Yuan society as go-betweens for the Mongol government authorities with members of the Persian and Arabic-speaking communities.

Zeng means Buddhist monk, *Dao* means Taoist priest, *Dashiman* means a person learned in the Islamic religion. In other words, these were leaders in their respective faiths, not simply believers. By the same token, *Yelikewen* (Christians), *Weiwuer* (Uygur), as used in the "Regulations," also meant leaders in those communities. Obviously, the "Regulations" requiring sale to the government of "seven stout horses each" could only have been directed at families of considerable position and wealth. The ordinary family would be lucky if it possessed even a single animal.

Who, then, were the prominent *Wotuo* referred to in the "Regulations"? In an article entitled *"Wotuo* Za Kao" ("A Study of *Wotuo*") which appeared in *Yen Jing Xue Bao (Yenching Journal of Chinese*

Studies), Beijing, June, 1941, Professor Weng explains why he rejects the claim that the *Wotuo* were Jews:

> Those taking this position predicate it on three reasons: That the sounds (of *Wotuo* and the German *Jude* or Greek *Ioudaia*) are similar; that the term is listed along with Buddhist, Taoist, Christian and Muslim (religionists); that they (the Jews) were shrewd merchants.
>
> These reasons are not very convincing. During the Yuan dynasty there were many complicated translations of foreign terms. To proceed solely from the sound, while unclear about the meaning and origin of a word, is a sure way to go wrong. Errors in the *Yuan Shi Yu Jie (Explanations of the Terms in the History of the Yuan Dynasty)* are examples of this. (The book was written during the Qian Long period of the Ching Dynasty.)
>
> It is true that *Wotuo* has, in some instances, been listed along with Buddhist monks, Taoist priests, Christian pastors, and Muslim mullahs. But it has also appeared in other lists which include the influentially wealthy, Tartars, Uygurs, Arabs, and Mongol officials. The inclusion of *Wotuo* in these lists is an indication of its special status and importance, and does not prove that it was a religion.
>
> The Jews were indeed shrewd merchants. But in Yuan times most of the wealthy businessmen were Muslims from the Middle East. The shrewd merchants referred to were not necessarily Jews.
>
> To learn who the *Wotuo* actually were requires much more detailed study and analysis.

Weng Tu-chien deals also with the contention by Zhang Xinglang that *Wotuo* could not come from the Mongolian *ortoq,* meaning merchant, since the Mongolian R sound was always represented when transliterated into Han Chinese. Weng quotes from Yuan Dynasty documents where the Mongol word *ordu,* meaning imperial tent, was at times also rendered as *wotuo,* without an R sound—to indicate that such renditions, though phonetically inaccurate and exceptions to the usual forms of transliteration, did occur.

He then sums up, in a note in English appended to the end of the article. It reads, in part, as follows:

> In the Chinese historical documents of the Yuan dynasty (the Mongol dynasty), particularly the *Yuan Dian Zhang (Yuan Laws and Regulations)* and the *Yuan Shi (History of the Yuan Dynasty),* there appears frequently the name *Wotuo.* From its general application we know that the name represents a special corps

of merchants, mostly Mohammedans, who, under the Mongol domination, had close connections with the Imperial house and the government, and enjoyed many privileges.

In the present article a few problems concerning the *Wotuo* are studied. Firstly, the wrong identification of the name with the Jews, which has been accepted by several Chinese scholars, is repudiated. Secondly, the fact that during the Yuan period the two Chinese characters *Wo* and *tuo* were also used, wrongly or exceptionally, to transcribe the Mongol word *ordu,* which means imperial tent, is pointed out. . . . Fourthly, the nature of the *"Wotuo qian,"* or *Wotuo* money, which is the money the Royal house or the imperial princes and princesses lent to the people through the *Wotuo,* is made clear. And, lastly, the origin of the name, which has its source in the Turkish word *ortaq,* is traced with new evidences and discussed in detail.

There the dispute among Chinese and Western scholars regarding the meaning of the word *Wotuo* stands today. If Hong Jun and Zhang Xinglang are correct, and *Wotuo* meant Jews, then the first mention of them in Chinese documents appeared in 1263, in Chapter 29 of the "Regulations Regarding Horses" in the Yuan *Administrative Code.*

If Pelliot and Lowenthal and Weng Dujian are correct, and *Wotuo* meant Muslim commercial organizations, then Jews were not mentioned in Chinese records until 1280, when they were called *Muhu (Zhuhu) Hui Hui* (Jewish Hui Hui) in Book 57 of the Yuan Dian Zhang *(Yuan Dynasty Laws and Regulations).* See Chen Yuan, p. 34, this volume, my comment.

All agree, however, that Jews were identified in Chinese official documents for the first time, whether by the use of one term or another, during the Yuan Dynasty.

Chen Yuan

A STUDY OF THE ISRAELITE RELIGION IN KAIFENG, 1920, REVISED 1980

The first Chinese scholar to discuss in depth the question of Jews in old China was Chen Yuan (1880–1971). An educator and historian of note, Chen Yuan held many academic posts over half a century, including Director of the Chinese Cultural Institute of Yenching University, President of Fu Jen University, President of Beijing Normal University, and Director of the Second History Institute of the Chinese Academy of Social Sciences.

His treatises on religions in China, written in the 1920's, have been compiled into Volume One of *Chen Yuan Xueshu Lunwen Ji (The Academic Theses of Chen Yuan)*, published by Zhonghua Shuju, Beijing, in 1980. It contains his classic "Kaifeng *Yicileye* Jiaokao" ("A Study of the Israelite Religion in Kaifeng"), and it is this essay we present in this volume.

Kaifeng had the largest Jewish community in China, the one which lasted the longest, and the only one which left substantial records of its own. These records, primarily three stellae, that is, stone inscriptions in Chinese commemorating various rebuildings of the synagogue, set forth considerable data regarding the community.

Chen Yuan begins his essay with a foreword reproducing texts of the inscriptions, and follows with twelve chapters analysing them and commenting upon Jews in Kaifeng, and other parts of China.

Here we offer extracts from the inscriptions, and portions of the first nine chapters. We omit the last three since they consist mainly of comments by 19th century foreign observers and a listing of religious quotation plaques, in Chinese and Hebrew, which had hung in the synagogue.

FOREWORD

The first inscription, entitled "Chong Jian Qing Zhen Si Ji" ("A Record of Rebuilding the Purity and Truth Synagogue"), is dated the second year of Hong Zhi, or 1489. Hong Zhi was the period title adopted by Ming dynasty emperor Li Zong, who reigned from 1488 to 1506. Momentous events during the course of an emperor's rule were sometimes marked by the adoption of a new period title. I have condensed Chen Yuan's reproduction of the 1489 inscription. It reads in part as follows:

> The Founder of the Israelite religion was Abraham, a 19th generation descendant of Pangu/Adam.

Pangu is the figure in Chinese mythology who is credited with having created the universe. As can be seen here, and in the other inscriptions, the composers went to pains to stress the similarity of their culture and beliefs to those of the Chinese Confucianists.

> In the 146th year of the Zhou dynasty (921 B.C.) Abraham established our religion, which has been carried on to this day.
>
> It was transmitted to Moses, Patriarch of the Correct Religion, in the 613th year of Zhou (454 B.C.). Intelligent, benevolent and righteous, he sought the Scriptures on Mount Sinai, where he fasted for forty days and forty nights. His earnest prayers moved God's heart, and that is how the Correct Scriptures, in 53 sections, originated. Meticulous and excellent, they inspire goodness in the good and expose the wickedness of the bad.
>
> The Religion was passed on to Ezra, another patriarch of the Correct Religion. His way of worshipping God fully manifested the mysteries of the ancestral Way. The Way has no shape or form, but is above all else.
>
> Our Religion was transmitted to China from Tianzhu. We settled in Kaifeng by imperial command. More than seventy clans named Li, An, Ai, Gao, Mu, Zhao, Jin, Zhou, Zhang, Shi, Huang, Li, Nie, Jin, Zhang, Zuo and Pai . . . arrived during the Northern Song dynasty (960–1127), bringing entry tribute of Western cloth.

Li, Jin and Zhang are listed twice. These are 15th century transliterations of names which no doubt were different in Hebrew, but could find only the same phonetic equivalents in Chinese. Tianzhu, above, is a reference to India, or the Middle East generally.

> The Emperor said: "You have come to our Central Plain. Preserve your ancestral customs and settle in Bianliang."

Kaifeng, then known as Bianliang, is located on China's Central Plain.

In the first year of the Long Xing period (1163) of Song emperor Xiao Zong, when *Wusida* Liewei was the leader of our faithful, the *andula* commenced the building of our synagogue. It was rebuilt in the 16th year of the Zhi Yuan period (1279) of Kublai Khan.

Wusida is a Chinese version of *usta,* a Persian word meaning master craftsman, which Persian-speaking Jews converted to indicate their Chief Rabbi. Liewei, of course, was Levi. Both Chinese scholars and foreign Sinologists disagree over *andula*. Some say it is also from a Persian term meaning supervisor. Others insist it is a person's name— An Dula. We shall hear from some of the contenders in the essays which follow.

During the Ming dynasty persons who were well-versed in the Scriptures and urged others to do good were designated *manla*. They preached our religion. Thanks to their efforts, today all of our people observe the law, worship God, venerate their ancestors, are loyal to their sovereign and filial to their parents.

Jews in China were strongly influenced by their Muslim neighbors, with whom they lived in close proximity. *Manla* comes from the Arabic *mullah,* and was applied loosely to elders and lesser rabbis.

Physician An Cheng, in the 19th year of the Yong Le period (1421) of Emperor Cheng Zu, was presented with ceremonial incense and authorized by the Prince of Zhou, whose posthumous name was Ding, to rebuild the synagogue. An Cheng erected a plaque therein wishing "Long Life to the Emperor of the Great Ming Dynasty." In the 21st year of the Yong Le period (1423) his merits were reported to the throne, and he was rewarded with permission to change his name to Zhao, and by designating him a Major of the Brocaded Robe Security Corps, and later raising him to Lieutenant Governor of the Military Area of Zhejiang Province.

"Ceremonial incense" here means money. Chinese-American Sinologist Fang Zhaoying contends that An Cheng never existed, that he was actually a cover-up for another person named An San, who was rewarded for reporting a treason plot by the Prince of Zhou. Chinese historian Li Jixian strongly disagrees. We present both views later on.

In the 10th year of the Zheng Tong period (1445) Li Rong and Li Liang rebuilt the temple's Front Hall of three sections with their own money. . . . In the 5th year of the Tian Shun period (1461) floods swept everything of the synagogue away except its foundations. . . . Permission was obtained to rebuild. . . . Li Rong again supplied funds, and construction began of a brand new temple decorated with gilt and many colors.

In the Cheng Hua period (1465–1488) Gao Jian, Gao Rui, and Gao Hong rebuilt the Rear Hall of three sections with their own money, painted it with colors and gilt, placed in it three scrolls of the Scriptures, and connected it by an esplanade to the Front Hall—a contribution of lasting value. This, then, is the story of the various constructions of the synagogue.

In the Tian Shun period (1457–1465) Shi Bin, Li Rong, Gao Jian and Zhang Xuan went to Ningbo and brought back a scroll of the Scriptures. Zhao Ying of Ningbo brought another scroll to Bianliang (Kaifeng) and respectfully presented it to our temple. . . .

Our religion and Confucianism differ only in minor details. In mind and deed both respect Heaven's Way, venerate ancestors, are loyal to sovereigns and ministers, and filial to parents. Both call for harmony with wives and children, respect for rank, and for making friends. In short, nothing less than the Five (Confucian) Relationships. . . .

This Tablet was erected on a propitious day in the fifth lunar month of the 2nd year of the Hong Zhi period (1489) by Jin Ying of Ningxia and Jin Li of Kaifeng, both descendants of the (religionists of the) Purity and Truth Synagogue. . . .

On the back of the 1489 tablet is a second inscription dated the 7th year of the Zheng De period (1512). It is entitled "Zun Chong Dao Jing Si Ji" ("A Record of the Synagogue Which Respects the Scriptures of the Way"). The latter is a Sinified term for the Five Books of Moses, or the Torah. The inscription reads, in part, as follows:

> Zuo Tang of Jiangdu (Yangzhou) . . . composed this inscription. . . .

> As to the religion of the Israelites, its first ancestor was Adam, and it originated in Tianzhu, Xiyu. By Zhou times its Scriptures were being transmitted. They are each in four parts and contain a total of fifty-three sections. Meticulous in principle and excellent in method, they are as veneration-worthy as Heaven.

> Founder of the Religion was Abraham. Transmitter of the Torah was Moses. Then, in Han times, the Religion entered China. A synagogue was erected in Kaifeng in the first year of the Long Xing period (1163) of Song emperor Xiao Zong.

The Song court had fled to Hangzhou, south of the Yangtse, in 1127, and Kaifeng in 1163 was in the hands of the Nuzhen Tartars who ruled as the Jin, or Golden, Dynasty. But the Israelites who remained in Kaifeng continued to calculate their calendar in Han Chinese dynastic terms. Chen Yuan explains the significance of this further on.

> The synagogue was rebuilt in the 16th year of the Zhi Yuan period (1279, under Kublai Khan) of the Yuan Dynasty. . . .
>
> Members of the Religion are found not only in Kaifeng, but all over. And wherever they are, there is none who does not venerate the Scriptures and the Way. . . .
>
> They give alms to widows and orphans, the afflicted and the lame, and provide them with shelter. They give funds to those otherwise too poor to marry, or who cannot afford funeral expenses. They refrain from meat and wine when in mourning and from extravagant funeral ceremonies, following prescribed ritual and rejecting superstition. They maintain accurate scales and measures, and never cheat their fellow man.
>
> Today, we have among us those who have sat for the Imperial Examinations and who have gained wide fame, those within or outside the administration who serve their sovereign and benefit the people, those who loyally support the Emperor in defeating enemy aggression, and those whose moral qualities and goodness are an example to the entire countryside.
>
> Our farmers till their fields and pay their taxes. Our craftsmen produce a plentitude of articles for the public. Our merchants, ranging far and wide, are well-known in commercial circles. Our traders adhere to principle, and seek profits in markets everywhere. . . .
>
> Graven images and gaudy pictures, impetuous actions and empty writings, things which dazzle the eyes and ears—these are heretical and unworthy of mention. But the true value of the Scriptures is appreciated by all who venerate them!
>
> These Scriptures had their origin. After the world was created, Adam transmitted them to Noah, who transmitted them to Abraham.

A peculiar error. Both the 1489 inscription, and this inscription itself some lines earlier, state that the first transmitter of the Scriptures was Moses.

> Abraham gave them to Isaac, who gave them to Jacob, who gave them to the Twelve Tribes, who passed them on to Moses, who transmitted them to Aaron, who gave them to Joshua, who transmitted them to Ezra. And from that time on, the religion of the Patriarchs glowed with renewed brilliance. . . .
>
> This synagogue was rebuilt in . . . the seventh year of the Zheng

De period (1512) of the Great Ming Dynasty. An, Li, Gao, and Jin Pu of Weiyang (Yangzhou) contributed a Torah scroll and constructed a Second Gateway to the temple. Jin Run of Ningxia erected a pavilion to house the tablet. Jin Zhong wrote the inscription. . . .

A third inscription, on a second tablet, also entitled "Chong Jian Qing Zhen Si Ji" ("A Record of the Rebuilding of the Purity and Truth Synagogue"), but dated the 2nd year of the Kang Xi period (1663) of the Qing Dynasty, is quoted by Chen Yuan. It reads, in part, as follows:

The Israelite religion was established in the distant past. It began with Adam, a 19th generation descendant of Pangu, and was continued by Noah and then by Abraham.

According to Chinese mythology, Pangu created the universe and human society. All races of the world were deemed to have descended from him.

After the Religion had been handed down for many generations, the holy Patriarch Moses was born. . . He received the Scriptures on Mount Sinai. . . In fifty-three sections, they are simple and easy to understand. They urge men to virtue and warn against evil. . . . Although written in ancient language with strange sounds, they are entirely in conformity with the principles of the Six (Confucian) Tenets.

The Religion started in Tianzhu. It was transmitted to the Central Plain during the Zhou Dynasty. Centuries later, a temple was built in Daliang (Kaifeng). Many changes occurred during the Han, Tang, Song and Ming Dynasties which followed, but the members of the Religion continued scrupulously to observe its teachings, which were as necessary to them as drink and food and clothing.

The *andula* (supervisor) started building the synagogue in the first year of the Long Xing period (1163) of Song Emperor Xiao. The *wusida* (Chief Rabbi) rebuilt it in the 16th year of the Zhi Zhong [should be Zhi Yuan] period (1279) of the Yuan Dynasty. A Yellow River flood inundated the synagogue in the 5th year of the Tian Shun period (1464) of the Ming Dynasty, and Li Rong, Li Liang, Gao Jiang and Gao Rui contributed money for its restoration. . . .

Near the end of the Ming Dynasty in the 15th year of the Chong Zhen period (1642), Chuang the Brigand rebelled and laid siege to Kaifeng three times. . . . After six months, for want of a better plan, Chuang diverted the waters of the Yellow River and flooded the city. The synagogue was destroyed and the scriptures were sunk beneath the waves.

"Chuang," meaning a powerful rushing force, was the nickname for Li Zecheng, leader of a peasant rebellion. He captured Kaifeng in 1642, took the capital Peking in 1644, and proclaimed himself Emperor. Wu Sangui, a general of the Ming armies, enlisted the aid of the Manchus of Northeast China, and the combined forces defeated Li in the open field. He retreated and disappeared. Once in Peking, the Manchus established their own rule, the Qing Dynasty.

> Only two-hundred some-odd families of the congregation managed to get across to the north side of the river. For a time they wandered about, but as soon as they settled down, they began planning to recover the Scriptures. Gao Xuan, a Gong Shi scholar, acting on orders of his father . . . made several trips back to the ruined synagogue and recovered a number of Torah scrolls, plus 26 Miscellaneous Writings. . . .

Civil Service examinations were conducted every few years on county, provincial, and national levels. Successful candidates in the county exams were called Xiu Cai. They were eligible to take the provincial tests. If they passed, they were called Ju Ren, and could compete in the national (Imperial) exams. Those who achieved high grades in the Imperial examinations were called Jin Shi, those with slightly lower marks were called Gong Sheng and were usually appointed to the post of magistrate. The top first, second and third scorers in the national tests were entitled Zhuang Yuan, Fang Yuan, and Tang Hua, respectively. All of these exams were tests only of cultural—primarily literary—attainments, not competitions for specific posts. But appointments were usually made on the basis of the grades received.

> By the time restoration of the Torahs was completed, they were as good as new. They were placed in a large house which the congregation rented, and where they gathered and conducted services as before. Thus, the Scriptures were not lost and the Religion was preserved. . . .
> In 1653 public discussions were held regarding raising money for the rebuilding of the synagogue. The entire congregation gladly contributed, and construction started. When it was finished, the synagogue was more complete than the earlier temples, and all who saw it were filled with admiration. . . .
> I (Liu Chang) have been asked to compose this permanent inscription in stone, lest men forget. I am a native of Kaifeng and am familiar with the religion of the Israelites. Moreover, Major Zhao Chengji, Assistant Treasurer Zhao Yingcheng, and Official Physician Ai Xiansheng (leading members of the Jewish community) are my intimate friends, and so I can report the facts in

detail. With these supplementing the older records, I am able to trace the origins of the Religion. I have set all of this down so that those seeing the restored synagogue—Repository of the Scriptures—will remember always the meritorious deeds of the religionists. . . .

Chen Yuan concludes his foreword by listing the tangible evidence he has seen or has on hand. He says in 1917 a Mr. Shi of the Anglican Mission in Peking sent him recent rubbings of the 1489 and 1512 inscriptions. Seventy or more characters of the 1489 inscription had been obliterated, with a resultant loss of personal and place names, Chen says, though the damage to the 1512 inscription is somewhat less. However, he subsequently acquired early 18th century rubbings which are flawless.

He says he also has a rubbing of the 1663 tablet, which has the names of contributors on the back, and which also is called "Chong Jian Qing Zhen Si Ji" ("A Record of the Rebuilding of the Purity and Truth Synagogue"). He notes that while the Muslims also use the term Qing Zhen Si to designate their mosques, "Judaism is not Mohammedanism." The 1663 tablet has vanished.

Chen Yuan says that in 1912 the Canadian Church of England in China bought the ruins of the Kaifeng synagogue and site, and moved the tablet bearing the 1489 and 1512 inscriptions to the churchyard of Kaifeng's Trinity Cathedral, and that this tablet is still in Kaifeng.

I saw it in 1983 in the Kaifeng Museum, its present repository, together with a tablet entitled "Ci Tang Shu Gu Bei Ji" ("A Tablet Record of the Ancient History of Our Ancestral Hall"), dated 1679, belonging to the Zhao Clan. Chen adds:

> I have also seen the writings, in over two hundred volumes, of Israelite Zhao Yingcheng of the Shun Zhi period (1644–1662) . . . Moreover, I have acquired articles written by Chinese and foreign scholars since the Kang Xi period on the results of their research in this matter, and on the origin of the parchment Scriptures.

He then proceeds with his analysis, which we present in the form of a summary of his first nine chapters.

I. VERIFICATION OF THE HONG ZHI (1489) TABLET INSCRIPTION

> The writer of this inscription was Jin Zhong. His name is distinguishable on the rubbing I recently obtained. Jin Zhong was an Israelite. He was still alive in 1512. On the 1512 inscription he is mentioned as having composed the 1489 inscription. This latter states that when the Israelites first arrived in Kaifeng there were seventy clans (although only 17 of them were actually listed). On

the later rubbings only Li, Ai and Jin are still legible. All the others have been obliterated. This is because of the Muslim uprisings in the Tong Zhi period (1862–1875) and the Boxer Rebellion (1900) . . . The descendants of the Israelites hoped in this way to avoid trouble.

Local people often confused the Jews with the Muslims, because of their physical and religious similarities. For several years in the 19th century the Muslims were engaged in bloody clashes with the Han Chinese. By then all of the Kaifeng Jews had adopted Chinese surnames, and most had become fully integrated as Han Chinese. Some did not want their names to appear on any public listing which would identify them as Jews, since this might leave them open to attack by persons who mistook Jews for Muslims.

During the Boxer Rebellion of 1900, the invasion and pillaging of China by the troops of thirteen foreign countries engendered a widespread anti-foreign revulsion. By the turn of the century the Kaifeng Jews had been in China for nearly 800 years. Although they certainly were no longer "foreigners," some thought it safer to remove reminders of their foreign origin. These fears proved groundless. Contrary to the experience of Jews in other countries, those in China were never subjected to racial or religious persecution.

For a number of years there has been speculation regarding the accuracy of the statement in the 1489 inscription that when the Jews first arrived in Kaifeng they comprised seventy clans. Only seventeen clan names are listed, and "seventy" ("qishi") might have been a scribal error for "seventeen" ("shiqi"), that is, the same two characters written in reverse. Chen Yuan mentions the dispute without resolving it.

Actually, the question was answered in 1912 with the discovery of the Zhao clan tablet of 1679, which Chen Yuan had not seen. It was embedded in the rear wall of a Zhao family house formerly adjoining the synagogue. The tablet also outlines the history of the Jews. When they came to Kaifeng, it says, ". . . there were 73 clans and over 500 families . . ." This confirms the "seventy" figure as correct. Chen Yuan next discusses their place of origin.

> Both the 1489 and 1512 inscriptions said they ". . . came from Tianzhu . . ." Later, these words were obliterated, as if later generations considered them to be in error and wiped them out. Tianzhu is an ancient term. As used here it simply represented a place far to the west. In the same way Adam is compared to Pangu. The purpose in both instances was to make the text comprehensible to people today. No one in China ever heard of Youtai (Judah, Judea) before the fifteenth century. If the Kaifeng Jews had written that they came from Youtai no one would have known

where it was. The scribe couldn't invent a new word, nor was he aware of the fact that during the Yuan Dynasty (13th century) there were already terms for Jews such as *Zhuhu* and *Wotuo*. So there was nothing wrong at the time in using Tianzhu to represent Judea. In the 1512 inscription, immediately after Tianzhu, the word Xiyu appears. This is a more suitable term.

Xiyu, literally the Western Regions, as used in Chinese historical material embraces a vast area running all the way from China's Xinjiang to the westernmost end of West Asia, including India and the entire Middle East.

The most serious mistake was dating Abraham in the 146th year of the Zhou Dynasty (921 B.C.) and Moses in the 613th year of Zhou (454 B.C.). It arose from an erroneous comparison of the Chinese and Western calendars. But it is not entirely wrong, for placing Moses some 400 years after Abraham is not necessarily incorrect.

The 1489 inscription says the synagogue was built in the first year of the Long Xing period (1163) of Song Emperor Xiao Zong. This is the same as the third year of the Da Ding period of (Golden Tartar) Jin Emperor Shi Zong. By 1163 the Jin had been in occupation of Kaifeng for 38 years. Kaifeng people describing Kaifeng affairs of that time should have used the Jin Dynasty calendar. The fact that the Jews did not, shows that they held orthodox concepts (regarding legitimacy of rule). It is like people today using the Western calendar in dating Chinese history. A common practice, not at all peculiar. Both the 1512 and 1663 inscriptions, in referring to building the synagogue under the Golden Tartar occupation, also follow the same dating system . . .

For more on the significance of the continued use of the Han Chinese calendar under the Golden Tartar occupation, see the article by Wu Zelin entitled "An Ethnic Historian Looks at China's Jews," p. 165.

II. VERIFICATION OF THE ZHENG DE (1512) INSCRIPTION

Chen Yuan says this inscription deserves special study for a number of reasons: Why does it call the temple the Synagogue Which Respects the Scriptures of the Way (the Torah) rather than the Purity and Truth Synagogue, as did the 1489 inscription? Was Zuo Tang, the composer of the inscription, an Israelite? What does it show about the relationship between the Jews of Kaifeng and those of Weiyang, as Yangzhou was then known, an important commercial city on the Yangtze River? Regarding the first question, Chen Yuan explains:

The 1489 inscription says: "The Way originates in Purity, Truth and Worship—the Purity being absolute, the Truth being orthodox and not heretical . . ." The inscription in conclusion refers to the descendants of the Purity and Truth religionists. This gives the impression that the Israelite religion is no different from that of the Muslims. To correct this impression, the 1512 inscription rigorously avoids the term Purity and Truth. It is not used once in the entire inscription . . .

In Yuan times (13th century) the synagogue was called Gu Cha Qing Zhen Si (Ancient Temple Synagogue of Purity and Truth). In early Ming (14th century) the same name was used in an application to rebuild. This is stated in the 1489 inscription.

But the 1512 inscription avoids the term Purity and Truth, and speaks only of the Ancient Temple. The aim was obvious. At that time the Muslims called their mosques Qing Zhen Si (Temples of Purity and Truth). Zuo Tang, the composer, deliberately chose the term Zun Chong Dao Jing Si (Synagogue Which Respects the Scriptures of the Way) to prevent any confusion.

As to the identity of Zuo Tang, Chen Yuan has no doubts. Zuo was one of the seventeen clan names listed in the 1489 inscription. Zuo Tang, who had qualified as a Jin Shi in the Imperial Examinations in 1496, came from Jiangdu (Yangzhou), a city which contained a Jewish community. Also, at the end of the 1512 inscription, he refers to "our descendants. . . ," clearly identifying himself as an Israelite. Further, in relating the transmission of the Torah by the Patriarchs subsequent to Abraham, he demonstrates a more detailed knowledge of Jewish history than the composer of the 1489 inscription, who mentions only Moses and Ezra.

The Jews of Kaifeng and Yangzhou, also known as Weiyang, says Chen Yuan, were closely related:

> The composer, the calligrapher of the text, and the calligrapher of the caption in ancient style, were all from Weiyang. So was the man who brought a Torah scroll to Kaifeng and those who contributed money for the rebuilding of the synagogue. There were Israelites in Weiyang. This inscription fortunately is proof.

Chen Yuan is puzzled by the failure of Ming writers to make any mention of the earlier Kaifeng synagogue. He says:

> During the Jia Jing period (1522–1567) of the Ming dynasty a native of Kaifeng named Li Lian wrote an essay entitled "Bian Jing Yi Ji Zhi" ("Notes on Ruins of the Bian Capital"). He described structures long since gone, of which only the names re-

mained, in order, he said, that gentlemen in future times who were interested in antiquities might know of them.

He included more than ten former structures in and around Tu Shizi Jie (Local Products Market)—such as the Huang Jian Compound to the southeast, the Guang Hui Compound on the east side of the southern end of the market, and the Dawani Temple northeast of the market. All had been destroyed, and all were listed. But the Israelite synagogue which had stood to the southeast of Local Products Market was the only building he did not mention.

Li Lian wrote his essay in the 25th year of the Jia Jing period (1546), only thirty-four years after the 1512 inscription. He should have known from the inscripton of the old Israelite synagogue. Very strange.

Not strange at all if by "Bian Jing" Li Lian meant literally the capital of Northern Song, in Kaifeng. Song fled to Hangzhou in 1127, and the synagogue was not built until 1163, by which time Kaifeng was no longer "Bian Jing," and so the old synagogue could not have been among the Bian Jing ruins.

III. VERIFICATION OF THE KANG XI SECOND YEAR (1663) TABLET

This tablet is called "Chong Jian Qing Zhen Si Ji" ("A Record of the Rebuilding of the Purity and Truth Synagogue"), which is the same as the title of the 1489 inscription. The inscription of the 1663 tablet covers both the front and back of the stone. This, and the 1489 and 1512 inscriptions, formerly stood in the synagogue courtyard.

Chen Yuan says it is not known where the original tablet has gone, but that a rubbing made by a Roman Catholic priest exists today in the library of the Zikaway Mission in Shanghai. The inscription was composed by Liu Chang of Kaifeng. Liu states that he is a native of Kaifeng, that he is familiar with the Israelite religion, and that he is an intimate friend of three prominent members of the congregation.

The tablet is in effect a history of Kaifeng Judaism prior to Emperor Kang Xi, who reigned between 1662 and 1722. Without it we would not know how Judaism flourished after the Sheng De period, which ended in 1521, and before the Qing Dynasty, which commenced in 1644. Neither Liu Chang, the composer of the 1663 inscription, nor Li Guangzuo, the calligrapher of the ancient style caption, nor Hou Lianghan, the engraver, were Israelites.

It was a common practice to seek the participation of prominent figures in the creation of a tablet, to lend prestige to the occasion. They

were not necessarily members of the group of persons doing the commemorating.

The inscription describes Adam as a 19th generation descendant of Pangu. This is based on an erroneous reading of the 1489
inscription which says that Abraham was a 19th generation descendant of Pangu/Adam. The statement that the *Wusida* (Chief
Rabbi) rebuilt the temple for the first time in the 16th year of the
Zhi Zong period (1365) of the Yuan Dynasty should read the 16th
year of the Zhi Yuan period (1279) of the Yuan, which is what
both the 1489 and the 1512 inscriptions say. The error of a single
character makes a difference of nearly eighty years.

Liu Chang was not an Israelite. He based his inscription on the
earlier tablet, as he himself said, and he made a few mistakes. For
that he can be forgiven.

In describing Israelite religious ceremonies the tablet uses a lot
of Confucian terminology. It is more detailed than the 1489 and
1512 inscriptions regarding the Day of Atonement. "At the end of
autumn," it says, "they (the Jews) close their doors and meditate
all day. They neither eat nor drink, but cultivate their innate
goodness."

Yom Kippur, or the Day of Atonement, is the most ancient and most
important of Jewish religious holy days, Chen Yuan notes. Its rites are
very solemn. It comes on the tenth day of the seventh month of their
calendar, starting at sunset the previous day and ending at sunset of the
day itself. Quiet and fasting and silent contemplation of their sins are
essential to all who observe the rites. They atone profoundly to seek
God's forgiveness.

Although the Kaifeng Jews today no longer have a temple
where they can observe this holy day, they still fast and mourn
without fail on the tenth day of the seventh month. The description of the rites in this tablet indicates that Liu Chang was not
entirely ignorant of the Israelite religion.

It is doubtful whether there still were Jews in Kaifeng observing *Yom
Kippur* in the 1920s when Chen Yuan wrote this. There certainly is no
such observance today. Some individuals know they are of Jewish
descent. But racially they are thoroughly integrated, and they no
longer practice their religion.

IV. WHEN THE JEWS CAME TO KAIFENG

Judaism is a racial religion, says Chen Yuan, different from other
religions which may be practised by many different races at the same

time. Wherever the Jewish race went, there the Jewish religion was practised. To know when the Jews entered China is to know when their religion arrived.

Opinions vary as to the time. The 1489 inscription says Song (960–1279), the 1512 inscription says Han (206 B.C.–220 A.D.), the 1663 tablet says Zhou (1066–256 B.C.). But the statement on the 1663 tablet that the religion was transmitted to the Middle Kingdom in Zhou seems to be based on a remark to that effect in the 1489 inscription, and is not necessarily correct.

According to European and American scholars the Jews began their travels a long time ago. The Russian Alexei Vinogradov (19th century) claimed the Jews reached China at the time of the Kingdom of Israel. He alleged that an ancient poem by a Chinese Jew tells of how King Hiram of Tyre presented to King David the gift sent to him by Chinese Emperor Zhao (1000–976 B.C.) of the Zhou Dynasty.

David reigned over the United Israelite Kingdom from approximately 1010 to 970 B.C. Regarding a Zhou Dynasty entry, see Pan Guandan, Chap. IV.

Others say the word "Sinim" in *Isaiah,* Chapter 49 of the Torah, means China, and is proof of contacts between the Jews and China in ancient times. Isaiah's dates correspond to the reign of Emperor Ping (770–719 B.C.) of the Zhou Dynasty, and this supports the allegation that Jews came to China at that time.*

Still another argument is that they arrived after the slaughter of many Jews in Babylon in 34 A.D. Or after the destruction of Jerusalem in 69 A.D. Since the 1512 inscription says the Jews came to China in Han, and the dates of later Han (25 to 220 A.D.) and the massacre correspond, such a view is not without logic.

But, says Chen Yuan, the Jews were slaughtered more than once, and Jerusalem was destroyed more than once. There is some reason in contending that on these occasions Jews migrated to Persia, Afghanistan and Central Asia, and from there to China, he maintains. Yet in more than one thousand years from Han to Yuan if there were long term settlements of Jews, why haven't they left a single trace of any person, event, or structure?

Chen Yuan queries: Why does the 1489 inscription place the transmission of the religion in Song, and not before? The claim that the Kaifeng Jews are descended from those who came to China in Han is not credible. It is possible that some Jews reached China even before Han, but the Kaifeng Jews could not possibly be descended from them. This would be like saying the (Roman Catholic) Christians in Yuan

*Cf. Pan Guandan, p. 67, this volume.

(1279–1368) were descendents of the Nestorian Christians who arrived in Tang (618–905). Or that Matteo Ricci and his brethren were descendants of the Christians who thrived for a time during Yuan.

During the Tang Dynasty travel between Europe and Asia gradually expanded. Nestorianism and Islam came to China, and the Jews followed. According to Arab traveller Aboul Zeyd al Hassan, during the Huangchao Rebellion toward the end of Tang (Chen Yuan sets the date at 879 A.D.), 120,000 Muslims, Jews, Christians, and Parsees were killed while in Guangzhou on business. A clear evidence of a Jewish presence in China during Tang. But they were here for commerce, and had come by sea. They were only temporary, not long term, residents. These are two different things.

See Pan Guangdan, p. 60–61 regarding dates and places of the "Guangzhou" massacre.

A number of facts prove the Jews could not have come to Kaifeng prior to Song. In his *Dongjing Ji (Glimpses of Dongjing*—meaning the Eastern Capital, another appellation for Kaifeng during the Song Dynasty before the move to the south), writer Song Mengqiu describes the temples then existing in the city, even including Ning Yuan Fang—a Persian Zoroastrian temple. But he makes no mention of any Israelite synagogue.

Zhang Bangji, in his *Mozhuang Man Lu (Casual Notes From Mozhuang)* also records the existence of the Zoroastrian Temple in the northern part of the city. But of an Israelite synagogue, he too says not a word.

In the Yong Zheng period (1723–1736) of Qing, Zhou Cheng of Jia Xing wrote a twenty-nine volume treatise on Kaifeng, the Eastern capital in Song times, based on over 390 items of information culled from Song sources. Not one of them mentions the Israelites. Nor is there any record confirming the statement in the 1489 inscription that the Israelites brought tribute of Western cloth in Song times, and that the emperor directed them to respect their ancestral customs and settle in Bianliang.

See Gao Wangzhi, p. 120. He also questions the authenticity of the "imperial pronouncement," allegedly made before the court moved south to Hangzhou. For the name of the emperor and an exact date of arrival in Northern Song, cf. Chen Changqi, p. 142.

This shows that no one can testify to their presence in Kaifeng during the Northern Song. As to the contention that they arrived before Song, we can definitely say this isn't so.

Cf. Gao Wangzhi regarding an arrival date, possibly in Tang. As to a lack of records concerning the first Jewish synagogue, it was built in 1163, by which time Kaifeng was in the hands of the Golden Tartars, or Jin. Events transpiring under an alien administration would not have been noted in Southern Song Chinese records.

After the Mongols conquered China and established the Yuan Dynasty (1279–1368) there were many mentions of Jews in the official records.

> In the *Yuan Shi Wen Zong Ji (Regarding Emperor Wen Zong in the History of the Yuan Dynasty)* it is noted that a decree was issued in 1331 stating that Buddhist monks, Taoist priests, Christian pastors, *Zhuhu,* and Muslim *mullahs* who engage in commerce shall pay the same taxes as they did before. *Zhuhu* means Jews. The *Yuan Shi Yu Jie (Explanation of Terms in the History of the Yuan Dynasty)* says *Zhuhu* is the same as *Zhuhe* (Jews).
>
> Yuan Dynasty Jews lived in a number of places. The *History* also notes a decree issued in 1354 requiring "All wealthy Muslims and *Zhuhu,* wherever they may be, to report to the capital for military service."

Zhuhu were also called *Zhuwu* and *Zhuhu.* This last has the same sound as the first *Zhuhu,* but is written in different Chinese characters.

> In 1340, *Shutuer,* the Imperial Censor recommended that ". . . Muslim mullahs, Arabs and *Zhuhu* be prohibited from marrying their brothers' widows."
>
> Yang Yu (Yuan Dynasty) wrote in his *Shan Ju Xin Hua (Fresh Comments From a Mountain Retreat):* "All the officials in the Hangzhou Sugar Bureau are rich *Zhuhu* and Muslims." *Zhuhu* and *Zhuwu* are the same. None of these terms appeared before Yuan.
>
> Marco Polo in his *Travels* says both Beijing and Hangzhou had many Jewish inhabitants. He was in China in 1279 when the synagogue was being rebuilt. The Jews had arrived not too long before then and had not yet adopted Chinese surnames. Marco Polo needed only one look to recognize them. It wasn't until after Yuan that the Jews gradually changed to Han names.
>
> In the early fifties of the 19th century a register of names in both Hebrew and Chinese was purchased in Kaifeng by a foreign missionary. The 1489 inscription states that Li, An, Ai, and others arrived during the Song Dynasty bringing a tribute of Western cloth, and that the *andula* began construction of the synagogue. These facts no doubt appear in the register and stand as clear evidence.

Actually, the register says nothing about the history of the Jews in Kaifeng. It seems to have been completed after the 1642 flood, and is a list of persons of earlier generations. The name An does not appear at all, possibly because An Cheng, the physician, was permitted by imperial decree to change his family name to Zhao in 1423, and the name An was abandoned. Chen Yuan obviously never saw the register.

> When the Jews first came they still had clan names, but between Yuan and Ming they changed to Chinese names. An Dula, who built the synagogue in Song, must have been a Jewish name.

Chen Yuan assumes this to be the name of a person. Had he seen the Zhao clan tablet of 1679 he would have noted that ". . . our *andula* who built the synagogue was appointed a Major of the Brocaded Robe Security Corps . . ." This could only have referred to Physician An Cheng who, according to the 1489 inscription, received that honor and was also permitted to change his family name to Zhao, a Han Chinese surname. *Andula* was therefore a designation, such as supervisor. Another suggestion is that the word may come from the Persian *adela,* meaning righteous man. In any event, whatever its derivation, it had no connection with the family name An. By Ming, says Chen Yuan, many Jews had adopted Chinese names.

> In 1423 An Cheng the physician was, by imperial decree, permitted to change his family name to Zhao, after which the name An was seen only rarely. An, Li, and Gao are written in the 1512 inscription—just the surnames, no given names—and these persons are not emphasized. From this we can see evidences of the transition to Chinese names of the Kaifeng Jews.
> Let's look at the name Li. There were a great many Li's at the beginning of Ming. The position of High Priest, or Chief Rabbi, had always been held by a member of the *Liewei* (Levi) clan. Rabbi *Liewei,* referred to in the 1489 inscription as heading the Israelite religious order when the synagogue was first built in 1163, was such a person. *Liewei* is today translated in Chinese as Li Wei. Of the fourteen *manla*s at the start of the Ming, nine were of the Li clan. In the 17th century repair of the flood-damaged scriptures was entrusted to a Rabbi Li. Li was the Han Chinese family name chosen by the Levi clan at the beginning of Ming.
> The circumstances, the persons involved, and the pronunciation of the names, prove that the adoption of Chinese names could not have occurred too long after the Jews settled in Kaifeng.

Chen Yuan notes that the term *Yicileye,* meaning Israelite, was first used in the middle of Ming. *Rudeya,* or Judea, appeared at the end of

Ming and the beginning of Qing. *Yutai* was used for Jew only after 1821. *Zhuhu* we find in Yuan. He points out that in *Yuan Shi Yi Wen Zheng Bu (Annotations to the Chinese Translation of the Yuan Annals)* by Hong Jun, published in 1897, it says the term *Wotuo* in the Yuan Dynasty *Jing Shi Da Dian (Administrative Code)* means Jews. The word also appears in the new compilations of the *Yuan Shi Zu Ji (Yuan Imperial Annals)* and the *Yuan Dian Zhang (Yuan Laws and Regulations)*. But whether the *Wotuo* were Jews is not clear, says Chen Yuan. Certainly the term was unheard of before Yuan.

> By early Song (10th century) the Jewish homeland had been occupied by the Arab Muslims for over 300 years. After the Arabs came the Turks, and this gave rise to the Crusades (11th to 13th centuries). Most of the Jews had migrated by then. Their permanent residence in China began in Song.
>
> No one can say whether they came by land or by sea. Both the 1489 and the 1512 inscriptions state they came from Tianzhu. An examination of their scriptures, in page rather than scroll form, reveals Persian type Hebrew letters on apparently Persian-made silk paper. Both Ningbo and Weiyang (Yangzhou) have such scriptures.
>
> Sea routes between East and West were open during Song. The Jews probably came with the Persian merchants from the Persian Gulf, across the Indian Ocean, to the various provinces of southeast China.
>
> Some Westerners say customs in Henan and Jiangsu provinces are very similar to those of the Jews. For example, local marriage ceremonies, and the prohibition against weaving wool and flax together.

Xia Nai, Director of China's Institute of Archeology, says the latter more likely was a conservative peasant reaction against anything new. Local people used cotton padding, or silk floss if they were rich, to keep warm. Wool is not a product of those parts. Coming from the Northwest, it was literally "outlandish," and therefore unpopular.

> In Xuzhou, Jiangsu Province, there is an "Adam and Eve Temple" which seems to be connected with the Jews.

For months, I tried in vain to track this story down. No one ever heard of such a temple. Recently, by chance, I met a Xuzhou scholar, and asked him about the "*Yadan* and *Xiawa* Temple." "*Xiawa*" is the Chinese transliteration of the Hebrew word for Eve. He puzzled over this a moment, then laughed. Xuzhou has no "*Yadan* and *Xiawa* Temple," but it does have the site of what had been called "Xia Wang Miao," meaning the Temple of the King of Xia. Yu the Great, first king of the ancient Xia Dynasty, who reigned some 4000 years ago, is reputed to have regulated the floods. He was subsequently defied as a god of harvests. Evidently a mispronunciation of "Xia Wang" was heard by someone familiar with the Chinese language Bible as "Xia Wa," or Eve, and thus the error spread.

Chen Yuan finds persuasive the statement in the 1489 inscription that the Kaifeng Jews brought tribute of Western cloth. He considers this substantial evidence that they came by sea. By then there was sea trade in cotton cloth from India, which China did not yet produce.

After the Arabs conquered Palestine, in 636 A.D., the Jews scattered throughout Central Asia and India. There were many of them in both areas, says Chen Yuan. The Jin family, prominent for generations in Ningxia, which abuts Central Asia, say they came along the road skirting the southern foothills of the Tian Mountains. This was the branch of the Silk Road which traversed the Middle East and India. Chen Yuan agrees that such land travel was also possible.

V. DIFFERENCES FROM AND SIMILARITIES WITH ISLAM, AND HOW THE NAME SINEW-PLUCKING RELIGION ORIGINATED

Chen Yuan says that though Judaism and Islam are different, the Chinese often confused them. The problem was in appearances. The Muslim mosque was called Qing Zhen, or Purity and Truth. So was the Israelite synagogue. For this reason, the composer of the 1512 inscription avoided using the term.

While very different from the Han Chinese, the Kaifeng Jews were similar to the Muslims in many ways. Both believed in one God, both had a weekly day of rest. The Muslims prayed five times a day, the Israelites three. Both practised circumcision, both abstained from pork. The Muslims call their literate men *mullah,* the Israelites called those well-versed in the Torah *manla*—the Chinese pronunciation of the same word. The 1512 inscription lists as Israelite forebears Adam, Noah, Abraham, Isaac, Jacob and Moses—and the Muslims name the same men as their patriarchs. No wonder those outside these religions are confused.

The people of Kaifeng called the Israelites "Lan Hui Hui" ("Blue Muslims"), or "Lan Mao Hui Hui" ("Blue Hat Muslims"), because for their religious ceremonies they wore blue turbans and boots, as distinguished from the Muslims who wore white.

"Hui Hui" in Tang times meant Arab or Persian believers in Islam. By Yuan the term embraced all "se mu ren," that is "people with colored eyes" from the "Western Regions"—Central and Western Asia—including Jews.

In a decree dated 1280 in the *Yuan Dian Zhang (Yuan Dynasty Laws and Regulations)* Kublai Khan prohibited the ritual slaughter of sheep by "*Muhu (Zhuhu)* Hui Hui" ("Jewish Hui Hui") and "*Musuluman* Hui Hui" ("Muslim Hui Hui").

Another general term was "*Bosi* ren," or "Persians." This too was loosely applied to all "persons with colored eyes" from the "Western Regions." To the Chinese it meant not only Persians, but Arabs and Jews as well.

As early as Song, Ningbo had a *Bosi* Xiang, or Persian Street, on which stood a *Bosi* Tuan, or Persian Hotel, which was, in fact, a residence for all foreigners from the West. Jews by then had been living in Persia and Arabia for centuries, and must have been quite assimilated racially. Some came, no doubt, with the other Persian and Arab merchants seeking China trade.

The Hotel is long since gone, but the street, which I visited in 1982, remains. It is known today as Che Jiao Jie, Nan Xiang (Cart and Sedan Chair Street, Southern Lane). See "Ningbo Gang Kao Lue" ("Notes on the Port of Ningbo") by Yuan Yuanlong and Hong Keyao in *Hai Jino Shi Yanjiu (Studies in the History of Sea Traffic),* an annual magazine, 1981, Fujian. Says Chen Yuan:

> Both Islam and Judaism have a common origin, though they developed differently. The Israelite faith is much older. After the rise of Islam, the sons of the Kingdom of Israel were conquered time and again. The *Zhuhude* referred to in the Koran were in fact the Judeans, or Israelites.

Chen Yuan repeats the famous biblical story, found in Isaiah, of how Jacob sustained an injury to a thigh sinew while wrestling with an angel, and was named Israel. To commemorate the event, says Chen Yuan, the Israelites extract the sinews of the cattle and sheep they slaughter.

> Kaifeng Israelites, after a thousand years in China, still maintained this custom. It is said that originally there was a courtyard on the north side of the temple building where the sinews were extracted. The name Sinew-Plucking Religion was given by the locals to distinguish it from the Muslim faith. The Jews did not eat pork, and earned their living mainly as butchers of cattle and sheep.
>
> They lived among the Muslims of Kaifeng and did not intermarry with the Hans. In later years, however, they took Muslim brides.
>
> Their families were badly off financially. For a long time they

had no rabbis or *manla*s. In order to be able to hear scriptures and pray, many joined Islam. But they were not really the same as the Muslims.

VI. A SUMMARY OF IMPORTANT FIGURES

Here Chen Yuan lists Jews who rose to positions of prominence and power. They were not identified as Jews when their names appeared in official records prior to Ming (1368–1644) or after the Kang Xi period (1662–1723) of the Qing Dynasty. He gives as examples Zuo Tang who was noted in the Weiyang *Gazette* for the Jia Jing period (1522–1567), and Zhao Yingcheng, who is mentioned in the Fujian *Gazette* for the Dao Guang period (1821–1851), but says no one would have known they were Israelites were it not for the appearance of their names on the two Kaifeng tablets as well. Today, he adds, we can search out Jews in the Xiangfu *Gazette*—Xiangfu is the county in which Kaifeng is located—by checking names against those inscribed on the tablets. Otherwise, all we would know is that they were residents of Kaifeng.

The gazettes were records kept by local governments, from county up to province, and included everything from small town news, to weather, to events of local importance. They have proved to be valuable sources of historical information.

Chen Yuan quotes the 1512 inscription to the effect that some of the Israelites took the imperial examinations and earned glory for their families and themselves; some, within and outside the royal court, benefitted the sovereign and the people; some, in defeating enemy aggression, proved their utmost loyalty to the nation; others, by their high moral qualities, were models for the entire countryside; while artisans for their skill, and merchants for their diligence, were famed far and wide.

Followers of the religion were not limited to Kaifeng, Chen Yuan points out. Obviously, by mid-Ming the Israelites were thriving. Unfortunately, the tablets were unable to list each and every one of them, and no one composed a compendium of prominent Israelites. Future historians will not have much to go by, he says, and so, with the tablets as his source, he makes the following summary:

> The Li's were the most flourishing Chinese Israelite family at the beginning of Ming. Well-versed in the Scriptures, and able to read Hebrew, nine of them were *manla*s (rabbis).
>
> Li Jung helped repair the synagogue in both the Zheng Tong (1436–1450) and the Tian Shun (1457–1465) periods, and contributed a large sum of money. He was active in bringing a Torah scroll from Ningbo during the Tian Shun period. An extremely able man, he lived a long life.

When the flood destroyed the Scriptures in 1642, Chief Rabbi Li Zhen, in collaboration with *Manla* Li Chengxian, collated and restored the damaged scrolls. A record of the Li family still exists after hundreds of years.

Aside from the rabbis and the *manla*s, the Li family also had scholars such as Li Fatian, Li Chengjun, Li Hui and Li Yuxiu. All were active in synagogue affairs at the beginning of Qing.

The Li family were leaders, both among the clans listed in the 1489 inscription and the seven clans listed on the 1663 tablet. In the previous chapter I stated that Li was the Han Chinese name adopted by the *Liewei* (Levi) Israelites.

Secondly, there was the Ai family. Two of them were *manla*s— Ai Duan and Ai Jing. There was also Ai Jun, who passed the provincial examination with the grade of Ju Ren in 1447. Ai Jun was named Chief Secretary of the Prince of Dezhou Prefecture.

Ai Tian, who also qualified as a Ju Ren, was appointed a county magistrate. Matteo Ricci noted that people from the land of Judea practised the ancient Heavenly Religion in a temple in the capital of Henan province, meaning Kaifeng, and that one of their number, a scholar named Ai, visited him in the capital Beijing. Ricci showed him the Bible—both the Old and the New Testaments— written in Hebrew, with a Western language translation appended. Ai was able to chant some of the Scriptures, and was very happy to see this Bible. Scholar Ai was, of course, Ai Tian, who could recite the Scriptures, although he couldn't read Hebrew.

Toward the end of the Dao Guang period (1821–1851) a Westerner copying wooden tablets in the synagogue came across a couplet composed in Chinese by Ai Tian, which his grandson Ai Xiansheng had re-engraved on a new tablet.

Ai Tian's son Ai Yinggui is included in the Xiangfu *Gazette* for the Qian Long period (1736–1796). He was a member of the literati and a fine doctor. Excellent at taking pulses, he could cure many ailments.

Xiansheng followed in his father's footsteps and also became a physician. His younger brother Dasheng was a *manla* in the synagogue. Another brother, Fusheng—there were five in all—in 1688 composed many couplets which were hung in the synagogue.

Also listed in the Xiangfu *Gazette* is Ai Shide. When he was still young, an official banner of honor was flown at his door because he returned money he had found to its original owner. He is mentioned on the reverse side of the 1663 tablet, along with several other Ai's who contributed to the synagogue's reconstruction.

Next, there was the Zhao family. In early Ming they were not particularly prominent, but in the Tian Shun period (1457–1465) Zhao Ying of Ningbo presented a Torah scroll to the synagogue in Kaifeng. Earlier, in 1423, the Israelite physician An Cheng was permitted by royal decree to change his family name to Zhao, was designated a Major of the Brocaded Robe Security Corps, and was subsequently appointed Lieutenant Governor of the Military Area of Zhejiang Province. It is impossible to say whether Zhao Ying was his descendant (although Ningbo is a city in Zhejiang Province).

The Zhao family achieved considerable fame in early Qing. Zhao Yingcheng scored a Jin shi grade in the imperial examinations in 1646. He is mentioned in both the revised edition of the Henan *Gazette* and in the 1829 Fujian *Gazette.* I have his original examination papers in my possession. He was only twenty-eight when he sat for the Imperial Examinations in 1647 and qualified as a Jin Shi, having already become a Ju Ren in the 1645 tests. He was born in 1619, and so was forty-four at the time of the 1663 tablet.

In 1650, when he was Secretary of the Board of Punishments, he was sent to the Zhang Nan Circuit of Fujian Province to serve as Investigating Judge. When the people heard lessons being recited in schools again after years of strife, it was as if the stars had emerged again amid happy clouds.

Zhao Yingcheng put down local Fujian bandits who were exploiting eight ethnic tribes, built schools for the populace, and settled long-pending criminal cases.

On returning to Kaifeng to mourn the death of his mother, he contributed generously to the restoration of the synagogue and the damaged Torahs. It was then he wrote the *Sheng Jing Ji Bian Ji (History of the Holy Scriptures)* to record the events of his day.

I have recently discovered that Zhao Yingcheng also wrote a book in 240 sections entitled *Si Zhu Tang Ji Wei (The Hall of the Four Bamboos Record of Wonders).* Although there is no mention of it in the Kaifeng *Gazette* of the Shun Zhi period (1644–1662), it is noted in the supplement to the section on literature and art in the Kaifeng *Gazette* of 1739. A work of that size should not have vanished quickly. Why wasn't it listed in the Qian Long *Encyclopedia* published only fifty years later? Perhaps some old Kaifeng family still has a copy. It would be good to get hold of it, since it should have evidence of the origins of the Kaifeng Jews. We could add this to the already existing Chinese material.

Early in the Kang Xi period (1662–1723) Zhao Yingcheng was

assigned to head the Hunan-Hubei provincial Flood Prevention Bureau. He subsequently died in office.

His younger brother Zhao Yingdou was a county magistrate in Yunnan Province. He contributed to the repair of the synagogue, and wrote a book of ten chapters entitled *Ming Dao Xu (An Introduction to an Understanding of the Way)* and composed several of the synagogue couplets.

Brother Zhao Yinggun qualified in the local examinations.

Another brother, Zhao Yingfu, died young. But his wife gained fame by not remarrying for the remaining forty-odd years of her life. This deed was recorded in the Xiangfu *Gazette*.

In feudal male chauvinist China there was no onus attached to the man who married again after the death of his wife.

The father of these men, Zhao Guanyu, because two of his sons had become officials, was given the same titles. He contributed the plaque hung on the entry arch in front of the synagogue.

Zhao Chengji was Defence Commander of the Kaifeng Area and formerly a field officer in Guyuan County in Shaanxi Province. In early Qing he was the main organizer in the restoration of the synagogue. It was he who invited Liu Chang to compose the inscription for the 1663 tablet.

Then there was the Jin family. Though not very numerous, they were the most widely spread. In the late 15th century the two brothers Jin Xuan and Jin Ying, both of Ningxia, were patrons of the restoration of the temple. One of their ancestors had been Court President of State Banquets, and their great-uncle had commanded a battalion of advance guards.

The Xiangfu *Gazette* mentions Jin Zhong and Jin Li. Jin Zhong, who qualified in his local examinations, was the composer of the 1489 inscription. Jin Li was one of the patrons of the tablet.

During the Zheng De period (1506–1522) Jin Run of Ningxia erected the kiosk which housed it. Jin Pu of Weiyang (Yangzhou) presented the synagogue with a Torah scroll and built the Second Gateway.

Thus, Ningxia, Kaifeng and Weiyang all had Israelites named Jin. In early Qing a Jin Zhifeng erected a Wan Sui alcove. Jin Yingxuan, along with others in the clan, repaired a portion of the Torah scrolls.

The alcove was a special pavilion inside the synagogue building containing a tablet wishing "Wan Sui" ("Long life") to the emperor.

Clearly, the Jin family was still in existence at the beginning of the Qing Dynasty.

Editor Jin Xiaojing only recently discovered that her family is of Jewish descent. See her article "I Am a Chinese Jew" in the quarterly *Bai Ke Jishi (Universal Knowledge)*, IV of 1981.

And finally there were the Gaos. Gao Nian, who qualified as a Gong Sheng in the Xuan De period (1426–1436), was appointed a magistrate of Qixian county in Huizhou prefecture, Anhui province, during the Zheng Tong period (1436–1450). In the Tian Shun period (1457–1465) Gao Jian fetched a Torah scroll from Ningbo. Gao Rui and Gao Hong, during the Cheng Hua period (1465–1488), contributed funds for the construction of a Hall of Scriptures.

When a flood destroyed the synagogue in 1642 and the congregation fled to the opposite side of the river, Academy graduate Gao Xuan, at the urging of his father Gao Dongdou, made repeated trips across the river to the wrecked synagogue and rescued several Torah scrolls. This provided reliable material for the repairing and collating—an admirable achievement.

There were also the brothers Gao Weiping, an Imperial Academy graduate, and Gao Dengkui. Both supervised the rebuilding of the synagogue from start to finish.

Chen Yuan sums up by saying that seventeen surnames are mentioned in the three inscriptions. These include fourteen different persons named Li and fourteen named Ai. Ten different Zhao's are listed, nine persons named Gao, eight named Jin, three each named An and Zhang, two named Shi, and one each named Zuo and Zhou. Zuo was Zuo Tang, composer of the 1512 inscription. There were no further references to the names Mu, Huang, Nie and Bai, after their first appearance among the seventeen in the 1489 inscription. In the 1663 inscription only seven clan names appear—Li, Zhao, Ai, Zhang, Gao, Jin and Shi.

VII. SUCCESSIVE CHANGES IN THE SYNAGOGUE AND ITS CONDITION AT THE END OF THE KANG XI PERIOD

Chen Yuan notes that the synagogue was first constructed during the Jin Dynasty (1115–1234), when the Golden Tartars ruled over northern China. It was rebuilt in Yuan (1279–1368), and again in Ming (1368–1644)—a total existence, by Qing, of some five hundred years. It was restored ten times. This was mainly necessitated by floods, but it was also connected with the advance and decline of the religion. Chen Yuan enumerates:

The first synagogue was erected in 1163 in Kaifeng, under the Jin Dynasty of the Golden Tartars. It was first rebuilt during the reign of Yuan emperor Kublai Khan in 1279. The tablet above the portal read: "Gu Cha Qing Zhen Si" ("Ancient Temple Synagogue of Purity and Truth").

The next reconstruction was in 1421, under the sponsorship of the Prince of Zhou, posthumously called Ding. The prince, who was generally known as Zhu Su, was the younger brother of Ming emperor Chen Zu. During the Hong Wu period (1368–1399) the prince was appointed Governor of Kaifeng prefecture. He had considerable medical knowledge and compiled two treatises: *Jin Huang Ben Cao (Materia Medica for Epidemic Diseases)* in eight sections, and *Pu Ji Fang (Prescriptions for Common Ailments)* in 426 sections.

Accused of plotting treason, he was summoned to the capital, then in Peking, in 1421, where he was confronted with the evidence. The prince bowed his head and requested the death penalty. But the emperor took pity on him and dropped the charge. The prince returned to Kaifeng and gave up his three guards divisions.

He directed that Israelite physician An Cheng be presented with ceremonial incense (money) and be permitted to repair the synagogue. A tablet was erected inside wishing Long Life to the Emperor of the Great Ming Dynasty.

I don't know what An Cheng did to earn the prince's favor. But the Israelite was an established physician, and he undoubtedly helped with the compilation of the *Prescriptions For Common Ailments.*

Fang Chaoying, a Chinese-American Sinologist, disputes this version of the events, and is in turn refuted by a historian in the Chinese Academy of Social Sciences. See the article by Li Jixian later in this volume.

The third rebuilding was in 1445. The fourth was in 1461 after a flood. The fifth was in the Cheng Hua period (1465–1488) when a Hall of Scriptures was added. The sixth was in 1489, which was the time of the first inscription. The seventh was in 1512, and the eighth in 1663, for both of which there were inscriptions.

The synagogue was rebuilt for the ninth time in 1679. A foreign missionary discovered a badly defaced stone tablet in the synagogue compound (at the end of the 19th century). It was entitled "Ci Tang Shu Gu Pai Ji" ("A Tablet Record of the Ancient History of our Ancestral Hall"), and told how the Zhao family rebuilt the Purity and Truth Synagogue. The date of the tablet, 1679, is still decipherable, and this coincides with what the wooden tablets and couplets inside the synagogue indicate as the time the synagogue was restored.

The tenth and final rebuilding was in 1688, a fact attested to by many new vertical plaques.

Chen Yuan relates the findings of Portuguese Jesuit missionary Gozani, who went to Kaifeng in 1702. Gozani reported the presence of a Jewish synagogue, restored under a permit from the Henan provincial government, and a congregation of two or three thousand who described themselves as members of the Sinew-Plucking Religion. On every Sabbath they chanted and prayed in their temple. They still practised circumcision, and observed Passover and the Feast of the Tabernacles.

Gozani stated that in the center of the temple was a tablet wishing Long Life to the Emperor, with plaques in Hebrew on either side. The one on the left said: "Hear, O Israel, your God Jehovah is the only God." The one on the right said: "Your God Jehovah is the Master of all spirits and the King of Kings, a great and mighty and terrible God."

In front of the Emperor's Tablet was a tall chair called the Chair of Moses. On it was an embroidered cushion on which the rabbi rested the scrolls when reciting the Torah. In the middle of the synagogue the Torah scrolls were kept, as well as the books of the prophets Malachi and Zechariah.

Chen Yuan acknowledges that the sketches of the interior and exterior of the synagogue, made by French Jesuit missionary Domenge in 1722 were of great help to him. He knew from the 1663 tablet that there had been a Hall of Patriarchs, a Hall of Sages, an Ark of the Scriptures, a North Lecture Hall, a South Lecture Hall, ancestral halls, and dwellings, but had been unable to figure out their exact location. Domenge's drawings made everything clear. Chen Yuan proceeds, based on this information, to describe the synagogue layout in the 17th and 18th centuries.

> The synagogue compound was about four hundred feet in depth and a hundred and fifty feet wide, and faced east, surrounded by an enclosure wall. (The worshippers faced west, in the direction of Jerusalem.) Entering the compound through the east street door, the visitor first saw a large memorial arch on which was hung a board reading: "Venerate Heaven and Bless the Country." This led to the Main Gateway.
>
> Flanking the Gateway were decorated walls, and beyond it was the Second Gateway, which provided entry to a large courtyard. In the middle of this was another memorial arch, with kiosks to left and right housing the tablets—the 1489/1512 tablet to the

right, the 1663 tablet to the left. On both sides of the courtyard were doors leading to ancestral halls and dwellings.

Behind the kiosks were stone lions and a bronze incense burner. These were part of the approach to the Front Hall. Between them and the building itself was an imposing Moon Terrace enclosed by a stone balustrade. On either side of the courtyard were the North Lecture Hall and the South Lecture Hall. West of the North Lecture Hall was the Kitchen.

Left and right of the Front Hall, also facing east, were the Hall of the Patriarchs and the Hall of the Sages. Behind the Front Hall was an esplanade leading to the Rear Hall. The Front Hall, where the religious services were conducted, was sixty feet in depth and had windows on either side. Immediately inside the doorway was a ceremonial table and candlesticks. Beside it was a drain for washing the hands. Next was the Chair of Moses on a raised dais. Then came the Dragon Pavilion, housing the Long Life to the Emperor plaque.

Behind this, and deepest into the synagogue, was the Ark of the Scriptures, which contained, when the drawings were made, one of the most ancient Torah scrolls, newly repaired. Beautiful drapes screened the Ark. On either side were racks of twelve tabernacles for housing Torah scrolls—still being repaired.

On the walls to left and right, written in letters of gold, were the Ten Commandments given to Moses. The ceiling of the building had a latticed dome.

This was the situation in the early years of the Kang Xi period.

In the Xiangfu *Gazette* for 1739, Chen Yuan discovered an old city map showing a Synagogue of Purity and Truth west of the Tong Yue Buddhist Temple. The map is a copy of an earlier one which appeared in the *Gazette* of 1661. It showed the synagogue, then newly repaired.

It had been built southeast of a crossroads called Tu Shizi Jie (Local Products Market) in early Yuan (13th century). In the mid-19th century the lane leading to the synagogue was named Tiao Jin Jiao (Sinew Plucking Religion) Lane. But in the 1920's the Kaifeng Police Department thought the name was too undignified, and changed it to Jiao Jing (Scripture Teaching) Lane.*

VIII. ORIGIN OF THE SCRIPTURES AND THEIR PRESENT LOCATION

Chen Yuan notes the reference in the 1489 inscription to a Torah of 53 chapters, namely, the Five Books of Moses. The first of these was

*Cf. Pan Guandan, footnote, p. 50, this volume.

Genesis, which Moses compiled, dealing with the earliest times. Then came Exodus, Leviticus, Numbers and Deuteronomy, all received by Moses in a revelation from God. This was some time between the 18th and 13th centuries B.C., says Chen Yuan. Moses ordered the High Priests of the Jews to place these Scriptures beside a holy cabinet and recite from them on every Sabbath to the people of Israel.

Their descendants divided the Torah into 54 chapters. One to twelve comprised Genesis. Exodus was thirten to twenty-three. Leviticus was twenty-four to thirty-three. Numbers was thirty-four to forty-three. Deuteronomy was forty-four to fifty-four. But in the 1489 inscription it says fifty-three, Chen Yuan observes. Why was the chapter division different?

Persian bibles had 53 chapters as against the European 54. Some scholars believe this is an indication of the Persian origin of the Kaifeng Jews. Chen Yuan continues his review of the Kaifeng Torahs.

Kaifeng had only one Torah scroll in its synagogue prior to the Tian Shun (1457–1465) period of Ming. But during that period, Shi Bin, Li Rong, Gao Jian and Zhang Xuan went to Ningbo and brought another. Zhao Ying, of that same city, also delivered one. That made three.

During the Cheng Hua period (1465–1488) the Rear Hall was built and became a Torah repository. Jin Bo of Weiyang (Yangzhou) presented a fourth scroll in the Zheng De period (1506–1522). All of this information is contained in the 1512 inscription. Both Jin Bo and Zuo Tang, who composed the text, are from Yangzhou.

After the Zheng De period the religion flourished, and the Scriptures increased from four to thirteen scrolls, a sign of how the congregation also grew.

Then came the flood of 1642, and the Torah scrolls were immersed in the waters. Gao Xuan retrieved seven of them, and Li Cheng recovered another three, but they were very blurred. Thanks to the efforts of Chief Rabbi Li Zhen and *Manla* Li Chengxian, three scrolls were collated and restored.

Later, the families of Ai, Zhao and Gao repaired two more each, and the Jin, Shi, Li and Zhang families each repaired one. Thus, all thirteen scrolls were returned to their original condition.

Although the 1663 tablet speaks of 13 Torah scrolls, today we can account only for the 10 bought by Europeans and Americans. There are still another three. Has someone else bought them? Are they still in Kaifeng? Were they destroyed in a later flood? Only future investigations can supply the answer.

IX. THE SQUARE PAGE SCRIPTURES AND THE MISCELLANEOUS WRITINGS

The 1663 tablet states that the synagogue had several dozen sets of what it calls Square Scriptures and Miscellaneous Writings, says Chen Yuan. These were not mentioned in either of the two previous inscriptions. In general they were religious laws, doctrines, rites, and prayers, as well as Jewish calendars, holy days, and a genealogical record of Kaifeng Jews. None of these were really scriptures, but were called that because they were passed on and reverently chanted and preserved.

> Both the Torahs and the Miscellaneous Writings were inscribed on parchment in ancient scroll style. They were wound around sticks at either end, with handles top and bottom to facilitate rolling.
>
> The Square Scriptures were bound volumes of heavy paper, much the same as books today. Most were ruined by the flood of 1642, and even those which survived were too badly mildewed for use.
>
> But the Torahs and the Miscellaneous Writings were not all swept away. Because they were of more durable material, namely parchment, it was possible to collect some and restore them.

When Gao Xuan returned to the synagogue after the 1642 flood he was able to rescue seven Torah scrolls and 26 scrolls of Miscellaneous Writings, Chen Yuan adds. Li Chengjun managed to save another three Torah scrolls. But nothing has been said of bringing back any of the Square Scriptures, for the reasons given above.

Later on, not only were 13 scrolls of the Torah repaired, but some of the Square Scriptures and Miscellaneous Writings were also gradually restored to their original condition.

> The genealogical record of deceased Kaifeng Jews is a scroll divided into male and female sections. The names are written in Hebrew. Many have Chinese names appended as well. At the end of the scroll is a prayer: "May God protect those named here and allow them to ascend to Heaven and sit with the Seven Sages." These are Abraham, Isaac, Jacob, Moses, Aaron, Elijah, and Elisha.
>
> Included in the religious rites were services performed in the synagogue, ceremonies conducted during holy days, and various prayer ceremonies. There was also a Jewish calendar scroll, and another dealing with ceremonies and prayers for Purim. There were also prayers for every day.

Purim celebrates the saving of the Jews in the fifth century B.C. by Esther, Jewish queen of King Ahasueras (Hebrew form of Xerxes) of Persia, from persecution by Haman, the prime minister.

The compilers of the Miscellaneous Writings were devout men, says Chen Yuan. Each scroll ends with the statement that it has been worshipfully recorded, and gives the name of the scribe.

Although a few items of information which Chen Yuan used were inaccurate or incomplete, and while he apparently never visited any of the places which formerly hosted Jewish communities, his treatise, over-all, is excellent. The first comprehensive Chinese survey of Jews in ancient China, it exercised a profound influence on later research.

Pan Guangdan

JEWS IN ANCIENT CHINA—A HISTORICAL SURVEY, 1953, REVISED 1983

Born in 1899, Pan Guandan was a professor at the Central Institute of Nationalities when he died in 1967. After taking his Master's degree at Columbia University in 1926, he taught at Beijing's Tsinghua University and the Southwest Associated University in Kunming. His books include *Problems of Chinese Families* and *Principles of Eugenics.*

Pan specialized in studies of Jews in ancient China, particularly Kaifeng. During his lifetime he wrote articles in excess of 100,000 Chinese characters on the subject. He condensed these into a book of roughly 50,000 characters, plus a lengthy bibliography, with comments, in 1953. But it was not until 30 years later, in 1983, that Beijing University Press finally published Pan's *Zhonggue Jing Nei Youtairen de Ruogan Lishi Wenti (Jews in Ancient China—a Historical Survey).*

It consists of six chapters, dealing mainly with the Jews of Kaifeng. But it also discusses Jews in other parts of China, and explores such questions as when they left their homeland, the routes they followed, and the dates of their arrival.

An introduction by Wu Zelin analyzes the reasons for the assimilation of the Chinese Jews, as contrasted to their survival as communities in other countries. We present it as a separate article elsewhere in this book.

Here, then, is Pan's comprehensive treatment. The numbers in parrentheses refer to bibliographical sources listed at the end of this section.

I. NAMES OF THE RACE AND THE RELIGION

In his introductory remarks Pan tells us of a Jewish colony in Kaifeng, the capital of Henan province in south-central China. Over

46

the centuries the Jews there ranged in number from the hundreds to the thousands, he says, though only one or two hundred remain today. Like Jews in other parts of the world they stem from the same race and same religion. Pan asserts that, generally speaking, all members of the Jewish race believe in Judaism, and all who practise Judaism are members of the Jewish race.

The question "Who is a Jew?" is still being widely debated in the West. But few would contend, whatever their opinions, that the Jews, after centuries of dispersal and assimilation in many different countries, are members of a single race. Pan is on surer ground when he talks of terminology. He says:

> The word "Jew" came into being relatively late, particularly in China, where it was transliterated as *Youtai*. The Jews living in Kaifeng probably left their homeland—Palestine in Western Asia—very early. Even by the end of Ming (1368–1644) they still had never heard the word *Youtai*. They did not know they were *Youtai*, or that their religion was *Youtai Jiao*, the current term for Judaism (49, 87). They were known by various other names. Some were of their own choosing. Some were imposed by others, but came to be accepted with the passage of time. Still others they did not accept, or flatly rejected.

They did not know *Youtai*, a Chinese word for Jew, until it was introduced by the Jesuits in the 17th century, but they certainly knew they were Jews. *The Book of Esther*, which they possessed, uses *Yehudi*, the Hebrew word for Jew, repeatedly. See Pan p. 88. They also knew the Chinese renditions of the Arabic Djuhud, such as *Zhuhu*, used in 14th-century Yuan records. See Pan, p. 52. Pan lists five terms in the first category, of their own choosing:

> 1. *Yicileye,* that is, Israelites. This is the most ancient and most formal term. It was used in at least three of the four inscriptions on stone tablets passed down through the generations by the Kaifeng Jews (6, 7, 14). I say "at least" because the fourth (15) is so badly defaced that many words cannot be distinguished.
>
> The first inscription, dated 1489, opens with the words: "The founder of the Israelite religion was Abraham, a 19th-generation descendant of Pangu/Adam" (6). The second, dated 1512, also starts with a reference to the Israelites. And the first sentence of the third inscription, dated 1663, reads: "The Israelite religion was established in the distant past." As late as the mid-19th century Kaifeng Jews told visitors they always used the term "Israelite" when talking about their synagogue, although they hadn't written it on the entrance plaque.

Pan goes into a detailed recital of how Jacob was given the name Israel by the angel he wrestled with, how all of his descendants were thereafter known by that name, and how, shortly before the ninth century B.C. it became the name of their country. In China, right up to the latter half of the fifteenth century, says Pan, it was also used as the term for their religion.

He scoffs at those who tried to find significance in the Chinese rendition of the word.

> *Yicileye* is simply a transliteration, a combination of characters which happen to be readable sequentially as a phrase. Foreigners who visited Kaifeng, although they knew this perfectly well, stressed the meaning of the characters and went into elaborate gyrations to transform them into a Western phrase. They said *Yi* (one), meaning "God," plus *ci* (bestow) equals "Bestowed by God," etc., etc. (93, 102).

Pan goes on to other appellations which the Jews themselves chose.

> 2. Gu Jiao, that is, the Ancient Religion. A Catholic Jesuit visiting Kaifeng in 1704 was told by the Jews that they formerly used this term (53). Gu (ancient) and jiu (old) are similar in meaning, and so some people used the term Jiu Jiao (78, 220). The Israelite religion is of ancient origin. The 1489 inscription refers to the "Ancient Temple Synagogue of Purity and Truth" (6). We believe the term Ancient Religion was one used by the Jews themselves. The Old Religion was a misnomer applied by others. It was rejected by the Jews and never became an accepted term.
>
> 3. Hui Hui Gu Jiao, that is, the Ancient Hui Hui Religion. This name was reported by a Protestant missionary, William C. Milne, in the mid-19th century (98). Like the term Gu Jiao, mentioned above, I believe this name was also chosen by the Kaifeng Jews themselves. Their aim was to distinguish themselves from the Hui Hui believers in Islam who lived all around them. They added Ancient to the term Hui Hui to emphasize that their religion was much older than the relatively "new" religion of Islam, which was partly derived from Judaism.

See also Chen Yuan, p. 33 and 34, this volume.

> 4. Tian Jiao, or, the Heavenly Religion. Also reported in the early 18th century by the Catholic Jesuit mentioned above. Its use was not widespread.
>
> 5. Tian Zhu Jiao, or, the Indian Religion. This term was not seen in Chinese documents until after the mid-19th century. The Jews told visitors they used this term prior to the adoption of the

appellation Tiao Jin Jiao, meaning the Sinew Plucking Religion. American Missionary W. A. P. Martin who visited Kaifeng in 1866 speculated on the reason for the change (102). He said the Jews stopped in India for a time during their migration to China from the West, and adopted the name Indian Religion to commemorate this period. Later, the Roman Catholics came to China in large number. They also called their religion Tian Zhu Jiao, meaning Religion of the Lord God. Although the "Zhu" is written differently [i.e. different characters] it is pronounced the same. Because of the confusion this caused, the Jews acceded to their religion being called Tiao Jin Jiao. This sounds reasonable.

Pan here gives two terms used by others which the Jews came to accept, and another term about whose acceptance he is not sure.

6. Tiao Jin Jiao, or, the Sinew Plucking Religion. From what we know of Chinese records to date, this term appeared for the first time in late Ming or early Qing in a book called *Ru Meng Lu (As in a Dream),* author unknown. (12). It says: "East of Tu Jie (Local Products Market) . . . is the temple of the Sinew Plucking Religion." Just this one sentence.

The name originates in *Genesis* and the story of Jacob wrestling with the angel. Because the sinew in the hollow of Jacob's thigh was injured, Jews do not eat the thigh sinews of animals they slaughter for food. The so-called "sinew in the hollow of his thigh" is the sciatic nerve. (See Adolphe Lods: *Israel From Its Beginnings to the Middle of the Eighth Century,* London, 1932, p. 248) Their Law provides only specially designated Jews may do the slaughtering, and only in a certain prescribed manner. Persons outside their religion, observing this and not understanding the reason, named their faith the Sinew Plucking Religion. Originally, it was merely a nickname, but with the passage of time, it became commonly used by the Chinese. It was much easier to say than "Yicileye Jiao."

Most observers agree with this thesis (102, 160, 191). But a few feel the Jews chose the name themselves. S. M. Perlmann, an English Jew, for example, says the Jews have many traditions. Why take the sinew removal in slaughtering as the basis for a name? Perlmann believes it was to differentiate themselves from their Muslim neighbors—who also list Abraham and other biblical figures as their "patriarchs"—by stressing their descent from Jacob from whom the sinew tradition is derived (168).

Others point out that Muslims also abstain from pork, and eat only beef and mutton, and that the sinew plucking name helps to avoid confusion (27).

In any event it was the most widely used term, and lasted 276 years, roughly corresponding to the period of the Qing dynasty. (1644–1911). We have not heard of it being employed before then, nor has it appeared in any of the writings by the Jews themselves—such as the tablets commemorating the rebuilding of the synagogue.

But starting with *As in a Dream* (12, ibid), and especially in the 18th century, at least in foreign reports, it is used frequently. In 1900, two Kaifeng Jews who went to Shanghai said that while they no longer removed the sinews before eating, the name still prevailed (211).

7. Jiao Jing Jiao, or, The Scripture-Teaching Religion. Some say the Jews selected this name themselves, since they had not been removing sinews from slaughtered animals for nearly a hundred years. Moreover, the Sinew Plucking Religion was an inelegant title. Why not simply discard it and adopt a name like Scripture-Teaching Religion (220, vol. 1, p. 12)? Others say the Kaifeng Jews never accepted it; they still said they were adherents of the Sinew Plucking Religion. This is what Ai, a Jewish descendant, told an American Jewish businessman who visited Kaifeng in 1932 (200).

But the real story probably is this: By the first year of the Republic, 1911, the Israelite faith was very feeble, the community had drastically shrunk, no one was observing the religious practices. The Jews were no longer considered a social force. And so the municipal government changed the "inelegant" name of the lane abutting the synagogue from Sinew Plucking Religion Lane to Scripture-Teaching Religion Lane.* The name of the religion was then also changed to correspond with the lane's new name, although the alteration was absurd. What religion doesn't teach scriptures? But the Jewish community no longer had the strength to resist, and the new name stuck. This, therefore, was another imposed title.

8. Youtai Ren (Jews) and Youtai Jiao (Judaism). Ever since the early years of the 17th century when the Jesuit Matteo Ricci met with an Israelite from Kaifeng, Westerners, whether writing about them in Latin, Italian, French, Spanish, Portuguese, English or German, have always referred to them as Jews and their religion as Judaism. In our country the Chinese term "Youtai" did not appear until after the start of the Dao Guang period in 1821, in the Qing dynasty. To the best of our knowledge it was never

---

*The lane was already designated as Jiao Jing (Scripture Teaching) Lane on a map in the Xiangfu County Gazette of 1898, as pointed out by Chen Changqi in a letter dated October, 1980, to the compilers of the Pan Guangdan book. We don't know which was changed first, the name of the lane or the name of the religion.

applied to the Kaifeng Jews until 1924, when it appeared in the Commercial Press edition of the first *China Year Book* (29, p. 1977). We still don't know whether they were aware of the term or accepted it.

Pan next itemizes appellations he says were definitely unpalatable to the Kaifeng Jews, and were only used behind their backs.

9. Qing Hui Hui (Blue Muslims). Lan Mao Hui Hui or Lan Maozi Hui Hui or Lan Mao Huizi (all meaning Blue Hat Muslims). The name originated from the custom of Jewish men wearing blue turbans during religious services. The Muslims, during their services, wore white turbans. The terms were used to differentiate the two.

Three years after Matteo Ricci's meeting with an Israelite in the early 17th century, as stated earlier, he dispatched another Jesuit to Kaifeng to investigate. The emissary found not only White Hat Hui Hui (Muslims) and Blue Hat Hui Hui (Jews), but also was told of Shi Zi Hui Hui (Hui Hui of the Cross). This was a term used for Nestorian Christians before the arrival of Jesuits (49). In the 18th century the Jesuits also referred to the Jews as "Hui Hui" (56, 58). But, of course, they never used the term Shi Zi Hui Hui since it applied to persons of the same faith as theirs. Hui Hui is a disrespectful term for Muslims.

The Jews never liked the name Blue Hat Hui Hui. For example, at the beginning of this century when Kaifeng Jews who had gone to Shanghai were asked about the term they said they never heard of it. They knew only that they were followers of the Sinew Plucking Religion (168). Obviously, they considered the name Blue Hat Hui Hui somewhat contemptuous. But it was used in Xian, perhaps having spread west from Kaifeng, as late as twenty years ago (i.e., 1933).

10. Qi Xing Hui Zi (Seven Clans Hui Zi). Near the end of the Ming dynasty, in 1642, a disastrous flood released by the ruling class struck Kaifeng.

The authorities are alleged to have breached the Yellow River dykes in an inept attempt to block the forces of peasant rebels besieging the city.

Many Kaifeng residents perished. Those who managed to escape included something over two hundred Israelite families bearing seven different clan names (14). When they returned after the flood subsided, their non-Jewish neighbors dubbed them the Seven Surnames Hui Zi. For the past few hundred years the local Israelites have had only seven surnames, according to clan. By 1910, these were reduced to six, the Kaifeng Jews say, because many left the city. How long the *Seven Surnames* appellation persisted thereafter in the non-Jewish community, we don't know.

11. Moxi Jiaotu (Disciples of Moses). This name does not appear in any of the writings of the Kaifeng Jews. But some people probably used it regarding Jews generally in various parts of China, and others borrowed the term from them (103, quoting 48). It was never accepted by the Jews. They worshipped only one God, and opposed all idols. To name their religion after Moses would, in effect have been idolizing him, when he was merely one of the major patriarchs. The Kaifeng Jews called him "Mieshe" (6, 7).

With a bow to Chen Yuan's seminal work (27), Pan notes that while there are not many mentions of Jews in Chinese records, there are some. He lists and documents them, thus:

1. *Zhuhu.* The earliest written reference in Chinese history to Jews within China's borders. The term is used at least twice in the *History of the Yuan Dynasty.* First, in a 1329 decree stating that "All Buddhists, Taoists, Christians, *Zhuhu* and Muslims who engage in commerce shall pay the same taxes they did before" (3). The second is a 1354 decree requiring that "All Ningxia sharpshooters and wealthy Muslims and *Zhuhu,* wherever they may be, report to the capital for military service" (4)

"Jew" in Hebrew is "Yehudi." In Arabic it is "Djuhud." Palladius was the first to point out that *Zhuhu* was the Chinese transliteration of the Arabic word for Jew (113).

2. *Zhuhe* (*Yuan Shi,* "Yu Jie," that is, *History of the Yuan Dynasty,* "Explanation of Terms")

3. *Zhuwu.* In 1346 it was written thus in the decree proposed by the Imperial Censor: "Mullahs, Arabs and *Zhuwu* should be prohibited from marrying their brothers' widows" (4). Younger brothers sometimes married the widows of deceased elder brothers if they died without a son, in order to carry on their family line.

It is not known whether this recommendation ever became a law. Unless Marco Polo was mistaken, it would appear to be inconsistent with the customs of the Mongols who then ruled China. In the Everyman Library edition of *The Travels of Marco Polo* he says, in Book One, Chapter XLVII, p. 126: "Upon the death of their brothers they (the Mongols) can marry their sisters-in-law." Or the error could be in the rendering of the Yuan records into Chinese from Mongol. The translations were notoriously bad.

4. *Zhuhu* (pronounced the same but written differently from "1," above). Yang Yu, a Yuan dynasty writer from Yangzhou, in his *Notes from a Mountain Retreat* says: "All the officials in the Hangzhou Sugar Bureau are wealthy *Zhuhu* and Muslims" (5).

5. *Zhuhude* This was the term for Jews in Chinese translations of the Islamic scriptures. It was a direct rendering of the Arabic word Djuhud.

Pan sums up the five terms by saying they all are Chinese renditions of Djuhud, the Arabic word for Yehudi. But he notes that Laufer claims that Djuhud or Djahud was New Persian, current during the Yuan dynasty, while in the earlier Middle Persian the word was Yahud or Yahut, corresponding to the Hebrew Yehudi (194). Pan says he himself is not qualified to judge whether the Chinese terms came via the Arabic or Persian versions, but he is definite that all of the Chinese transliterations mean Jew.

He refers also to the argument over the meaning of *Wotuo,* and the varying contentions of Hong Jun, Chen Yuan and Lowenthal as to whether this also was a term for Jew. He concludes that the question needs further study.

He disputes the assertion of W. Y. Chen (not Chen Yuan), supported by Godbey (193), that another term for Jew is *Dashiman.* Pan says Qing dynasty historian Hong Jun already proved in his *Annotations to the Chinese Translation of the Yuan Annals* (23) that it means Mullah. He sees no basis for the Chen and Godbey claim. (cf Hong Jun, p. 4, this volume)

Pan notes that the word *Rudeya* (Judea) was brought in by the Jesuits, and was first employed by Chinese writers in late Ming and early Qing. He doubts whether the Kaifeng Jews were familiar with it. They knew only that they were from the Western Regions and from "Tian Zhu." Pan says:

> In the broadest sense the Western Regions, or for that matter Tian Zhu, can be deemed to have embraced Judea. When people in Ming spoke of the Western Regions, they certainly included Arabia (see *Ming Hui Dian,* and *Da Ming Yi Tong Zhi*). But it is not likely the Kaifeng Israelites were aware of these concepts.

II. WHEN THE JEWS ARRIVED IN KAIFENG

Pan starts by examining the question of when the Israelites left their homeland and when they entered China. He points out that these are two different things. In view of travel conditions and the international situation in ancient times, they might have halted en route for several hundred, or even a thousand, years in some other country, he says.

What's more, although they ultimately settled in China, it was not necessarily according to some pre-arranged plan, but more a case of "Since we're here, we might as well stay."

Moreover, he adds, because they didn't arrive directly from the Jewish homeland but via other countries in which they stopped, they could have crossed the Chinese border at any number of places. Nor did they enter China just once, in a single group, but several times in different groups, entering through various border towns and seaports. Kaifeng, says Pan, was only one of several cities in which they settled, temporarily or permanently. But it probably was the final and longest lasting of their communities. Even to Kaifeng, he notes, the Jews probably did not all come at the same time.

> But the main group—the one which played the decisive role in obtaining approval for permanent residence and the construction of a synagogue and in establishing a regular religious life—most likely arrived in Northern Song. The main proof of this appears in the 1489 Ming dynasty inscription, which reads: "Our Religion was transmitted from Tianzhu, arriving by imperial command . . . We came during the Song dynasty, bringing entry tribute of Western cloth. The Emperor said: 'You have come to our Central Plain. Preserve your ancestral customs and settle in Bianliang (Kaifeng).' In the first year of the Long Xing period (1163) of Song emperor Li Zong, when *Wusida* Liewei (Levi) was the leader of our faithful, the *andula* (supervisor) commenced the building of our synagogue . . . It was rebuilt in 1279 during the reign of Zhi Yuan (Kublai) . . ." (6)

Pan analyzes the inscription, which he says is the most ancient of all the Jews' own written evidence. It appears on the tablet entitled "A Record of Rebuilding the Purity and Truth Synagogue," and recalls the construction of the first synagogue in Kaifeng. Although that happened more than 300 years before the tablet was written, says Pan, it was fresher in the minds of the Jewish community, and therefore more reliable than the later tablets. He examines what he considers some of the key words in the inscription.

> 1. "entry tribute." This shows they had come to China for the first time. If the Jews already had a community in Kaifeng, and were politically and socially acknowledged by the Chinese people, there would have been no necessity for them to present "entry tribute."
>
> 2. "Western cloth." In 1851 two Chinese Protestants were sent to Kaifeng by the Church of England to investigate. In their report, one of them says he was told by a local Jew more details

than appears in the inscription about the "Western cloth." According to this man, the tribute consisted of "multi-hued cotton, and cotton cloth in five colors" (93). These commodities were not current then in China. They could only have been brought in from abroad by this band of Israelites, who must have come in fairly large number. In ancient times it was unthinkable for people to travel in small groups. This ties in with our belief that this group was the main contingent, and the one whose influence was decisive.

3. The emperor's words of welcome. We don't know which emperor he was, only that he was a monarch of the Song dynasty, and Northern Song at that. His statement: "You have come to our Central Plain" indicates that, whether or not all the Israelites had reached Kaifeng at that time, at least these latest arrivals were a representative group, an "entry tribute"-bearing group, and therefore obtained the recognition of the highest ruler in the land.

4. Although the first synagogue was built during the Jin (Golden Tartar) dynasty (1115–1234), the memorial tablet gives the date according to Song dynasty period calculations. This fact is clear evidence that a portion of the Kaifeng Jews first arrived and established a community earlier, during Northern Song (960–1127). The synagogue construction date is given as the first year of the Long Xing period (1163) of Song emperor Li Zong. By that time more than 30 years had elapsed since the removal of the Song court to Linan (Hangzhou) south of the Yangtse. Kaifeng was then in the hands of the Jin, and had become their capital. Logically, and according to custom, the construction date should have been stated in terms of Jin dynasty periods, but the 1489 tablet gives the date according to Southern Song calculations.

Chen Yuan thinks this is because the Kaifeng Jews had "orthodox" concepts (27). There is something in that. But we believe it is because even by the Ming dynasty the Kaifeng Jews still were grateful to the Song emperor who had accepted their tribute and welcomed them to "settle in Bianliang." This was before the move to the south. And most likely funds for the building of the synagogue were also granted by the ruling Northern Song monarch (221, p. 551). Later, though the ruling house was changed, the gratitude of the Jews continued for many years thereafter.

5. *Liewei Wusida.* The first synagogue was built in Kaifeng and the Chief Rabbi was chosen at the same time. He was *Liewei,* the Chinese rendering of Levi, the *wusida.* When the temple was rebuilt in Yuan times, the *wusida* was also a Levi. We know from the Old Testament that Levi was a clan name (25, 27). But what

was an *wusida?* It meant a master of one of the trades or crafts—such as carpentry, ironwork, masonry, etc. This kind of person in Persian is called an *usta*—transliterated into Chinese as *wusida* (220, White quoting Godbey's letter to him, Book I. p. 148; see also 193, Godbey). Otherwise, how could we have one *wusida* constructing the synagogue in 1163, and another rebuilding it in 1279, after a lapse of 116 years? In other words, we have two *wusida*'s, not one. We will elaborate on this later on.

Here, we call attention to the term because it helps substantiate the contention that the Jews could not have arrived in Kaifeng earlier than the late years of Northern Song, not too long before the imperial court moved to the south. The proof is, first, that the Jews employed mainly their own people—such as the *wusida*—when the first synagogue was constructed, as demonstrated by the typically Jewish layout of the various buildings. Non-Jews could not have planned it. The fact that they had to take charge of their own construction shows that they were not yet well acquainted with local people in the building trade—also evidence that they had arrived relatively recently.

Second, they were still using their original names and terminology, although transliterated into Chinese—words such as Levi, *wusida* and *andula*.

6. Wherever Jews congregate in large number and live any length of time, they construct a synagogue. This is agreed upon by Jews and gentiles alike (220 p. 10, also p. 140 quoting 193). As the 1489 tablet says: "In 1163 . . . we commenced building our synagogue." We can prove that none existed before.

Pan repeats Chen Yuan's quotations from two writers in the mid-years of Northern Song (960–1127) who were investigating Kaifeng temples to show that they make no mention of any synagogue. Had there been one, says Pan, they would not have missed it. The 1163 construction presupposes an earlier arrival, but not too much earlier. Pan sums up by saying:

> We have reason to believe that the bulk of the Kaifeng Jews came and settled down in the 50 or 60 years intervening between the middle of Northern Song and the Court's southward move in 1126. Cf. Chen Changqi for exact date of arrival, p. 142.

III. JEWS IN OTHER PARTS OF CHINA

In addition to Kaifeng, says Pan, several other places contain traces of Chinese Jews. Some were settlements of fairly substantial numbers. Otherwise, people would not have noticed them, and there would be no mention of them in history. He quotes from the 1512 tablet: "Members of the religion are found not only in Kaifeng, but all over" (7). Pan goes on:

> This was during the Ming dynasty. But even as early as Yuan, references to *Zhuhu* and *Zhuwu,* quoted above from decrees in the *History of the Yuan Dynasty,* convince us that the Jews must have been widely dispersed. If not, why would the imperial court feel impelled to issue the decrees in the form of a "General Notice?" Moreover, the 1354 decree is directed to all Jews "wherever they may be."
>
> If Hong Jun is correct, the *Wotuo* mentioned in the Yuan *Administrative Code* were also Jews. Aside from the province of Henan, the Code places *Wotuo* in Dongping (Shandong) and Daming (Hebei). Of course Henan includes Kaifeng (23).
>
> Godbey believes one of the reasons the Kaifeng community was able to last so long is that the Jews had many settlements in China which nourished and sustained it. And not only on the Central Plain—they had religious centers in Xinjiang (formerly Chinese Turkestan) and Mongolia, as well. Godbey says because of this at least one place, Kaifeng, was able to survive (220, Book I, p. 147 quoting 193). I am inclined to agree.

Pan then itemizes, according to the material he has been able to gather, the places other than Kaifeng which contain traces of Jewish communities. He lists them in order of their founding.

> 1. Luoyang. Probably the earliest Jewish settlement. In 1926 Frenchman Georges Prevost published photographs and rubbings of three stone fragments found near Luoyang, which he claims are written in Hebrew, together with his translation and notes. We don't know when these fragments were discovered or by whom. But Prevost draws certain conclusions, namely: that they were probably part of an Eastern Han tablet, inscribed in the second century A.D. At that time, the Syrian region in Western Asia was already trading with China and had a "tributary" relationship, says Prevost, and among the merchants were Syrian Jews. The largest country in the Syrian region was the Kingdom of Kushana, whose capital was in Palmyra, and the Hebrew on the tablet was in the Palmyrian style script (220 p. 193 quoting 189).
>
> That one of the Jews coming from Palmyra to Luoyang should leave such a tablet, whether he was a merchant or a "tribute emissary," proves that they were not casual visitors but longtime, perhaps even permanent, residents. We have no way of knowing. The so-called Palmyrian script was Hebrew in the final stage be-

fore it evolved into the square-shaped letters used in the scriptures of the Kaifeng Israelites.

We have not seen Prevost's translation, only a brief condensation of it by others. We therefore cannot offer any detailed analysis.

I have been more fortunate, having found both the stone fragments and Prevost's tract—two fragments in the vaults of Beijing's Museum of History, a third in the Archeology Department storeroom of Beijing University, and the tract in the Shanghai Library Repository.

Georges Prevost was a priest of the Lazaristes missionaries in Peking. He says the fragments were found in the outskirts of Luoyang amid the ruins of the ancient Han capital. He thought they might be part of a tombstone, since Chinese graves are always placed outside the city. He says the writing is Palmyrian script Hebrew, used by Syrian Jews only between the first and third centuries A.D.—corresponding roughly to the time of Eastern Han—the language being a branch of Aramaic, the lingua franca of Jews in Western Asia generally. Only three of what had been four fragments remain. Prevost interprets them as follows:

> 1st fragment. The first verb means "died a violent death." The subject is missing. The name of a person? This is followed by ". . . died for the sake of his (her?) co-believers . . ."
>
> 2nd fragment. ". . . although in good health . . . Sarah (or Sared) died . . ." Both names are Palmyrian.
>
> 3rd fragment. ". . . from Anath . . ." A place name, a person's name (III. Judges 31), a clan name, the name of a goddess?

Prevost notes that the 1512 tablet in Kaifeng dates the arrival of the Jews as during the reign of Han emperor Ming Di, who ruled from 58 to 76 A.D. This is within the first to third century A.D. period when Palmyrian script was the current form of Hebrew writing in Syria. He says according to historical records the Jews had a synagogue in Palmyria. Many of them were merchants. The city was a big trade center between Antioch—which had a population of 600,000 and wove silk from the Orient for the Roman market—and India and Ferghana, then in the neighborhood of Tashkent and just west of China's Xinjiang province today. Jewish merchants may have joined caravans trekking all the way to Luoyang. Roman coins of several emperors have been discovered in Shanxi province. The Palmyrians were wide-ranging travellers. Their inscriptions have been found in Egypt, Rome, England and Germany.

John Brough of England offers another view. His article "A Kharoshti Inscription from China" appears in the *Bulletin of the School of Oriental and African Studies,* vol. XXIV, 1961, part 3, pages 517–530. He says the fragments are part of the rim of a well, probably built by a Kharoshti speaker from northern India, then one of the many foreigners in Luoyang during the late 2nd and early 3rd centuries engaged in translating Buddhist scriptures into Chinese. It was the custom in northern India to inscribe Buddhist sentiments around well rims, and Brough believes this Indian abroad may have had a similar well built for him in Luoyang.

Xia Nai, Director of the Institute of Archaeology of the Academia Sinica, was good enough to reply to my plea for his appraisal of these conflicting views. In letters to me dated April 2 and 5, 1983, he says:

> I have read John Brough's article and have learned that the inscription is in Kharoshti. Brough says, judging from the script, the inscription was made between late Eastern Han and the Wei-Jin (220–313) period, and was both written and incised by a Buddhist monk from the Western Regions (including India). I find Brough's arguments convincing.
>
> You ask whether there could be some connection because Kharoshti is derived from Aramaic, a language then spoken by the Jews. Actually, Kharoshti is a written form of Prakrit, an Indo-European language, whereas Hebrew is a Semitic language. Even if the Kharoshti script was a development of the Aramaic script, that would not make it a Semitic language, any more than writing Chinese in the Roman alphabet would make Chinese a Latin language.
>
> . . . The inscription is a Buddhist formula for good deeds, such as the building of a well for common benefit.
>
> . . . I have met Professor Ji Xianlin (head of the Oriental Languages Department, Beijing University) and asked him about the inscription. He authorized me to tell you that "Brough's conclusion is right." The inscription is written in Kharoshti, not Hebrew, and is a Buddhist formula. It has nothing to do with the Jews.

Clearly, Brough and the Chinese specialists are in general agreement. Both unequivocally refute Prevost's speculations about the Luoyang stone fragments.

The next city Pan lists is in the far Northwest, in the province of Gansu.

2. Dunhuang. Early in the present century British and French archeologists Stein and Pelliot stole a great many cultural relics from China, including some relating to the Jews, at least two of which are fragments written in Hebrew script. In Dandan-ui-liq,

which is northeast of Hetian and northwest of Luopu, in Xinjiang province, Stein discovered a business letter from Persia. The words are Persian but the script is Hebrew. Experts date it at 708 A.D.

In the Cave of a Thousand Buddhas in Dunhuang, Pelliot found a Hebrew prayer written on paper, which the experts also date as 8th century (122). Because only China had paper at that time, it must have been made in China. At least it was written by a Jew within China's borders, since it couldn't have come from the outside.

These two artifacts prove that in Gansu and Xinjiang along the Silk Road between Asia and Europe there are traces of Jews in a number of cities, especially in Dunhuang.

3. Guangzhou (Canton). Toward the end of the Tang dynasty, that is, toward the end of the ninth century, Islamic traveller Aboul Zeyd al Hassan, also called Abu Zaid visited India and China (40). He wrote: "During the Huang Chao rebellion near the end of Tang, 120,000 Muslims, Jews, Christians and Parsees in Guangfu (Chen Yuan's rendition of the French "Khanfu") on business, were killed" (27 p. 29). Neither the *New* nor *Old Tang History* mention this event, though they do say that Huang Chao occupied Guangzhou in 879, and that he withdrew the following year, the reason for the pull-out being that ". . . a great plague destroyed four out of ten of the population." All of this is in the records. Whether the deaths were due to a massacre, or to a plague, or to a combination of both, we have no way of knowing.

There is also some discrepancy in dates. Renaudot's translation from Arabic into French (40) states the deaths occurred in 877, two years before the *New Tang History* date. But his "in Khanfu on business" corresponds with the observation in *New Tang History* that "shipping and commerce flourished in the southern seaport." The Parsees were Persian Zoroastrians, no doubt about it.

What is in doubt is which city is Abu Zaid talking about? Renaudot translates the Arabic as Khanfu, whereas Yule in his notes on the *Travels of Marco Polo* (41, p. 158) renders it as Canfu. Do Khanfu or Canfu mean Guangfu, that is, Guangzhou? We will leave this for discussion a bit further on.

At this point we can definitely say this much: That in the ninth century at the latest, a city on the southeast coast of China, whether Guangzhou or some other port, harbored a number of Jews. They were probably there on business, and in fairly large number. That being so, they were not merely temporary residents. The figure of 120,000 deaths is no doubt exaggerated. But we may take it for granted that there was a substantial community of each of the four faiths mentioned.

4. Ganpu and Hangzhou. Many writers, such as Finn (87), Chen Yuan (27), Wieger (150) and White (220), believe Khanfu means Guangzhou. Chen Yuan says the Japanese *General History of China* is in error to translate it as Ganpu. He himself renders it as Guangfu (27, ibid.). I am inclined to think Ganpu is correct.

Why not Guangzhou, as Canton was called in Tang times? In *The Travels of Marco Polo* the Venetian calls Canton "Kangiu" (41 p. 316). "Giu" is much nearer to "zhou" in sound than it is to "fu." Guangzhou did not become known as Guangfu until the Ming dynasty. Guangfu was short for Guangzhoufu (Guangzhou prefecture). Chen Yuan was a 20th century Cantonese, and accustomed to the term Guangfu. That is why he assumed that Khanfu meant Guangfu, and considered the translation Ganpu an error. I imagine Finn and White's mistake was due to never having heard of a place called Ganpu.

Why does Khanfu probably mean Ganpu? First, while today it is a small sea port in the southern part of Haiyan County in the province of Zhejiang, it wasn't small in ancient times. It was the home of the "Ganpu Naval Fleet," a ship-building center, and a major seaport during Southern Song. Marco Polo places it 25 *li* northeast of Kinsai (Hangzhou), and says it was a fine seaport harboring merchant ships from the Middle East (41 p. 308).

During Song and Yuan, Ganpu was not outstanding, but earlier, in Tang, it was an important seaport, linked with the nearby city of Hangzhou, and served as an entry for the merchandise brought by foreign vessels. In other words, the Khanfu of ninth century Abu Zaid was the Ganpu of thirteenth century Marco Polo. The translation from Abu Zaid should be rendered as Ganpu, not Guangzhou. To interpret it as Ningpo is also incorrect (41 p. 308).

Second, toward the end of Tang, Huang Chao's army attacked twice in Zhejiang province. The first time was before his entry into Guangzhou in 879, the second was after his withdrawal in 880. The history books tell plainly of the "invasion of Hangzhou (and) . . . , the attack on Linan (Hangzhou)" during the second incursion into Zhejiang.

The first assault on Zhejiang was in 878, which is close to the 877 date given by Abu Zaid, and certainly prior to Huang Chao's attack on Guangzhou in 879. We therefore believe that Huang Chao's slaughter of the Jews took place in the Ganpu-Hangzhou area, and not in Guangzhou.

Third, and particularly important: While we have no reliable written records, other than Abu Zaid's, of the presence of Jews in the Ganpu-Hangzhou area during Tang, in Yuan we have many, both Chinese and foreign. Already mentioned is Yang Yu's comment that rich Jewish merchants were officials in the Hangzhou Sugar Bureau (5). In addition, Wu Zimu, a native of Hangzhou in late Song and early Yuan, tells in his book *Meng Liang Lu (A Dream of Kaifeng)* of a hostel for foreigners who came on the big ocean-going vessels, of ginger-flavored meat prepared in the butcher shops for the "Persians," of the vast variety of goods the foreigners brought on their "tall-masted great ships," of how some of them were "kind to orphans and the afflicted, respectful to the old and solicitous of the poor . . ."

Wu makes no mention of Jews, but they must have been there. Both he and Yang Yu plainly indicate that these foreign merchants were not just temporary residents. Godbey quotes the famous Islamic traveller Ibn Batuta, who wrote in 1346 of his visit to El Khansa, meaning the Capital, and called Kinsai by Marco Polo. (Hangzhou was China's capital during Southern Song, but the name hung on for a time even after the capital returned north during Yuan.) According to Godbey, Batuta said the city's Second District was given over to Jews, Christians, and sun-worshipping Turks, with the Muslims living separately in another section (46, as quoted in 193).

Batuta's own words are slightly different. The way he put it was: "We entered a subsidiary town (Ganpu?) of the capital through a gate in the town wall known as the Gate of the Jews. In this town dwell a great many Jews, Christians and sun-worshipping Turks" (46, quoted in 218). The name "Gate of the Jews" indicates that they were numerous and wealthy, which is probably what enabled them to be among those who were "kind" and "solicitous," as Wu Zimu noted. This is only a guess on our part.

The Hangzhou Jewish community lasted at least till the final years of the Ming dynasty. In 1605, Ai Tian, a Kaifeng Jew, told Jesuit Matteo Ricci in Beijing that Hangzhou had more Jews than Kaifeng, and a synagogue as well. This was also true of Guangzhou. Were there any Jews in Guangzhou during Tang? Very possibly. After all, before the development of Shanghai, Guangzhou was the largest seaport in southeast China and closest to the foreign sea routes. However we have no evidence of Jews in Guangzhou subsequent to Tang.

By the beginning of the 18th century Hangzhou's Jews seemed to have approached a vanishing point. They no longer communicated with their co-religionists in Kaifeng. Jesuits visiting Kaifeng at that time were told by Jewish residents that, so far as they knew, theirs was the only Israelite community left in Asia (58).

5. Ningbo. There were Jews in Ningbo, and they probably arrived very early. Because the city is a river port quite near the sea, and because it is not far from Ganpu-Hangzhou, Yule mistook Ganpu for Ningbo. In any event, Ningbo had Jews. We have positive proof in Ming, with the 1489 Kaifeng tablet inscription. It reads: "In 1461, when the synagogue was rebuilt, Shi Bin, Li Rong, Gao Jian and Zhang Xuan went to Ningbo and brought back a scroll of the Scriptures. Zhao Ying of Ningbo brought another scroll to Bianliang (Kaifeng) and respectfully presented it to our temple." This shows that there were members of the faith in Ningbo, and Zhao Ying was one of them. Also, that they had more complete sets of the Scriptures, indicating that the Jews and Judaism of Ningbo probably had a history no shorter than their Kaifeng counterparts, plus a considerable prestige.

6. Beijing.

Here, Pan repeats the Marco Polo stories of how Kublai Khan reproached the Jews and Muslims for deriding the Nestorian Christians who were defeated in battle in 1287, and of the respect the monarch showed for the religious celebrations of the Christians, Muslims, Jews and Buddhists (41 p. 157–159). Pan says that somewhat later Franciscan priests from Rome—Monte-Corvino in 1305 and 1306, and Marignolli from 1342 to 1347—wrote back mentioning Jews in Beijing. Marignolli says he debated religious matters with them (103). Many still remained at the end of the 16th century. Benedict Goes (48) claims he met a Muslim trader from Kashgar, who told him he had encountered several "disciples of Moses" in Beijing. These, of course were Jews, says Pan (103, quoting 48). He continues:

But by the early 18th century, at the latest, Beijing no longer had any Jewish community. The same was true of Hangzhou and Ningbo, mentioned above, and Ningxia which I will discuss below. The main reason is that most of the Jews became Muslims (220, Part I. p. 52 quoting 58). Others moved to Kaifeng where they joined their fellow-religionists.

For example, the family of Li Guangdian, author of the *Defense of Bian* (11), moved from Beijing to Kaifeng in 1368 during the Ming dynasty. Kaifeng Jews in the 17th century told Jesuit missionary Gozani that a book depository in Beijing still had copies of the Five Books of Moses, although the Jews themselves were gone. But a later search by Jesuits proved in vain (220 Part I.

p. 51). Are there any writings, or other proof today of the former existence of Jewish communities in Beijing and other places? That is a question which merits further research.

7. Quanzhou. Regarding Jews in Quanzhou we have only one piece of evidence. In 1326, Andrew of Perugia, who served as Catholic "Bishop" of Quanzhou, wrote a letter to his superiors in Rome, complaining: "We are able to preach freely and unmolested, but of the Jews and Saracens none is converted" (44). Like Guangzhou, Ningbo and Ganpu, at that time Quanzhou was also a large seaport. It is reasonable to assume there were Jews in all of these places.

8. Ningxia. Both the 1489 and 1512 Kaifeng inscriptions testify to the presence of Israelites in Ningxia. The first told of how Jin Xuan, when the synagogue in Kaifeng was rebuilt after a flood, gave an altar, a bronze censer, vases and candlesticks. His younger brother Jin Ying contributed to the funds used to buy the synagogue site, and for the inscribing and erection of the 1489 tablet (6). In 1512 Jin Run built the kiosk which housed it (7). All three were from Ningxia. The 1489 tablet also mentions that one of the ancestors of Jin Xuan and Jin Ying had been Court President of State Banquets, and that their great-uncle had been a high military official. Clearly, the Jin family had a long history in China extending back to early Ming or late Yuan.

9. Yangzhou. The 1512 inscription, relating how the synagogue was rebuilt, says that An, Li, and Gao of Kaifeng, and Jin Pu of Weiyang (another name for Yangzhou) ". . . contributed a scroll of the Scriptures and constructed a second gateway of the temple." This is ample evidence of the presence of Israelites in Yangzhou.

10. Nanjing. Toward the end of Ming, certainly not later than 1641, Alvare de Semmedo, a Portuguese Jesuit, met a Muslim in Nanjing who said the city formerly had four Jewish families, but they all had recently joined Islam. These were the last of them. There must have been more before. But as their numbers diminished their religious teachers couldn't hold the community together (87 quoting 51).

The existence of Jewish communities in the foregoing ten cities is thus, to a greater or lesser extent, attested to by the materials available.

Pan disagrees with Chen Yuan's conjecture than an "Adam and Eve Temple" in Xuzhou was in some way connected with the Jews (27 p. 32). He says Chen Yuan fails to give the sources of his information. Such a temple, if it existed, would surely have idols of Adam and Eve, and this would violate the strict Israelite injunction against the worship of graven images, Pan insists and so, it would not prove a former presence of Jews in Xuzhou. (211, 87 p. 25). See also Chen Yuan, p. 32–33, this volume.

He observes that during the past century there were large numbers of Jews in commercial centers like Shanghai, Tianjin and Harbin, but these were all relatively recent arrivals and not within the purview of his inquiry.

As to communications among the Jewish settlements in ancient times, Pan says he has already shown the closest rapport between the Jews of Kaifeng and those in Ningxia, Yangzhou and Ningbo. There probably also was liaison during late Ming and early Qing with co-religionists in Hangzhou and Beijing, although Pan admits he is unable to prove it.

Pan examines some of the wilder conjectures advanced by various observers. He cites Perlmann's speculation that there are Jews among the Tibetans, that they are, in fact, "descendants of the Ten Lost Tribes of Israel" (168, 193). Pan also quotes the comment of Britisher Thomas Manning that the Tibetans look more like Jews than Mongols (168 p. 30, 31).

Another English missionary, Thomas Torrence, "discovered" descendants of the Lost Tribes among the Qiang people, an ethnic minority in western Sichuan (218 quoting 213). Pan finds his contention that they arrived in China several centuries before Christ absurd.

On the other hand Pan agrees with the statements of certain Japanese scholars—mentioned but not named by Lowenthal (218)—that there had been Jews in Gansu province who earned their living by money-lending. He cites Broomhall, a British expert on Islam in China, to the effect that there had been Jewish communities in northern Anhui (218 quoting 163 p. 222), and says this is possible. Pan elaborates:

> Since there were Jews in Henan and northern Jiangsu, and these communicated with each other, why not in northern Anhui which lies virtually between them? Many of them could have migrated from Kaifeng. We know that during the Kang Xi period (1662–1723) of the Qing dynasty a Jew named Jin died in Chuzhou in northern Anhui. A maternal nephew of his named Ai brought his body back to Kaifeng (16, Vol. 27, p. 21 "Persons," "Filial Piety"). Clearly, there was communication between Jews in Kaifeng and northern Anhui and this could conceivably have led to settlements in the latter area.

IV. WHEN THE JEWS IN GENERAL ENTERED CHINA

Pan notes the disparity of opinions and the difficulty in fixing dates, then proceeds with an analysis of the various schools of thought.

We have already told, in Chapter II., of when the Jews came to Kaifeng. But of all those who migrated to that city, only the group which brought entry tribute and exercised a decisive influence in establishing a Jewish community came directly from abroad. The rest were probably people whose fathers, or grand-fathers, or even more remote ancestors, arrived in China much earlier and gradually moved to Kaifeng from other cities.

As we saw in Chapter III., there were Jews in several other cities, and a few, such as Hangzhou and Ningbo, probably pre-dated Kaifeng in hosting Jewish settlements. People moving from those cities probably contributed to Kaifeng's population.

Which leads to the question; when did the Jews arrive in China? Can we fix a first entry date? Many opinions, and not a few guesses, have been expressed. Naturally, the earlier the dating, the more guesswork we encounter, and the less substantiation. The theories vary widely, from pre-Zhou to Song. Even the Kaifeng Jews were not able to agree on the times of their arrival. Let us examine the different contentions, one by one.

1. Pre-Zhou (before 1066 B.C.). There was only one proponent of this view—Alexei Vinogradov, a leader of the Greek Orthodox Church in czarist Russia. Building on meanings he alleged were implied in the 1489 Kaifeng tablet, he claimed the Jews came to China before the time of Moses.

The Jews themselves, S. M. Perlmann for example, describe this assumption as "improbable" and "daring" (168 p. 21–27 quoting 120). See also Chen Yuan, p. 28, this volume.

2. Zhou Dynasty (1066–256 B.C.). The 1663 Kaifeng tablet says: "The religion originated in Tianzhu. It was transmitted to the Central Plain during the Zhou Dynasty." Central Plain means Henan, where the Jews are alleged to have lived from Zhou to Song, and thereafter. Chen Yuan points out that this 1663 statement is due to a misreading of the 1483 and 1512 inscriptions which refer to events in Israelite history as occurring at times equivalent to certain Zhou dynasty dates, not that they came to China at that time.

Nevertheless, a number of foreign Sinologues accepted the Zhou theory as fact. The earliest of these was French Jesuit Gaubil (74). This was commented upon by Tobar (142 p. 89). Next was French Roman Catholic Sionnet (85). Finn thought the Jews came to China in Zhou, but moved to Kaifeng in Han (87 p. 58). Vinogradov, mentioned above, after originally claiming a pre-Zhou entry, subsequently changed his mind and settled for Zhou (120). Other supporters were Bainbridge (158) and Perlmann (164). Perlmann was convinced the Jews arrived prior to 700 B.C. (168 p. 29). Godbey (193) was more cautious. He said merely that in the 8th century B.C. the Israelites already had commercial dealings with China. Noye thought that while the Jews came later, by Solomon's time (1082–975 B.C.) they and China were conducting trade (207).

Is there any documentary evidence for all this?

Pan disposes of Vinogradov easily. The Russian had founded his contention of Zhou contacts with Palestine on a quotation from 2 Samuel 5:11 reading: "King Hiram of Tyre sent a trade mission to David; he provided him with cedar logs . . ." According to Vinogradov, a traditional verse among Chinese Jews says that Hiram presented David with gifts sent him by the emperor of China. Says Pan:

> The Bible does not reveal whether the cedar logs came from China. As to the "traditional verse," no one except Vinogradov seems to have heard about it.

Perlmann, says Pan, bases his Zhou dating on the famous prophesy in Isaiah 49:12 that the Jews would one day return from "Sinim," which Perlmann identifies as China. Pan notes that in the Greek, or Septuagint, translation of the Bible the word is rendered as "Persia," while in the Latin, or Vulgate, edition of the Roman Catholic Church, it is called "a land to the south." Rabbi Manasseh ben Israel, a Dutch Jew in the 17th century, was the first to translate the word as "China," says Pan, and Perlmann thought he was correct (168 p. 6–7).

See also my comments in Zhang Xinglang, "Foreign Documents." Isaiah pre-dated the Qin, or Chin, dynasty, of which Sinim is alleged to be a transliteration, by 500 years. Pan continues:

> The supporters of the "China" for "Sinim" theory were not only numerous, but indeed unanimous in their acclaim. They included Jewish Orientalist Mollendorff (127), and French Catholic Noye (207). Moreover, in the *Complete Bible,* Chinese edition, used by Christians for more than 100 years, "Sinim" is translated as "Qin Guo" (Land of Qin, or Chin).
>
> All of this bolsters the adherents of the claim that the Jews arrived in China during the Zhou dynasty. Isaiah made his prophesy in the latter half of the eighth (some say the sixth) century B.C., which would correspond to the reigns of Kings Ping and Huan of Eastern Zhou. Therefore, goes the theory, by the end of Western Zhou at the latest there were Jews in China.

Pan comments sarcastically on the reasoning of Rabbi Manasseh. Didn't ten of the twelve tribes vanish between the exodus from Egypt and the Assyrian conquest? Where could they have gone? For some at least, according to Manasseh, the answer was China!

Pan describes the views of Sionnet as "even more specious." Sionnet offered three reasons for his belief in a Zhou migration of the Jews to China. One, resemblances between Jewish and Chinese history during the Zhou dynasty. Two, similar folklore, such as: references to Paradise, the Tree of Knowledge of Good and Evil, the Rainbow After the Deluge, the Seven Years of Famine, the Stopping of the Sun, etc. Three, and most preposterous of all according to Pan, a mention of Jehovah in the *Dao De Jing (Canon of Virtue)* of 6th century B.C. Chinese philosopher Lao Zi, and the conclusion that he had learned of Jehovah from Israelites in China (85).

Two other theories offered to support an early arrival, although not necessarily as early as Zhou, says Pan, seem on the surface to have some merit. First, the prohibition against weaving wool and linen together, found in Deuteronomy 22:11, exists also in China, particularly in Tibet. Second the Israelite custom of the younger brother marrying the widow of his deceased older brother in order to "carry on the line" is alleged to be fairly common in Jiangsu and Henan. Perlmann was much impressed by these two "identical" items (168 p. 31–35). Says Pan:

> Actually the weaving prohibition was first mentioned by Finn (87 p. 65–66). Most impressed by the second point was Vinogradov. He was sure the custom was brought into Henan by the Jews (168 p. 31 quoting 120), and said it proved that they had migrated to Kaifeng much earlier than originally believed. Chen Yuan refers to both of these contentions (27 p. 32).

See Xia Nai's comment about the weaving in Chen Yuan, this volume, p. 32. Regarding remarriage of widows, see my note, Pan, above, p. 52.

> But even if China does have these customs, how prevalent are they? Are there any other nationalities which also observe the same customs? Even if there are not, could they have originated spontaneously among the Israelites and the Chinese at more or less the same time? Until we can obtain good answers to these questions, we will have to consider the foregoing arguments as forced and far-fetched.

Pan notes Godbey's allegation that the Israelites were using silken articles in the 8th century B.C., at which time only China produced silk. As evidence, Godbey offers the statement in *Amos* 3:12 to the effect that the Israelites of Samaria were reclining on couches of *dmsk,* that is, damask, according to famous contemporary translator Robert Moffat. Damascus, says Godbey, was then Assyria's major city, and this proves that the Semites of that region, including the Israelites, were importing Chinese silk to the West (220 p. 136 quoting 193).

It seems to Pan that only Godbey's reasoning contains a shred of credibility in support of the contention that Jews first came to China in the Zhou dynasty. He observes that those who think they see resemblances among the Chinese to the "Ten Lost Tribes of Israel" of necessity must also claim a Zhou dynasty entry, since the dates of the vanishing of the Tribes and the time span of the dynasty approximately coincide. He promises a detailed discussion of this in Chapter VI.

3. Han (206 B.C. to 220 A.D.). The Kaifeng Jews themselves gave three different arrival dates. Their 1489 inscription says Song, their 1512 inscription says Han, their 1663 inscription says Zhou. The more recent the inscription, the more ancient the date of arrival.

According to the 1512 inscription ". . . in Han times, the Religion entered China" (7). This is the only written evidence the Jews have left us. But there is also a verbal tradition. In 1723, Jesuit priest Gaubil travelled from Beijing to Kaifeng, and asked about arrival time. He says the Jews told him it was 1,650 years previous (87 p. 57 quoting 223). That would make it during the reign of emperor Ming Di (58–75 A.D.) of the Eastern Han dynasty. Gaubil did not accept this statement, nor did he pay much attention to the 1512 inscription, since he himself was a proponent of the Zhou dynasty theory, as mentioned above.

But some 40-odd years later Brotier, another Jesuit, compiled his own letters and those of three other Jesuits into a volume entitled *Memoire Sur Les Juifs Etablis en Chine* in which he quotes Gaubil as saying: "The (Kaifeng) Jews stated they had come to China during the reign of Han emperor Ming Di . . . Several of them insist that this is the date of their arrival" (58, 77). Brotier does not doubt that the initial entry into China was in Han, although he believes the Kaifeng settlement occurred later on, in Song (58).

We have not seen Gaubil's original letter, but we are sceptical of the Ming Di story. It is not necessarily something the Kaifeng Jews said. More likely it was Gaubil's deduction (87 p. 57). In any event, this theory is widely accepted. Even the recent edition of the *Ci Yuan* encyclopedia repeats it.

In 1850 two Chinese Protestants were sent to Kaifeng by the London Society for Promoting Christianity Among the Jews to investigate. Their conclusion was that the Israelites had arrived in China 1,850 years before (93, 96). This places the date more than 70 years earlier than the Gaubil story, and has them entering China in the Ping Di period (1–6 A.D.) of Western Han.

Thus we can see that beyond any doubt many Kaifeng Jews in

their own minds and in their oral traditions really believed their ancestors came to China in the Han dynasty. We also have people like Brotier and many other writers, each of whom has his own speculations for specific dates.

Here Pan lists them in sequence of the arrival times they support: 217 B.C.—Murr (62 III), between 200 B.C. and 220 A.D.—Edkins (125), around 200 B.C.—Mishkovsky (210), before 164 B.C.—Noye (207), within the 2nd century B.C.—Ausubel (221 p. 550), within the 1st century B.C.—Ezra (147). Brotier, says Pan, found the destruction of Jerusalem by the Romans in 70 A.D. and the reign of Ming Di (58–75 A.D.) an irresistible coincidence, particularly since the 1512 Kaifeng tablet states that the Jews came to China in the Ming Di period of Han (58). Cordier also thought they arrived after Titus destroyed Jerusalem (225).

French scholar de Lacouperie claimed that survivors of the slaughter of the Jews in Babylon in 34 A.D. fled to Parthia (northeast Persia today). Subsequently, merchants among them travelled to China and settled down, their numbers being constantly replenished by new arrivals from the West (224).

Tobar agreed with Brotier, Cordier and de Lacouperie. He believed that Kaifeng Jews had indeed told Gaubil their ancestors had arrived at the time of Ming Di. He stressed the importance of this "statement" (142 p. 90, 91).

Wilhelm concurred with Cordier that the destruction of Jerusalem was the pivotal date. He thought that the first group to enter China settled in Kaifeng, Nanjing and Hangzhou, but that the last two communities no longer existed (188).

MacGillivray in 1917 said he accepted the theory that the Jews arrived in China 1,800 years before, which would place the date in the second century (173).

It was Godbey's contention that the Jews came after 50 A.D., via the northwest. But these were people who had moved to Central Asia much earlier, says Godbey. Their migration to China was not due to events in their former homeland. Pan promises a detailed discussion of this in Chapter V. He asks:

> What evidence have the supporters of the theory that the Jews entered China during the Han dynasty? Neither the 1512 inscription, nor the statements of the Kaifeng Jews, no matter how clear, no matter how some persons stress the value of oral legend—none of these are real proof. The only evidence is Prevost's French translation and preliminary analysis of the three fragments of a Hebrew inscription (184, 189), mentioned in Chapter III. As to place, they were discovered in Luoyang. As to time,

they may be Han dynasty, possibly 2nd century A.D.—we have only Prevost's guess. He says it is "possible."

Chen Yuan's comment is correct: "Yet in the more than one thousand years from Han to Yuan (it should read 'Song') if there were settlements of Jews, why have they not left a single trace of any person, event, or structure? Why does the Hong Zhi (1489) inscription place the transmission of the religion in Song, and not before? The claim that the Kaifeng Jews are descended from those who came to China in Han is not credible. It is possible that some Jews reached China before Han, but the Jews in Kaifeng could not possibly be descended from them" (27 p. 28).

Strictly speaking, we have no proof whatsoever of an entry of Jews into China either pre-Han or Han—no evidence of any Jewish person, or artifact, or contemporary document regarding them.

4. Tang (618–907).

Pan is inclined to believe the Abu Zaid account of the presence of Jews in Guangzhou, Ganpu and Hangzhou (40). He agrees that many of the foreigners slaughtered—whether in Guangzhou or Ganpu—in the ninth century must have been Jews. He notes that Mishkovsky puts the number at 40,000 (210). Although he feels the 120,000 figure is probably exaggerated, he observes that French priest Wieger, who lived in north China for many years, has pointed out that careful population registers were kept in Tang times for taxation purposes and could have been checked (150).

Pan lists the article by Schwab about the journey of a Spanish Jew to China in the 9th century (122), the account by Adler of the tenth century visit by a Jewish merchant (201), the Semitic-featured tomb figures unearthed in Tang dynasty graves (220), and the Hebrew documents of Tang date found in Xinjiang by Stein and Pelliot and discussed in Chapter III. Pan continues:

> Even without the foregoing, if we consider the heavy traffic during Tang between East and West, and the several Western religions which entered China at that time, we can state almost positively that a relatively large number of Jews arrived then, of whom at least a small proportion remained. Manichaeism and Zoroastrianism came even before Sui, and special governmental agencies were set up to govern them during Tang. Islam is said to have been introduced in Sui and flourished in Tang. Sui is too early, since Islam had not yet been created as a religion (227). By Tang, Nestorianism was firmly established in Changan (Xian), then China's capital.

These religions all came from the Near and Middle East. With the destruction of Jerusalem in 70 A.D. and the forced "Diaspora," the Jewish people spread widely over these areas in many cities. Most of them were merchants, and their lives were very unsettled. Because they were "a people without a country" they tended to be more mobile than their neighbors of other races and religions. That they should therefore form commercial companies of their own, or in conjunction with people of other faiths, and travel to China, is not only within the realm of logic, but a factual necessity.

Pan believes some of the Jews came to Kaifeng in Tang. While none of the tablets mention this, Kaifeng Jew Ai Tian, in his conversation with Matteo Ricci in Beijing in 1605, said there was a tradition among the Jews that ". . . when King Tamerlane conquered Persia he conquered China too, and there came with him many Moors (Muslims), Christians, and Jews, about 800 years ago . . ." (49).

Of course, says Pan, this is riddled with errors. Tamerlane lived in the 14th century, not 800 years previous to 1605, in the 9th. He never entered China, to say nothing of conquering it. The whole story is a hodge-podge. But:

> . . . two facts are correct. The first is "about 800 years ago," which would place the event in mid-Tang. The second is that the Jews arrived together with Muslims and Christians, exactly as we deduced above. Chen Yuan tells us: "During the Tang dynasty travel between Europe and Asia gradually flourished. Nestorianism and Islam came to China, and the Jews followed" (27 p. 29). According to Ai Tian's partially correct statement we may accept the premise that the ancestors of some of the Kaifeng Jews arrived in China in Tang.

Pan asserts that Ball believes the Jews came to China in the 7th century (148), Shyrock favors the 9th (197). White and Williams say in view of the Kaifeng Jews' calendar calculations (see Chapter VI, of Pan), it had to be prior to the 10th century (220, III. p. 108). Goodrich states it would be more correct to say they left Persia at that time, but entered China later (220, I. Roman numeral 17).

In any event, says Pan, all fix the entry time as Tang, or early Five Dynasties (907–960) at the latest. In other words, that was when a substantial number of Jews came to China, including some who settled in Kaifeng.

Pan admits that several writers consider it unlikely any sizeable number of Jews should have arrived in China before Song, whether it be in Kaifeng or any place else. He notes:

French Sinologist Chavannes asserts that only with regard to a Northern Song entry do we have any reliable material (151). Chen Yuan, while agreeing that some Jews came in Tang, adds "But they came for commerce. . . . They were only temporary, not long term residents. . . . The Jews could not have come to Kaifeng prior to Song" (27 p. 29).

Lowenthal's position was: "From the materials available so far, we have no reason to believe that there were large numbers of Jews taking up permanent residence in China prior to the 12th century. All theories to the contrary are either groundless or misinterpretations of the facts" (218).

Finally, Pan notes the attempt by Chinese writer Bai Meichu (233) to reconcile the difference in dates given in the Kaifeng 1489 and 1512 inscriptions, the first saying Song and the second saying Han. Bai's theory is that the Han referred to is the Posterior Han (947–948) of the Five Dynasties and means the time they left their homeland, and Song is when they arrived in Kaifeng. Pan's appraisal:

> Very clever. But although it solves the contradiction, it has absolutely no foundation in fact or legend. The early Han concept was at least put forward by some of the Kaifeng Jews.

V. THE COUNTRIES THEY CAME FROM AND THE ROUTES THEY FOLLOWED

Pan points out the inconsistency in the three Kaifeng inscriptions commemorating the rebuilding of the synagogue. The 1489 inscription says they came ". . . from Tianzhu" (6). The 1512 inscription says they ". . . originated in Tianzhu and Xiyu" (7). The 1663 inscription says: ". . . the religion started in Tianzhu" (14). According to Jesuit priest Gozani (52) they also knew they came from Judah, or Judea, which they conquered under Joshua's leadership after 600,000 of them left Egypt and crossed the Red Sea and the desert.

In which country or countries were they living before coming directly to China? In other words, what was their last stop on the way? Pan traces their long trek, going back into Jewish history. He says:

> The Jews differ from many other races. From 70 A.D. on they had no country of their own. Before that date, because their land was a crossroads between three continents—Europe, Asia and Africa—and international and racial relations were extremely complicated, with constant wars and large shifts in populations, they were unable to live and work in peace. And so, they were constantly on the move.

Even before they lost their country, a large number had already departed. After it fell to the Romans, still more of them dispersed in every direction, settling in many different lands. The words of the three inscriptions are therefore significant. Tianzhu is India. Xiyu is the Western Regions, as used in the broad sense subsequent to the Han dynasty. It embraced, at a minimum, the whole Persian empire.

But, Pan explains, although Persia had invaded and occupied the Jewish homeland from the middle of the sixth to middle of the 4th century B.C., by the time of the big dispersal in Han times after the Roman conquest in 70 A.D. Persia had been reduced to roughly the size of Iran today. So if Kaifeng Jews meant Persia when they told Gozani they came from the Western Regions, they obviously were not implying they knew they came from Judah as Gozani suggests, since in Han it was no longer part of Persia.

Of course, all Jews originated in Judah, Pan notes. They knew this not from memory or word-of-mouth legend, but from *Exodus* in their Bible. If they really knew they came to China directly from Judah, they would have written it clearly and unequivocally on all of the inscriptions, and not have said Tianzhu in one place and Xiyu in another.

The Jews spread in many directions after they lost their country. But before that, aside from a move by some to Egypt, they migrated mainly toward the east. To understand this, and lay a foundation for Chapter VI, says Pan, we must examine their folk tales and history. He offers a general review:

They originated on the west bank of the Euphrates in Mesopotamia, equivalent to present day Iraq. About 2,000 B.C., their patriarch Abraham, whom the Kaifeng Jews called *Awuluohan,* led them south into Canaan, that is, Palestine. Subsequently, in the time of Abraham's grandson Jacob, called *Yahejuewu* by the Kaifeng Jews, they moved to Egypt because of famine. Jacob had twelve sons, who later founded the Twelve Tribes.

Because the Jews were enslaved and mistreated by the Egyptian rulers, they fled the country after a stay of some two hundred—some say four hundred—years and reoccupied Palestine. Calculating according to legend, this was probably around 1,270 B.C.

Gradually they established a kingdom, producing several famous monarchs, such as David and Solomon. But in approximately 930 B.C. the kingdom split into two, with the north becoming Israel and the south becoming Judah. The powerful Mesopotamian country Assyria pushed south in the 8th century

B.C. and destroyed Israel, carrying off twenty-seven or twenty-eight thousand captives. This was in 722 B.C.

In 586 B.C. Babylonia, replacing Assyria, crushed Judah and took away even more prisoners, causing the historic "Babylonian Exile." Sixty or seventy years later, a small number of the descendants of the captives, thanks to the relatively lenient policy of the newly rising Persia which had conquered Babylonia, were allowed to return to their homeland. By the middle of the 5th century B.C. they had rebuilt the city of Jerusalem and the temple which was their central place of worship.

During the turbulent five or six hundred years from the time the Jews fled Egypt to the destruction of Israel, the ten tribes which had been living on the relatively flat Israel plains are believed to have been thoroughly scattered. This was known as "the loss of the Ten Tribes." Only the two tribes settled in hilly Judah remained intact. They were the tribe of Judah, whose people were the more numerous, and the tribe of Benjamin. These then, were the Jews who in the 5th century B.C. restored their homeland.

The restoration was more a union of religious sentiments than the formation of an organized government. Torn by internal strife and subject to constant outside harassment, the country was weak and never at peace. The Persian rulers were fairly enlightened, but in the hundred years between the middle of the 5th and middle of the 4th century B.C. they nevertheless caused the Jews to move several times from their homeland to Babylon and to Hyrcania, today known as Asterabad, on the southeast shore of the Caspian Sea.

Religious life developed. What we now know as Judaism took form in the middle or the end of the 5th century B.C. under the guidance of the prophet Ezra. The most important of the Israelite scriptures—the Torah, or Five Books of Moses, were composed in this period, marking the coming into maturity of the Jewish religion.

But the state never attained maturity. It was never more than a tributary, or simply a province, of one or another big nation. A series of big nations dominated Judah. Persia was followed by Alexander's Macedon, Ptolemy's Egypt, Seleucid's Syria, and Caesar's Rome. A number of national revolts, including the one led by Jesus, all ended in defeat, until finally, in 70 A.D., the military might of the Roman Empire destroyed Jerusalem and converted the Jewish temple into a Roman shrine. In 135 the Jews were prohibited from entering their holy city, or from even coming within sight of its walls, on pain of death. This added impetus to the mass Diaspora which had begun in the year 70.

Pan traces the eastward movement of the Jews from Babylonia and Persia, to which they had gone as captives. He says:

> East of Persia is Afghanistan, a country containing a complex mixture of ethnic nationalities. The main one is the Durani, who call themselves in Arabic Ben-i-Israel, meaning the Children of Israel. They say their ancestors were forcibly removed from Babylon and settled in the Media (northwestern Persia). From there, they migrated to northwestern Afghanistan.
>
> They claim they are descended from Saul, who preceded David as King of the Israelites. They say Saul's son Jeremy fathered a son named Afghan, and that the Jews who moved to Afghanistan from Persia are his descendants. Another story is that they departed the homeland in the time of Solomon, who expelled them.
>
> Although these tales are not entirely credible, there are one or two things about the Durani which are worth noting: First, their features, including their hooked noses, in general resemble those of biblical times Jews. This is especially true of their women. Second, their unwritten law, called Pukhtunwali, is very similar to the law of the ancient Hebrews, although it was modified somewhat by later Muslim influence.
>
> The Tajik people in the Badakshan area of northeast Afghanistan also resemble Jews. Up near the northern border is the city of Balkh, or Bactria, known in China in ancient times as Daxia, when it was an important Central Asian traffic artery. The city has a Jewish residential district of many years standing.
>
> North of Afghanistan, in Soviet Uzbekistan, is the city of Bokhara. It has a large Jewish district which is very old. There is also a considerable Jewish community in Samarkand, another important commercial hub in Central Asia.
>
> South and southeast of Afghanistan is India.

Some of the places Pan describes as Indian were in India in ancient times, such as Khairpur and Karachi, but are now part of Pakistan. Kashmir is claimed by both countries.

> The stages of Jewish migration through India are equally important with, if not more important than, those through Persia. The people of Kashmir, which borders on Afghanistan, closely resemble Jews. For this reason, some believe them to be descendants of the Lost Tribes of Israel.
>
> Travelling southwest across Punjab you reach Khaibar, also called Khairpur, or Khyrpoor, which is not far to the northeast of Karachi. As late as the first half of the 15th century the region had a small Jewish kingdom which could muster 300,000 troops. The

king, of course, was a Jew. The local people say they came after the first destruction of the temple in Jerusalem in the 6th century B.C. In other words, they are descendants of the Jews who were captured by the Babylonians.

Pan wonders whether it might not have been even earlier, such as the fall of Israel in 722 B.C. He quotes 2 Kings 18:11, which says: "The Assyrian emperor took the Israelites to Assyria as captives and settled some of them in the city of Halah, some near the River Habor in the district of Gozan, and some in the cities of Media." Pan suggests the Jews of Khaibar may have migrated from those places.

South along the Arabian seacoast is a whole string of areas and ports, large and small, closely connected with the Jews. Kolaba, known as Cheul in ancient times, is a seaport and district thirty or forty miles south of Bombay. The Jews here, with perhaps even more justification than the Durani, also call themselves Ben-i-Israel. Kolaba's heaviest concentration of Jews is in Junjira, a principality of ethnic peoples. In Kolaba and the Bombay Presidency generally the Jewish population exceeds 10,000.

Some say they didn't arrive until the 15th century. But their own tradition has it that they came in 175 B.C., after fleeing from persecution by Seleucid king Antiochus IV (Epiphanes), and travelling through Egypt and across the Red Sea. An examination of the development of their creed and religious practices leads us to believe their story is correct. At least it conforms with historical chronology (221 p. 540–541, and Haeem Samuel Kehimkar *The History of Bene-Israel of India*).

Craganore, much further south, once had a very large and very old Jewish community. In 1020 they received from their Indian rulers a bronze plaque inscribed with the many rights bestowed upon them. These included the grant of a large tract of land, the right to collect taxes from its tenants, and the right of Jewish leaders to ride in elephant howdahs, be sheltered by umbrellas, and when travelling to be preceded by ceremonial panoply and flunkies shouting to clear the way. This was the beginning of the 11th century, but the Jews surely had arrived much earlier. They must have long since established a firm foothold, or the local satraps would never have felt obliged to grant them such rare privileges (221, and David G. Mandelbaum *The Jewish Way of Life in Cochin*).

Part of the same district, and seaport for the area, is Cochin. The Jews there say they arrived after the 70 A.D. destruction of Jerusalem and the temple. According to Mandelbaum, he found nothing among them to contradict this statement (221 p. 558). But

Godbey believes the first of them came long before the Christian Era, and that their number was gradually increased by later arrivals (193). In any event, Cochin had a very large Jewish community, so much so that the Portuguese, in the 15th and 16th centuries, called the ruler of Cochin "the King of the Jews" (221).

The Cochin Jews have a record called the "Cochin History Roll." It includes events prior to their arrival which do not appear in any history written by Western Jews. Based on these events, Forster (119) contends that the "Ten Lost Tribes" divided into two bodies, the first advancing from Persia and Media into China, the second moving north and integrating with the Tartars to become the Khazars. Perlmann agrees, but thinks most of the "Ten Lost Tribes" remained in Afghanistan, and that this is borne out by existing evidence (168 p. 29–30).

The final port along the Arabian seacoast which contained a Jewish community, notes Pan, was Quilon, formerly known as Coulan or Koulam, near the southwest tip of India. In his *Travels,* Marco Polo says: "Upon leaving Malabar and proceeding five hundred (it should be two hundred) miles toward the southwest, you arrive at the kingdom of Koulam. It is the residence of many Christians and Jews, who retain their regular language" (41 p. 376–377). Pan also quotes from Southern Song writer, Zhou Qufei, who, in his *By Way of Reply from Beyond the Mountains,* wrote in 1178: "In that country live many fan ke from Dashi." Says Pan:

Dashi meant Arabia. Fan ke in the strict sense meant Muslims. But Zhou naturally wouldn't have been able to distinguish among the various religions and races from abroad. There were many different kinds. So far as Koulam was concerned, they were all "fan ke," including the Jews. And as in Kolaba and Cochin, they certainly had arrived well before the 12th century, as their history attests.

Pan observes that inland in southern India one can still find a fairly ancient Jewish settlement in the small city of Chentamangalam, and that the island of Ceylon, to the southeast of India, also has many Jews. This was noted by a 10th century Arab traveller (221 p. 557).

As can be seen from the foregoing, says Pan, the Jews travelled east from their homeland. But from Persia and Afghanistan, some migrated east, and some went south. East to Bukhara and Samarkand, to Balkh in Afghanistan, then across the Pamir mountains into Kashgar, known as Sule in the Han and Tang dynasties. That was the route the Jews gradually followed east. We are clear on that, Pan alleges.

But that still doesn't answer our question: What was the last country they resided in before entering China? Directly from Persia and Afghanistan? Or did they move first to southwest India and then east to China? If they migrated directly east, they had to have travelled by land. If they went first south and then east, they would have come by sea.

Pan proposes an examination of four different possibilities: 1) from Persia, 2) from India, 3) by land, and 4) by sea. The Kaifeng Jews said they came from "Tianzhu" and from "Xiyu." Of course these were the two main routes. Xiyu had to mean Persia, and Tianzhu could only be India. Were the Kaifeng Jews suggesting these to future researchers as the main avenues for investigation? Pan proceeds:

1). From Persia.

a) People who have seen the Scriptures of the Kaifeng Jews say some of the letters are written in the Persian style (27, p. 32). They suspect the writer may himself have been Persian (27, p 48). Others have discovered Persian words in the Scriptures (58). Still others have detected in Scriptures—other than the Torah— Jewish-Persian dialect (180).

b) The paper they used was thick, and came from Persia (27 p. 32, 48). This was for auxiliary scriptures. The Torah was written on parchment.

c) When they first arrived in Kaifeng a part of their vocabulary was still Persian, including words such as *wusida* (usta).

d) Godbey notes that the structure of the Kaifeng synagogue compound was clearly different from those erected by Jews in the West, and was of the general Semitic *mikdash* type. That is, a large rectangle, with buildings for various purposes arranged around it. The holiest Rear Hall was located at the far western end. Before that a Front Hall where the worshippers first gathered. When they prayed, in the Rear Hall, they faced west. This was typical of Semitic sanctuaries in the Persian areas (193).

e) We learn from what Kaifeng Jews told the Jesuits that they had frequent contact with the "Western Regions" after the construction of the synagogue in the Song dynasty. Brotier believes this means travel of Jews between China and Persia (58). Two Jews who spoke to Adler in the late 19th century were even more specific (133, 143). They said for the past three hundred years their religious practices had been influenced by the Persian Jews (168).

The problem with that is it omits the whole 13th to 16th century period. It would have been more accurate to say that this influence continued during the three hundred years following the erection of the synagogue in the 12th century, and that it subsequently declined. The Kaifeng Jews themselves admitted there had been no more travellers from the "Western Regions" for the last two hundred years, which is why their religious life had deteriorated. And they said this a hundred years ago.

We can therefore conclude that among the Kaifeng Jews there were some who came to China directly from Persia, and proceeded directly or indirectly to Kaifeng.

2). From India.

There are more supporters of a migration from Persia than from India, because there is more evidence. But French Sinologist Chavannes is a firm adherent of the India theory. He claims much of what is said of a Persian migration is unreliable. The Kaifeng Jews arrived in the Song dynasty from India via sea, bearing entry gifts, he alleges, and not by land across Central Asia (151).

Goodrich, based on Mandelbaum's findings, thinks a portion of the Chinese Jews are descended from Jews of Cochin, India, who came to sell cotton goods.

Chinese writers who confirm the Indian theory are the anonymous author of "Self Cultivation" (230) and the editor who included the article in the collection called *Avoiding Heterodoxy* (228). They say: "Jews of the *Wuhali* sect brought cotton and cloth of five colors as tribute in the Long Xing period (1163–1165) of the Song dynasty and thus . . . gained a foothold in China . . . The name of their faith was the Indian religion because *Wuhali* came from northern India."

We don't know whether these are the words of the writer or the editor. *Avoiding Heterodoxy* was published in 1861. "Self Cultivation" of course was written earlier. They have several extremely erroneous concepts of the Kaifeng Jews and their religion. For example, they lump Judaism and Christianity together, and say the Kaifeng Jews fabricated the famed Nestorian Tablet . . .

But between the 17th century publication of "As in a Dream" (12) and Hong Jun's *Religions of the Yuan Dynasty* (23) in 1897, we have found no other article in Chinese which goes into any detail on the Kaifeng Jews. And so they are worthy of our attention. This *Wuhali* they mention does not appear on the tablets or in any of the writings of the Kaifeng Jews. Where, precisely, he came from, needs more investigation.

Pan says we have only two proofs the Kaifeng Jews travelled directly from India, but both are fairly solid. The first is the statement in the 1489 inscription that they brought Western cotton cloth as entry tribute

(6). Southwest India was the first region in the world to raise cotton, Pan alleges, and he quotes Herodotus to the effect that Indians were wearing garments of cotton cloth in the 5th century B.C.

Before the development of Western textile machinery, Indian home-spun was famous. Chinese records make no mention of cotton until the Six Dynasties and Tang. It was called "jibei," and had been brought in from India. But not until the end of the 13th century, Pan explains, did people like Huang Daopuo (Mistress Huang) start raising and weaving cotton in China. From Tang to the beginning of Yuan, says Pan, cotton cloth was a rare commodity, which is why it was worthy of ranking as an "entry tribute." He believes it came from the Arabian Sea coast of India, and that it was carried by Jews who travelled directly from Cochin or some other such port.

His second proof is linguistic. He observes that of the various Semitic languages Aramaic was the closest to Hebrew. Part of the Torah was written in Aramaic. At the time of Jesus, Aramaic was prevalent among the Jews, and was also spoken in Syria, Mesopotamia and Persia. In the 6th and 5th century B.C. when Darius conquered the Indus River area, he implanted speakers of Aramaic into Afghanistan and northwest India, where it evolved into a new language called Kharoshthi, which subsequently, Pan claims, spread into China's north-west. He says:

> Early in this century fragments written in this language were found in Dunhuang, brought in, very likely by Jews from north-west India. Godbey is of that opinion, and he further contends that Kharoshthi did not fully evolve in India until long after its earlier form was transmitted to northwest China—not by a scat-tering of traders but by a large scale migration from India's north-west.
>
> In 60 A.D. the flourishing Yueshi (Yueh Chih) people swept down into northwest India and established the Kushan kingdom. They encouraged the local residents, who spoke Kharoshthi, to move to the original homeland of the Yueshi—China's northwest. It is thus, Godbey asserts, that Jews and Judaism most probably entered China (193, 220 I. p. 137).

Another point for the school of thought which alleges the Jews first entered China in Han, remarks Pan. It even offers a bit of documentary evidence. But the evidence requires more detailed study: what specifically was the relationship between the Jews and Kharoshthi? Godbey believes Darius shifted into India's northwest Jews who had already been moved twice before, and as a result we now find traces of Judaism from the southeastern shores of the Caspian Sea all the way to the Punjab. This we can concede, says Pan. But can we say for sure that thereafter it was the Jews who brought Kharoshthi into northwest China?

He then takes up the dispute over whether the Jews came to China by land or by sea.

3. By Land

The road across Asia commenced taking shape at the start of Eastern Han at the latest, that is, the early years of the Christian era, and the ones who trod out this road were, for the most part, traders in silk. Before the 6th century only China produced silk and silk fabric. After Imperial Rome conquered the Mediterranean region and amassed huge wealth, she developed a great appetite for Eastern silk. To satisfy this demand, silk merchants came into being.

They travelled from west to east, from Antioch on the northeastern shore of the Mediterranean to Baghdad, to Merv (now in the Soviet Union), to Samarkand, across the Pamirs, and into China's Kashgar.

Among the silk merchants there must have been many Jews. The Jews like trade, and they are good at it. This was so before they lost their homeland, and even more so after. Constantly travelling the Silk Road, they naturally halted temporarily in various cities, large and small, along the way. Or they may have lived for a time in one place, and then moved on to another. In general, they travelled from west to east. For east was where silk and other merchandise was to be found. In those days production was more active in the east than in the west. Moreover, China was relatively peaceful, with little of the turmoil plaguing Central Asia.

The Jews of Ningxia undoubtedly arrived at that time along the Silk Road, and perhaps a portion of the Kaifeng community as well. The road between the two cities was well-travelled, and the Jews in both places maintained close relations. We can see this from the aid the Ningxia Jews gave in rebuilding the Kaifeng synagogue.

4. By Sea

Pan says sea traffic between Europe and Asia started later than travel by land. Most of those who came by land were Persians— Persians in the broadest sense of the word, which included Jews. "Arabian foreigners" were in the majority at the inception of sea travel from the west, and these too included Jews, although in the narrow sense the term meant Muslims. Pan notes the two western points of departure:

The Red Sea and the Persian Gulf. From both places ships crossed the Arabian Sea and entered Mangalore Bay in India.

From there, they wound through the South Sea Islands, and on to China.

To accommodate these vessels, and their own, starting in Tang the Chinese set up a Joint National and Municipal Directorate, with a few Maritime Bureaus in the major seaports along China's southeast coast. Some say only in Guangzhou. Others claim Quanzhou and Hangzhou also had them.

In Song all three places definitely had these Bureaus, and there was a municipal Maritime Office in Hua Ting, today called Song Jiang, which was the forerunner of the Maritime Bureau established in Shanghai in Yuan. Hangzhou included Ganpu, mentioned above.

From the Tang dynasty on, each of these seaports had its "Foreign District"—an area reserved for the residence of foreign traders. Clashes among them were settled according to the laws of their own countries. Disputes between foreigners and Chinese were adjudicated according to Chinese law.

Abu Zaid during the Tang dynasty, and Ibn Batuta writing in Yuan, both remarked on how large the populations were in the Foreign Districts. In Song a foreigner was appointed Supervisor of the District in Guangzhou. He controlled all the residents' civil affairs, and collected tribute from them on behalf of the government. This was noted by Zhu Yu, in Chapter Three of his *Pingzhou Chats*. His father was an important official in the city of Guangzhou, so his comment is believable. Hangzhou's "subsidiary town," referred to by Ibn Batuta as having a "Gate of the Jews," was undoubtedly a Foreign District.

Pan agrees with Chavannes and Goodrich that the Kaifeng Jews, or that portion of them who played a decisive role, probably came by sea from the west coast of India, perhaps on a ship from the Persian Gulf, perhaps on an Indian vessel, perhaps on a Chinese ship returning home. But he thinks they didn't necessarily set sail from Cochin, as Goodrich believes. Pan says they may also have started from Kolaba to the north, or from Quilon to the south.

He quotes Zhou Qufei, who stated in his *Ling Wai Dai Da (By Way of Reply from Beyond the Mountains)*: "Many Arabian foreigners live in Quilon . . . Some come to sell horses . . . Chinese merchants with cargo for Arabia must transfer it to smaller vessels in Quilon . . ." Pan recalls that Marco Polo had remarked on the presence of Jews in that city, and adds that the "Arabian foreigners" described by Zhou Qufei certainly included Jews. If Chinese merchants could go to Quilon, why couldn't Jewish merchants come to China? Of course they could, Pan asserts, and in large number. Otherwise, where did the Guangzhou and Hangzhou Jewish populations come from? Abu Zaid was speaking in the Tang dynasty, Zhou Qufei in Southern Song, and Marco Polo in Yuan. That conditions for sea travel were equally good in the intervening Northern Song period goes without saying. Pan continues:

> The Kaifeng Jews who brought cotton as "tribute" almost beyond any doubt came during the heyday of sea traffic from a port in southwest India—be it Bombay, Kolaba, Junjira, Cranganore, Cochin, or Quilon.
>
> Ceylon is another possibility. It had a considerable number of Jews in the 9th and 10th centuries. There is also the Persian Gulf region and the western shores of the Arabian Sea. But the Jews there were Persians and other Western Asians, not Indian Jews.
>
> A still more distant sea route might have been from the region of the Red Sea, particularly around Yemen in the southwest corner of Arabia. The Yemen Jews say they arrived there 42 years before the first destruction of the temple in Jerusalem, that is, the end of the 7th century B.C. (221 p. 547). In Adler's view the content and the style of many of the prayers of the Kaifeng Jews are similar to those of the Jews of Yemen (168 p. 17). We therefore must suspect a relationship between the two. But from all the material we have been able to examine thus far, we believe the contention that they sailed to China from the southwest coast of India is the most convincing.

Pan points out that although Persia and the land route, and India and the sea route, are closely linked, they are not identical. Sea voyages could have started in Persia, or the Red Sea, without touching India. Kharoshthi-speaking Jews from the Indus River valley, who entered Xinjiang at the commencement of the Christian era, travelled overland. Thus we see, says Pan, that Persian Jews may have come to China by sea, just as Indian Jews may have come by land. He sums up as follows:

> Jews who entered China before Tang—and there probably were not too many—came by land east from Persia. It is highly unlikely that any came by sea. From Tang onward, both routes were used. Many travellers, including Marco Polo, came from the west by land and returned by sea.
>
> So far as the Kaifeng Jews are concerned, the main body sailed from southwest India. This was also obviously the approach to the Ningbo, Hangzhou, Nanjing, Yangzhou area. But both before and after the main body arrived in Kaifeng a substantial number of Jews came by land, some directly from abroad, some via other Chinese cities, such as Ningxia and quite possibly Beijing. More study should clear this up fairly easily.

VI. WHEN THE JEWS LEFT THEIR NATIVE LAND

The time the Jews left their homeland and the time they entered China are not, and could not possibly be, the same, Pan asserts. None of the conditions existed for a direct migration, neither their knowledge of world geography, nor of China, nor of travel conditions. The gap between the two times, therefore, could be anything from a few score, to several hundred, to a thousand years. Pan says the material we have to date leads us to the conclusion that the thousand year lapse is the most logical insofar as that portion of the Kaifeng Jews who played a decisive role is concerned.

In accordance with major events outlined above in Jewish history, Pan goes on, plus the premises various writers have offered in this regard, we can divide Jewish history into four periods, and estimate in which of these periods it is most likely the Jews left their homeland. This is the only approach we can use, Pan insists, because we can find nothing at all about this in their records, either concerning the Kaifeng Jews or Jews in China in general. Although they do have a few comments about a time of entry, they say not a word about when they departed from their native land. Pan outlines the four historical periods as follows:

1. Before the time of Moses, that is, prior to 1,300 B.C.

2. From the exodus from Egypt to the conquest of Israel by Assyria, that is, from 1,300 to 586 B.C., a period of approximately 700 years during which the so-called Loss of the Ten Tribes allegedly occurred.

3. From the Babylonian exile to the Roman conquest, that is, from 586 B.C. to 70 A.D.

4. From the start of the Diaspora to the completion of the Talmud, that is, from 70 to 600 A.D. During this period there were two other developments worth noting. The first was the growth of the rabbinical system. The second was the replacement of a central Temple by scattered synagogues. These features help determine when the Kaifeng Jews left their native land.

Pan then examines the four historical periods in turn:

1. Before the Time of Moses. (Prior to 1,300 B.C.)

Alexei Vinogradov, the Russian, held that this is when the Jews entered China. A quite impossible premise. To reach China before Moses was born they would have to have left their homeland even earlier. But prior to Moses they had no homeland. The twelve tribes were still in Egypt. They had not yet become Jews, or even Israelites.

2. From the Exodus from Egypt to the Conquest of Israel by Assyria. (1,300 to 700 B.C.)

This can also be termed the Loss of the Ten Tribes period, for it was then that they left Palestine, one after another, and vanished. They are a mystery to Western Jews and Christians alike, and their disappearance has become a kind of myth. Beginning in the 9th century travellers in Europe, Asia and Africa increased, and many claimed they encountered persons who resembled Jews in various remote hamlets and isolated villages. Fired by religious fervor, they labelled them descendants of the Lost Tribes. Even a few Irishmen and Anglo-Saxons came forward to assert their right to the honor.

None of the Chinese Jews claimed to be descendants of the Lost Tribes of Israel. Kaifeng's Jews said only that their ancestor was Jacob, also known as Israel. They did not say they were descendants of any of Jacob's twelve sons—from whom the twelve tribes were derived—nor did they refer in any way to the story of the "loss."

Pan recalls that the earliest proponent of the Lost Tribes origin for the Chinese Jews was Manasseh ben Israel, in the 17th century. His theory was that the Ten Tribes first went to Central Asia, then were driven out and scattered by the Tartars. Those who fled the farthest became the American Indians. Another segment ended in China (221 p. 520, 521, quoting the Introduction to *The Hope of Israel* by Manasseh, published in Amsterdam in 1651). Perhaps Manasseh was influenced by the letters Matteo Ricci sent to Rome (49), says Pan, or he may have created the story out of whole cloth. Pan continues:

Most of the supporters of the theory that the first Jews arrived during the Zhou dynasty also allege, of necessity, that these Jews were members of the Ten Lost Tribes. Foremost among them are Sionnet (85), Forster (119), Bainbridge (158), and Perlmann (168). They offer three reasons. First, the Kaifeng Jews knew themselves only as Israelites, and were unfamiliar with the term Jew. This was clearly manifested, they say, by Ai Tian in his conversations with Matteo Ricci.

They consider this very significant. Israel became the name of the northern country after the United Kingdom split in two. The Jews living there were Israelites, comprising ten of the twelve tribes. The other two were in Judah to the south. In 722 B.C. Assyria defeated Israel and led its people off into captivity, settling some here and there and scattering others. Thus, the "Ten Lost Tribes." Naturally, they remembered only the name of their northern land, Israel. While their ancestors may have known of the southern country of Judah, whose people were called Judeans, or Jews, they had no relations with them; in fact they were enemies. And so they certainly would never have thought of themselves as Jews. With the passage of centuries, their descendants forgot about Judah and the Jews completely.

Second, the Durani in Afghanistan, who call themselves Ben-i-Israel, or Children of Israel; the Kashmiri, who Bernier de Nevilles guessed in the 13th century were descendants of the Lost Tribes; the people in the Habor River area where Jews of Israel were exiled by the Assyrian emperor in the 8th century B.C.; and the Jews in the Bombay area who also call themselves Ben-i-Israel, were all plainly from Israel, not Judah, and therefore descendants of the Ten Lost Tribes.

Third, Perlmann especially put great stress on the Isaiah prediction that the Jews would return from "Sinim," and insisted this meant China. Isaiah lived at the end of the 8th—some say the middle of the 6th—century B.C. during the reign of Persian King Cyrus. In any event, he had to know, or even witness, the dispersal of the Israelites, or he would not have been able to predict their return, Perlmann contends.

Pan concedes some merit to the first two reasons, but he questions the entire concept. If the Ten Tribes were scattered and lost, could they have retained folk and religious traditions recognizable as such centuries later? In recent years many people have come to consider the story of the Lost Tribes a myth, he says, which grew more vague with the telling. He cites Godbey (193), then gives his own viewpoint:

It would be more reasonable to say that in the period between the exodus from Egypt and the Assyrian conquest, since the religious structure was still unformed, and since Canaan, where the Jews had settled, was a crossroads open to attack from all sides, there was little cohesiveness and a strong tendency toward disintegration. Group by group, people drifted away, and some wandered ultimately to China.

Besides Godbey, the two who are in clearest opposition to the Ten Lost Tribes theory are James Finn and Edward Isaac Ezra (147). Finn and Godbey have their own theories.

3. From the Babylonian Exile to the Roman Conquest (586 B.C.–70 A.D.).

Pan lists the reasons offered by Finn for his belief that the Jews must have left their homeland after their return from Babylonia and not before, although how long after, Finn is unable to say.

First, Finn reminds us, in their commemorative tablets the Kaifeng

Jews hail Ezra as their "second law-giver," the first having been Moses. This means they knew of the rebuilding of Jerusalem and the Temple (5th century B.C.). Second, they possessed a few verses from *Daniel,* and all of *Esther,* whom they venerated as the "Great Mother."

Finn points out they were not unfamiliar with the word "Jew," as some have said. It appears in *Esther* several times, though "Israelite" is not mentioned once. Pan says this indirectly refutes the claim that since the Kaifeng Jews called themselves Israelites they knew nothing of Judah and the term "Jews," and must therefore have come to China as part of a migration of the "Ten Lost Tribes of Israel." Only Ai Tian in his talks with Matteo Ricci displayed an ignorance of the term "Jew." In his eagerness to get ahead as an official he may have forgotten the teachings of his ancestors, says Pan, but he was only speaking for himself.

Pan continues:

> The *Book of Esther* was written in the 4th or 3rd century B.C. *Daniel* is now believed to have been created around the middle of the 2nd century B.C., which would coincide with the rule of Antiochus Epiphanes, called Antiochus IV (175–164 B.C.). Finn does not spell this out, but we can do it for him. When his book was published in 1843, biblical research into the Old Testament had not reached the point of refinement it has today.
>
> Third, the *Haphtorah* of the Kaifeng Jews includes selections from prophets like Zechariah and Malachi, who lived in Jerusalem during the time of the Second Temple.
>
> Fourth, in their religious life the Jews of Kaifeng calculated according to the Era of Contracts calendar, which runs from 312 B.C. Not until 1015 did Western Jews adopt what is known as the Era of Creation calendar. The Era of Contracts calendar first came into use in the Jewish homeland in 198 B.C. during the reign of a Greek Seleucid king. This was the calendar the Kaifeng Jews were still using in the 17th century.

At the other end of the time frame, Finn thinks the Jews may have left their homeland before the time of Christ, Pan points out. For one thing, the Kaifeng Jews had never heard of him, nor did they manifest any revulsion to the crucifix, at least Ai Tian was unmoved when shown one by Matteo Ricci. Nor did they suffer from what Finn calls "rabbinical despotism." Pan goes a step further and says flatly they had no rabbinical system at all.

Turning to Godbey, Pan observes that he did not state when he thought the Jews left their homeland. He did, however, in reviewing the contentions of others, indicate a preference, according to Pan, for a time prior to the successful revolt by the Maccabees in 164 B.C. Pan says:

> Most Western Jews commemorate the restoration of national independence and freedom of religion resulting from the Hasmonean uprising in the sixties of the 2nd century B.C. by the Feast of Lights, known as Hannukah. The Kaifeng Jews did not observe this holiday, indicating that they did not know of this glorious page in their history, because it occurred after their departure.
> 4. From the Start of the Diaspora to the Completion of the Talmud. (70–600 A.D.)

There are many proponents of this theory, says Pan, but most can offer little in its support. All who believe the Jews left their homeland after the destruction of Jerusalem and the Second Temple and came to China during the Han dynasty fall within this category. Their reasoning is *à priori*. Since the greatest dispersal of Jews occurred at that time, that is when they must have migrated to China, they contend. But they offer nothing to evince either the objective conditions or the subjective desire for such a move, Pan maintains.

Pan agrees with Finn that the Jews may have left their homeland while the Talmud was in the process of being created. Finn thought that a list of rabbis appended to a Kaifeng copy of *Genesis* and the observance of rabbinical customs in the slaughtering of animals for food show a Talmudic influence. Also because the Kaifeng Jews hung a plaque in their synagogue reading "Israel, remember this: The Lord—and the Lord alone—is our God." Displaying this plaque, says Finn, was adopted by Jews in all Western synagogues subsequent to the creation of the Talmud.

Gozani, as a Catholic Jesuit, Pan notes, believed the Kaifeng Jews were Talmudists, since his examination of their Old Testament showed it to correspond with the European editions "tampered with" by the early Talmudists. Their ancestors, therefore, he concluded, must have departed Palestine while the Talmud was being compiled, or even later.

Pan then offers his own analysis:

> Our preliminary view is that the Jews left Palestine between the Babylonian exile and the Roman conquest, that is, between 586 B.C. and 70 A.D. From the synagogue of the Kaifeng Jews, their scriptures, and their religious practices we have reason to believe it was a considerable time after they returned from Babylon and built the Second Temple.
> From the fact that they used the Era of Contracts calendar, we know that it could not have been before 198 B.C., since that was

the year Seleucid king Antiochus III, who imposed this calendar, took control of their country. But that would be setting it too early. A period of confusion would be bound to follow the forced adoption of an alien calendar. At least nine or ten years would have to have elapsed before it became a customary part of their lives.

We must also bear in mind that during 198 and 197 B.C., under the reign of Antiochus III, they were granted certain privileges, including freedom of worship. They would feel no compulsion to leave. Their departure, therefore, must have been subsequent to 197 B.C.

By the time of Antiochus IV (176–164 B.C.) their situation had considerably worsened. He extorted their wealth and tried to force them to become Greeks, using cruel and tyrannical methods. We have no doubt that many Jews had no choice but to abandon their native hearths during these years of oppression.

But we can narrow the period of likely departure still further, for in 168 B.C. the Maccabees led a revolt against the Seleucid Greeks. In 164 B.C. they captured Jerusalem and rededicated the Temple to Jehovah. This is celebrated in the West every year by the Feast of Lights, or Hannukah. Since the Kaifeng Jews had not even a shadow of such a holiday, their ancestors must have set forth before the revolt began, but after the start of the oppression by Antiochus IV, in other words, between 176 and 167 B.C. The Kaifeng Jews would naturally know nothing of subsequent developments, such as the advent of Jesus Christ, the meaning of the crucifix, the conquest by the Romans, and the Diaspora which ensued.

Pan finds further evidence of a departure date in an examination of the Old Testament scriptures in the possession of the Kaifeng Jews. He notes that the first of these is the Torah, or the Five Books of Moses, which they called in Chinese the Scriptures of the Way, or the Great Scriptures. Second is the Prophets. Third is the Hagiographa.

Pan states that these three sections were declared canon at different times. The Torah was the earliest, in the 5th century B.C. Next, in the early part of the 2nd century B.C., came the Prophets. Hagiographa was last, around 100 B.C.

In the Scriptures Repository of the Kaifeng Jews the Torah was the only complete section, Pan says, and the most revered. At one time the Kaifeng temple was named after it—"The Synagogue Which Respects the Scriptures of the Way." But the Prophets was not complete, and the Hagiographa was virtually non-existent.

He asserts that the completeness of the Torah and the veneration which it enjoyed shows that the Jews must have left their homeland after the 5th century B.C. The nearly total absence of the Hagiographa demonstrates that they had already departed before 100 B.C. Their only partial possession of the Prophets indicates that they left while this section was still being edited into canon—which is why they couldn't possibly have obtained a full set, although they could and did have a copy of *Esther* and fragments from *Daniel.*

To Pan this confirms they could not have left Palestine at any time other than between the seventies and the sixties of the 2nd century B.C. as stated above.

Pan replies to the query of how was it possible for them to have materials appearing after the Diaspora, and showing Talmudic and rabbinical influences, thus:

> The influences were slight, and their connection with the Kaifeng materials is yet to be established. Even if these influences existed, they could have been introduced from the outside subsequent to their arrival and grafted on to their original religious customs and structure. They continued to have dealings with Jews from the West, who might very well have brought these influences in. This would still be the case even if it were found that they had the *Book of the Maccabees* although not celebrating Hannukah.

Domenge in a letter dated 1721 says he was told by the Kaifeng Jews that they had the first two volumes of *Maccabees,* but admits he did not see them. Pan asserts that even if they existed, the fact that the Kaifeng Jews had only one copy of each showed how little importance they attached to them. Regarding Esther, the situation was quite different.

> Were it not for her, the Jews of Babylon would have been slaughtered. In other words, *The Book of Esther* and the Purim holiday are very different from *The Book of the Maccabees* and Hannukah. Although they concern equally glorious events, the attitude of the Kaifeng Jews toward them, or at least toward the books about them, was obviously not the same. Their ancestors had been personally involved in the crisis of Esther's time, whereas the Maccabean war was something they heard about only many years later.

Pan returns to the Jews of India to put the final piece in place in the long trek between Palestine and Kaifeng. He believes the statement by the Kolaba Jews in the Bombay area is correct. Namely, that they arrived there in 175 B.C., having fled their homeland to escape oppression by Antiochus IV. Pan alleges three religious practices, identical among the Bombay and Kaifeng Jews, prove the link between them.

Both communities give much prominence to the prayer: "Israel, remember this! The Lord—and the Lord alone—is our God." It has been customary from earliest times among Jews the world over to recite this prayer. It appears in Deuteronomy 6:4, and well pre-dates the Talmud. Finn is wrong to cite the use of it as manifesting a Talmudic influence.

The synagogues in both places burned incense during their prayer services, a custom followed in Jerusalem only up to, but not after, the destruction of the Second Temple in 70 A.D.

Neither community celebrated the Feast of the Lights, namely, Hannukah. This is the most important reason because it substantiates the claim of the Bombay Jews that they left Palestine in 175 B.C.

While the Kaifeng Jews are not as specific, since their objective conditions before leaving their homeland and the customs they retained thereafter are identical to those of the Bombay Jews, their time of departure from Palestine would have to be the same. We therefore have reason to believe they were once part of the Jewish community in Bombay, and migrated from there by sea to China.

In summing up his treatise, Pan reaches the following succinct conclusion:

The Jews of Kaifeng played the most decisive role of all the Jews who entered China. They left their native land in the seventies of the 2nd century B.C. and settled in the Bombay district of India. There they remained for 1,100 years until the middle or the end of the 11th century, when they sailed for China and took up residence in Kaifeng.

They came for commercial gain and because they had some knowledge of and liking for China. Was there also some other reason within India which impelled them to leave? This question awaits further study.

Of course we are not saying that all the Jews of Kaifeng came in this manner. Some of them, probably a minority, may have come directly from Persia. We now understand why the Kaifeng commemorative tablets thrice state their origin as "Tianzhu" (India) and once as "Xiyu" (Western Regions, including Persia). This is entirely in keeping with both the facts and the proportion of migrants involved.

BIBLIOGRAPHY: CHINESE AND JAPANESE SOURCES

1) *Genesis,* Chapter 32, verses 28–32.
2) *Isaiah,* Chapter 49, verse 12.
3) *History of the Yuan Dynasty, Biography of Emperor Wen Zong,* the 2nd year of the Tian Li period.
4) *History of the Yuan Dynasty, Biography of Emperor Shun Di,* 6th year of the Zhiyuan period, (1340) 14th year of the Zhizheng period, (1354).
5) Yang Yu: *Shan Ju Xin Hua (Notes from a Mountain Retreat),* 1360, Zhi Bu Zu Chai Series.
6) Jin Chong: Chong Jian Ching Zhen Si Ji (Tablet), 1489.
7) Zuo Tang: Zun Chong Dao Jin Si Ji (Tablet), 1512.
8) Zhao He: *Weiyang Jun Sheng (The History of Yangzhou),* written in the Jia Jing period, Ming dynasty.
9) Zhang Weishu: *Taixi Lixi Tai Zi Zhuan (Biography of Matteo Ricci),* early 17th century.
10) Ai Rulue: *Taixi Lixi Tai Xiansheng Xing Ji (The Life of Master Matteo Ricci),* 1621, collated by Xiang Da of Beijing University and republished in Beijing in 1947, together with (9).
11) Li Guangdian: *Shou Bian Rizhi (The Defense of Kaifeng),* mid-17th century, republished in Henan province, 1899.
12) Author unknown: *Ru Meng Lu (As in a Dream),* mid-17th century, collated by Chang Molai and published by Official Books Bureau, Henan, 1852.
13) Zhao Yangsheng: Examination Paper written in Imperial Hall, 1646, Formerly in the possession of Chen Yuan, now stored in Library of Catholic Cathedral at Xujiawei, Shanghai.
14) Liu Chang: Chong Jian Qing Zhen Si Ji (Tablet), 1663.
15) Chao Yanggun: Ci Tang Shu Gu Bei Ji (Tablet), 1679.
16) Guan Jiezhong (ed.): *Kaifeng Fu Zhi (Kaifeng Prefecture Gazette),* 1695.
17) Ru Zengyu (ed.): *Xiangfu Xian Zhi (Xiangfu County Gazette),* 1739.
18) Zhang Jinsheng and others, (ed.): *Sichuan Tong Zhi (Sichuan General Gazette),* 1736.
19) Ah Si Ha and others (ed.): *Henan Tong Zhi (Henan General Gazette),* 1767.
20) *Liao, Jin, Yuan, San Shi Guo Yu Jie (An Explanation of the Ethnic Languages Used in the Histories of the Liao, Jin and Yuan Dynasties),* Qian Long period, Qing dynasty.
21) Yang Fangcan and others (ed.): *Sichuan Tong Zhi (Sichuan General Gazette),* 1815.
22) *Fujian Tong Zhi (Fujian General Gazette),* Daoguang period, Qing.
23) Hong Jun: "Yuan Shi Jiao Ming Kao" ("Religions of the Yuan Dynasty"), in *Yuan Shi Yi Wen Zheng Bu (Annotations to the Chinese Translation of the Yuan Annals),* Vol. XXIX, 1897.
24) Zhang Xiangwen: *Taliang Fang Bei Ji (On Reading the Kaifeng Tablets),* 1910; later in collection entitled *Nan Yuan Cong Gao,* Vol. IV, p. 8–9, published by Zhong Guo Dixue Hui, 1935, Beijing.
25) Ye Han: *Yicileye Jiao Bei Ba (Postscripts to the Israelite Tablets),* 1913.

26) Yamauchi Shina: "The Jews and the Chinese," in *China,* 1918, Tokyo, Vol. IX, No. 3, p. 19–21.

27) Chen Yuan: "Kaifeng Yicileye Jiao Kao" ("A Study of the Israelite Religion of Kaifeng"), 1920, Commercial Press, Shanghai.

28) Wei Weizhen: "Henan Youtai Ren Zhi Gaikuang" ("The General Situation of the Jews In Henan"), in *Zhong Hua Jidujiao Nian Jian (The Chinese Christian Almanac),* Shanghai, 1921, No. 6, p. 89–90.

29) Ruan Xiang and others (ed.): *Zhong Guo Nian Jian (China Year Book),* 1924, p. 1977–1988.

30) Zhang Xinglang: *Zhong Xi Jiaotong Shiliao Huibian (A Survey of Historical Material Regarding Contacts Between China and the West),* 1930, Fu Jen University series, No. 1, Vol. IV, p. 21–40.

31) Shen Gongbu: "Guanyu Kaifeng *Yicileye* Jiao Zhi Jiguang Pianyu" "Sketches of the Israelite Religion in Kaifeng," in *Sheng Jiao Zazhi (The Holy Religions Magazine),* Shanghai, 1931–1932, Vol. XX, No. 1, p. 14–20; No. 3, p. 141–143. Vol. XXI, No. 1, p. 16–25; No. 2, p. 75–82.

32) Huang Yi: "Zhong Guo Youtai Ren Kao" ("A Study of China's Jews"), 1935, Shanghai, in *Wenhua Jianshe (Cultural Construction),* Vol. I, No. 4, p. 74–78.

33) Wei Yiheng: "Kaifeng Youtai Jiao" ("The Jewish Religion in Kaifeng"), in *Henan Zhonghua Sheng Gong Hui, Hui Kan, (The Holy Catholic Church of Henan, China, Periodical),* May, 1936.

34) Xu Zongze: "Kaifeng Youtai Jiao Gai Lun" ("A Summary of Judaism in Kaifeng"), in the *Sheng Jiao Zazhi (The Holy Religions Magazine).* Shanghai, 1936, Vol. XXV, No. 4, p. 194–202.

35) Guan Bin: "Kaifeng de Youtai Ren" ("The Jews of Kaifeng"), Aug. 28, 1936, in Tientsin's *Da Gong Bao,* History Supplement, No. 100.

36) Fang Hao: "Zhejiang Zhi Youtai Jiao" ("Judaism in Zhejiang"), in *Guo Feng (National Winds),* Nanking, 1936, Vol. VIII, No. 9–10, p. 84–86.

37) Fei Laizhi (translated into Chinese by Feng Chengjun): *Ru Hua Yesuhui Shi Lie Zhuan (Biographies of Jesuits in China),* 1938, Commercial Press, Shanghai, p. 48.

38) Author unknown: "The Israelite and Islamic Religions in China," in *Muslim Affairs,* Nov. 16, 1938: (in Japanese), Tokyo, Vol. I, No. 3, p. 53–66.

39) Pan Guangdan: "Minzhu Guojia de Yi Bi Faxisi Zhang: Meiguo Fan Youtai Yundong Lue Shi" ("A Fascist Debt of a 'Democratic' Country: A Brief History of Anti-Semitism in America,") *Xin Guancha (New Observer),* December, 1950, p. 16–20.

WESTERN SOURCES

40) Aboul Zeyd al Hassan, late 9th century, *Ancient Accounts of India and China,* London, 1733.

41) Marco Polo, late 13th century, *Travels of Marco Polo the Venetian,* Everyman's Library, 1908.

42) Rashid-ud-din, 1304–1307, *The Complete History of the Mongols,* included in Yule (103), *Cathay and the Way Thither,* 1916, London, Vol. III, p. 108–110.

43) Giovanni di Monte Corvino, 1305–1306, *Letters,* in Yule (103), Vol. I, p. 197–221.

44) *Letters from Andrew, Bishop in Zayton in Manzi,* 1326, Yule (103), Vol. III, p. 74.

45) Giovanni di Marignolli, mid-14th century, *Recollections of Travels in the East,* Yule (103), Vol. III, p. 215.

46) *The Travels of Ibn Batuta,* mid-14th century, English edition by S. Lee, 1829.

47) *The Travels of Rabbi Benjamin, son of Jonah, of Tudela; through Europe, Asia and Africa; from the Ancient Kingdom of Navarre to the Frontiers of China,* Istanbul, 1543, in Hebrew, Eng. ed. London, 1783.

48) Benedict Goes, late 16th century, *Travels from Agra to Cathay,* Yule (103) Vol. IV, p. 175.

49) Matteo Ricci S. J., early 17th century, *Opere Storiche del P. Matteo Ricci,* S. I. Macerata, 1911–1913, Vol. I, p. 86–88, Vol. II, p. 290–293.

50) Nicolaus Trigautius, *De Christiana Expeditione apud Sinas,* Rome, 1615, p. 118–120.

51) Alverez de Sammedo, *Imperio de la Chine, i cultura evangelica en él* 1641–1642, Madrid, in Portugese, then Spanish.

52) Jean Paul Gozani, *Lettre sur les Juifs à Kai-feng-fu, 1701,* included in new ed. of (77), Vol. XXVII, p. 266–287.

53) *Lettre du Père Gozani au Père Joseph Suarez,* 1704, Welt Blatt, German, Vol. IV, p. 89.

54) Jean Baptiste Du Halde, *Description géographique, historique de l'empire de la Chine,* 1735, Paris, Vol. III, p. 64.

55) *Jablonski's Hebrew Bible,* 1730–1740, Preface, sec. 38.

56) M. de Guignes, *Histoire générale des Huns,* 1756, Paris, p. 26.

57) Lockman, *Travels of the Jesuits,* 1762, London, Vol. II, p. 11–22.

58) Gabriel Brotier, *Mémoire sur les Juifs établis en Chine,* 1770–1771, included in (77), new ed., Vol. XXIV, p. 56–100.

59) Brotier, *Tacitus,* 1771, Paris, Vol. III, p. 567–580.

60) Benjamin Kennicott, *Dissertio generalis in Biblia Hebraica,* 1776, Oxford, p. 65.

61) Johann David Michaelis, *Orientalische und exegetische Bibliothek,* 1775–1785, Frankfurt, Sec. 5, p. 70; Sec. 9, p. 40; Sec. 15, p. 15.

62) Ignaz Kogler, "Notitiae S.S. Bibliorum Judaeorum in Imperio Sinensi" in the *Neues Journal zur Allgemeinen Literatur und Kunstgeschichte,* 2nd ed., Halle, 1805; Sec. 7, p. 240–252; Sec. 9, p. 81–92.

63) Johann Gottfried Eichhorn, *Einleitung in das alte Testament,* 1780–1783, Leipzig, Vol. II, p. 131.

64) Grosier, *Description général de la Chine,* 1819, Paris, Vol. IV, p. 484.

65) Pierre Cibot, "Parallèlle des moeurs et usages des Chinois avec les moeurs et usages décrits dans le livre d'Esther," 1789–1791, Paris, in *Memoires concernant l'histoire, les moeurs, etc., des Chinois,* Vol. XIV, p. 309–516, Vol. XV, p. 1–207.

66) Cibot, "Digression sur le temps ou les Juifs ont passé en Chine," in *Memoires* (ibid 65), 1791, Vol. XV, p. 52.

67) Christopher Gottlieb von Murr, *Diarii Litterarii*, 1797, Halle, Sec. 1, p. 81, Sec. 2, p. 304.
68) Murr, "Nachtrag zu den Koglerischen Notitiis," 1798, Leipzig, in *Neues Journal* (62, ibid), Sec. 1, p. 147–149.
69) A. J. Silvestre de Sacy, *Notices et extraits des manuscrits de la Bibliothè-que Nationale*, 1799, Paris, Vol. IV, p. 592–625.
70) Olave Gerhard Tychsen, *Abhandlung von der Jahrzahlen der Juden*, early 18th century, p. 9.
71) Murr, *Versuch einer Geschichte der Juden in China*, 1806, Halle, p. 13–20.
72) C. L. J. de Guignes, *Voyage à Pekin, Manille et l'Ile de France, faits dans l'intervalle des années 1784–1801*, Paris, 1801, Vol. II, p. 334.
73) C. L. J. de Guignes, *Memoire de Litt. Tirés des registres de l'Academie des Inscriptions et Belles-Lettres*, 1801, Paris, Vol. XLVIII, p. 763.
74) Antoine Gaubil, *Traité de la chronologie Chinoise*, 1814, Paris, p. 264.
75) *The Jewish Expositer*, 1816, London, p. 101, 135, 414.
76) Henry Ellis, *Journal of the Embassy to China*, 1817, London.
77) *Lettres édifiantes et curieuses, écrites des missions étrangeres, avec les Annales de la propagation de la foi*, 1819–1854, Paris, in 40 volumes.
78) *Calmet's Dictionary of the Bible*, 1823, London, Vol. IV, p. 251.
79) *Delle Opere del Padre Daniello Bartoli della Compagnia di Gesu*, 1825, Turin, Vol. XVI, Part 2, sec. 202, p. 389–390.
80) *Walton's Polygot Bible*, 1825, London, v. 41, Conclusion, Chap. III.
81) De Sacy, *Notices et extraits des manuscrits de la Bibliothèque du Roi*, 1831, Paris, Vol. IV, p. 592. Vol. XII, p. 277.
82) Karl F. A. Gutzlaff, *A Journal of Three Voyages along the Coast of China, 1831, 1832, and 1833*, 1834, London, p. 287.
83) E. C. Bridgman, "Jews in China: Notices of Those in the East by Josephus, Peritsol, Benjamin of Tudela, Manasseh, and the Jesuits" in *The Chinese Repository*, Hong Kong, 1834, Vol. III, Issue 8, p. 172–175.
84) Franz Delitzsch, *Zur Geschichte der Judischen Poesie vom Abschluss der heiligen Schriften des Alten Bundes bis auf die neueste Zeit*, 1836, Leipzig, p. 58–62.
85) Sionnet, *Essai sur les Juifs de la Chine*, 1837, Paris.
86) T. Wright, *Israel in China*, 1842, London.
87) James Finn, *The Jews in China; Their Synagogue, their Scriptures, their History, etc.* 1843, London.
88) W. C. Milne, *Notice of a Seven Months Residence in the City of Ningpo, from December 7th, 1842 to July 7th, 1843*, in Hong Kong (83), Feb., 1844, p. 79.
89) *Archives Israélites de France*, 1844, issues I–V.
90) Henri Hirsch, *Les Juifs de la Chine*, 1844, Paris.
91) W. M. Lowrie, *On the Fulfillment of the Prophecy of Isaiah Concerning the Land of Sinim*, Sept., 1844, Hong Kong (83), p. 466–469.
92) *London Society for Promoting Christianity among the Jews, Annual Report for 1849*.
93) *Journal of Chiang Jung-chi*, 1850, Chinese and English manuscripts in Library of Cambridge University.

94) *Journal of Ch'iu T'ien-sheng,* 1850. This, and (93) included in (95). Both men were Chinese, but Pan treats their reports as Western since they went to Haifeng under the auspices of the London Society . . . See (96).

95) *The North-China Herald,* 1851, Jan. 18, published (93) and (94). Aug. 15 news of two Kaifeng Jews who came to Shanghai with Chiang and Ch'iu.

96) Smith and Medhurst, *A Narrative of a Mission of Inquiry to the Jewish Synagogue of Kaifeng Fu, on Behalf of the London Society for Promoting Christianity among the Jews,* 1851, Shanghai.

97) Israel Josef Benjamin, *Acht Jahre in Asien und Africa von 1846 bis 1855,* 1858, Hanover, p. 156–158, 160–163.

98) W. C. Milne, *Real Life in China,* 1858, London, p. 403–411.

99) "Juden in China," in *Ausland,* Aug., 1858, issue.

100) "China's Hebrews" in the Russian magazine *Zion,* 1861, issue 9, and 1862, issue 37.

101) Alexander Wylie, "Israelites in China" in *The Chinese and Japanese Repository,* London, July, 1863, p. 13–22; August p. 43–52.

102) W. A. P. Martin, "A Visit to the Jews in Honan" in the *Journal of the North-China Branch of the Royal Asiatic Society,* Shanghai, 1866.

103) Henry Yule, *Cathay and the Way Thither,* London, 1866. Vol. I, p. 197–221; Vol. II, p. 309–394. Revised by Henri Cordier in 1916, see (123).

104) "The Hebrews in China," in the *Truth Review,* Russian, 1864, Aug., p. 348–351.

105) "China's Hebrews," in *Gakarmelyo,* Russian, 1849, in issues 38–40, 43, and 45.

106) Pégralb, "Jews in China," in *Bulletin de la société de geographie,* October, 1869, p. 335.

107) J. Alexander, *The Jews,* 1870, London, p. 111 ff.

108) Joseph Edkins, *China's Place in Philology,* 1871, London.

109) Author unknown, "China's Hebrews," 1871, in the Russian magazine, *The Russian Hebrew Reporter,* in issues 32, 36 and 37.

110) Finn, *The Orphan Colony of the Jews in China,* 1872, London.

111) N. McLeod, *Epitome to the Ancient History of Japan,* 1875, Japan, p. 35–36.

112) Mollendorff, *Manual of Chinese Bibliography,* 1876, Shanghai, p. 221–222.

113) Palladius, "Elucidations of Marco Polo's Travels in North China drawn from Chinese Sources" 1876, Shanghai, in *Journal* (102), Number 10.

114) J. L. Liebermann, Title unknown, but in regard to Kaifeng Jews, *Jewish Chronicle,* London, July 11, 1879.

115) Liebermann, "Jews in China" in *Israel's Watchman,* 1879, London, August issue, p. 248.

116) N. McLeod, *Illustrations to the Epitome of the Ancient History of Japan,* 1879, Tokyo.

117) McLeod, *Korea and the Ten Lost Tribes of Israel,* 1879, Tokyo.

118) Richard Andree, *Volkskunde der Juden,* 1881, Bielefeld, p. 244–248.

119) Forster, "The Ten Lost Tribes" in *The Chinese Recorder,* January/February issue, 1885, Shanghai, p. 47–48.

120) Alexei Vinogradov, *A History of the Bible in the Far East,* 1889, St. Petersburg, in Russian.

121) A. Kingsley Glover, "The Tablet Inscriptions of the Chinese Jews discovered at Kai-fung Fu (China) in 1850," in the *Babylonian and Oriental Record,* 1891, June, p. 138–141; July, p. 161–164; August, p. 179–182; also March, 1893, p. 209–213.

122) Moise Schwab, *Itinéraire Juif d'Espagne en Chine au IXe siècle,* 1891, Paris.

123) Henri Cordier, *Les Juifs en Chine,* 1891, Paris.

124) A. K. Glover, "The Jews of the Extreme Eastern Diaspora," in the *Babylonian and Oriental Record,* 1893, issue unknown.

125) Joseph Edkins, *Religion in China,* 1893, London, p. 181–183.

126) A. K. Glover, *Jewish-Chinese Papers,* 1894, Wisconsin.

127) Mollendorff, "Das Land Sinim" in *Monatsschrift fur Geschichte und Wissenschaft des Judentums,* 1894, issue 38, p. 8–9.

128) Mollendorff, "Die Juden in China" in same periodical, 1895, issue 39, p. 327–331.

129) A. K. Glover, "The Tablet Inscriptions of the Jews of China" in *Proceedings and Transactions of the Scientific Association, Meriden, Conn.* 1895, Vol. VII, p. 13–31.

130) Adolf Neubauer, "Jews in China" in the *Jewish Quarterly Review,* Aug. 1895, p. 123–139.

131) W. A. P. Martin, *A Cycle of Cathay,* 1896, Chicago, p. 265–279.

132) Alexander Wylie, *Chinese Researches,* 1897, Shanghai.

133) Elkan Adler, Supplement to (130), 1897, Chap. XVI, p. 624.

134) Dennis J. Mills, article in *China's Millions,* March, 1898.

135) Lopez, *The Portugese in Malabar,* 1898, Lisbon, p. 82, English.

136) Lev Meizel, "Jews in China" in German, in *Israelitische Monatsschrift,* 1898, issues 1–4.

137) Menashe ben Israel, *Mikweh Israel,* in Hebrew, 1898, Amsterdam, in English the same year.

138) Lehmann, "Jews in China," in *The American Hebrew,* Jan. 12, 1900.

139) Albert Katz, *Die Juden in China,* 1900, Berlin.

140) Lev Maizel, "Jews in China," Russian translation, 1900, Warsaw.

141) W. A. P. Martin, *The Chinese,* 1900, New York, p. 287–306.

142) Jerome Tobar, *Inscriptions Juives de K'ai-fong-fou,* 1900, Shanghai, revised 1912.

143) Marcus Nathan Adler, "Chinese Jews," in *Jewish Quarterly Review,* English, October, 1900, Chap. 13, p. 18–41, also in German and Hebrew in book form.

144) Elijah Solomon, "Jews in China and India," in *Jewish Comment,* 1900, October 5, 12, 19, and 26, also in book form, same year, in Baltimore.

145) Karl von Scherzer, "Die Juden in China," 1901, Vienna, in *Gesellschaft fur Sammlung und Conservirung von Kunst und historischen Denkmalern des Judenthums,* fourth annual report.

146) Paul Pelliot, article in the *Bulletin de l'Ecole Francaise d'Extreme-Orient,* 1901, Hanoi, Vol. I, p. 263–264.

147) Edward Isaac Ezra, "Chinese Jews," in *The East Asia Magazine*, Shanghai, 1902, Vol. I, p. 278–296.
148) J. Dyer Ball, *Things Chinese*, 1925, Shanghai, p. 307–308.
149) R. Powell, "Chinese Jews," in *T'oung Pao*, Ser. 2, 1903, Vol. IV, p. 174–175.
150) Leon Wieger, *Textes historiques de la Chine depuis l'origine, jusqu'en 1912*, 1923, Xian County, China, Vol. II, p. 1507, 1623–1624, first published ca. 1903.
151) Ed. Chavannes, review of *Textes* (150), 1904, in *T'oung Pao*, Ser. 2, issue 5, p. 482–483.
152) Henri Cordier, *Bibliotheca Sinica, Dictionnaire bibliographique des ouvrages relatifs á l'empire Chinois*, 1904–1907, Vol. II, col. 1353–1360; Vol. IV, col. 3136; addenda Vol. I, col. 3779–3780.
153) Berthold Laufer, "The Jews in China," in *Globius*, Apr. 13, 1905, issue 87, p. 245–247.
154) Edward Harper Parker, *China and Religion*, 1905, London, p. 12, 151, 164–177, 179.
155) Paul Pelliot, "China and Religion" (154), reprinted in *Bulletin* (146), Hanoi, Issue 6, p. 413–414.
156) W. A. P. Martin, "The Jewish Monuments at Kaifungfu," in *Journal*, 1906, (102), p. 1–20.
157) Marshall Broomhall, *The Chinese Empire: A General and Missionary Survey*, 1907, London, p. 159, 428–432.
158) Oliver Bainbridge, "Chinese Jews" in *The National Geographic Magazine*, October, 1907, p. 621–632.
159) "China," in the *Encyclopedia Britannica*, 1910, 11th edition.
160) "Kai-feng Fu," ibid.
161) Philippe Berger, "Jewish Manuscript" in *T'oung Pao*, Ser. 2 1910, Vol. XI, p. 709–710.
162) "Intinéraire des marchands Juifs et Russes qui se recontrent dans les parages de la mer Caspienne," in *Revue du Monde Musulman*, 1910, Paris, June, p. 273–274.
163) M. Broomhall, *Islam in China*, 1910, London, p. 31, 50, 55 note, 175–176, 222.
164) S. M. Perlmann, *Hassinim*, in Hebrew, 1911, London.
165) "Judaism in China," in Russian, in *China Report*, 1911, vol. 5, p. 314.
166) Samoilov, *White-faced Devils in China*, 1911, Warsaw, in Russian.
167) Kaufmann and Kohler "Jews in China," in *The Jewish Encyclopedia*, 1912, New York and London, Vol. IV, p. 33–38.
168) S. M. Perlmann, *The History of the Jews in China*, 1913, London.
169) William Charles White, *The Jews of Kaifengfu, in Honan*, 1913, Shanghai.
170) B. Schindler, "Berichtuber die Juden in China," in *Die Erde*, Feb., 1914.
171) Robert Streit and Johannes Dindinger, "Bibliotheca Missionum," in *International Institut fur Missionswissenschaftliche Forschung*, 1916, Vol. I, no. 1029; 1929, no. 2110; 1931, no. 2854, 2878.5, 3490, 3526.3, in several languages.

172) Samuel Purchas, *Hakluytus Posthumous, or, Purchas, His Pilgrimes,* 16th, 17th centuries. Reprinted 29th century, Glasgow, 1915, amended Vol. VIII, p. 584. 1916, amended Vol. XII, p. 467–468.
173) D. MacGillivray, "The Orphan Colony of Honan," in *The Chinese Recorder,* Jan. 1917, p. 37–42.
174) Samuel Couling, "Benjamin of Tudela," in *The Encyclopedia Sinica,* 1917, Shanghai.
175) Couling, "Jews in China," in *The Encyclopedia Sinica,* ibid (173).
176) "An Attempt to Reorganize the Chinese Jews of Kai-feng," in *The Chinese Recorder,* Nov. 1919, Shanghai, p. 780–782.
177) White, an article regarding the purchase of the ruins of the Kaifeng synagogue by the Canadian Church of England, June, 1921, in the *Church Missionary Review.*
178) P. Pelliot, "Le Juif Ngai, informateur du P. Mathieu Ricci," in *T'oung Pao,* Ser. 2, Vol. XX, 32–39.
179) Adolph S. Oko, "Hebrews in China," in *The North-china Daily News,* May 14, 1924, Shanghai.
180) A. S. Oko, "Acquisition of Chinese-Hebrew MSS by the Hebrew Union College, Cincinnati, Ohio," in *The North-China Daily News,* May 19, 1924, Shanghai.
181) Oko, "Chinese Hebrews" in ibid (180), May 22, 1924.
182) E. M. Berthel, "Chinese Jews," in *The North-China Daily News,* May 22, 1924.
183) Berthel, "The Jewish Colony of Honan," in *The North-China Herald,* June 7, 1924, p. 371.
184) "Les inscriptions hébraiques du Musée de l'Université du Gouvernement Chinois à Pekin," in *Le Bulletin Catholique de Pékin,* Oct., 1924, p. 407–410.
185) Perlmann, an article about Chinese Jews, in *Hebrew Life,* Harbin, in Russian, 1924, issues 15 and 17.
186) Israel Cohn, *Journal of a Jewish Traveller,* 1925, London, p. 115–122.
187) Roeh Hayim Yacobs, *Hithgaluth Hayehudim Hassinim,* 1925, Jaffa, in Hebrew, 1927, Jerusalem ed.
188) Richard Wilhelm, "Die Juden in China," in *Der Morgan,* April, 1926, Berlin, p. 3–12.
189) Georges Prévost, "Les inscriptions sémitiques de Loyang," in the bulletin of the *Lazaristes,* 1926, Peking.
190) Arthur Sopher and E. I. Ezra, *Chinese Jews,* 1926, Shanghai.
191) D. MacGillivray, "The Jews of Honan, A Tragic story of Submergence," in *Journal* (102), 1928, p. 22–49.
192) M. Ben Menahem, "Mandschurei un die Jiden," in *Die Jid. Emigracie,* 1929, Berlin, in Yiddish, Issue 5, p. 6–8.
193) A. H. Godbey, *The Lost Tribes: A Myth,* 1930, Durham, N.C., p. 368–425.
194) Berthold Laufer, "A Chinese-Hebrew Manuscript—A New Source for the History of the Chinese Jews," in *The American Journal of Semitic Languages and Literature,* Apr., 1930, p. 189–197.
195) A. C. Moule, *Christians in China Before the Year 1550,* 1930, London.

196) Moule, a review of Laufer (194), in *T'oung Pao,* Ser. 2, 1931, Vol. XXVIII, p. 125–128, 176–177.

197) John K. Shyrock, *The Origin and Development of the State Cult of Confucius,* 1932, New York and London, p. 131.

198) Skachukov, *Chinese Bibliographie, 1730–1930,* 1932, Moscow and Leningrad, related books, numbers 3199, 5502, 5507, 5540, 6582a, in Russian.

199) Frances Markly Roberts, *Western Travellers to China,* 1932, Shanghai, p. 22, 44.

200) David A. Brown, "Through the Eyes of an American Jew," in the *American Hebrew and Jewish Tribune,* Jan. 27 to Mar. 10, 1933.

201) E. N. Adler, *A Jewish Merchant in China at the Beginning of the Tenth Century,* 1933, Vienna, in German.

202) B. Bleyhofer, "Chinesische Juden," in *Ostasiatische Rundschau,* Oct. 16, 1933, Hamburg, p. 449–451.

203) F. Jager "Zur Frage der Chinesischen Juden," in *Ostasiatische Rundschau,* April 1, 1934, Hamburg p. 160–164.

204) "The Chinese Jew," in *Asia,* December, 1934, New York, p. 712.

205) Maurus, a summary of (203) in the *Digest of the Synodal Commission,* July/August, 1935, Peiping, p. 638–645.

206) Henry James Coleridge, *The Life and Letters of St. Francis Xavier,* 1935, London, p. 378–379.

207) E. Noyé, "Les Juifs en Chine," in *Le Bulletin Catholique de Pékin,* Nov. 1935, p. 587–599; Dec. 1935, p. 649–652; Jan. 1936, p. 22–29; Feb. 1936, p. 77–88.

208) W. C. White, "Chinese Jews," in the *North China Star,* June 1–2, 1936, Tientsin.

209) J. J. L. Duyvendak, "Early Chinese Studies in Holland," in *Toung Pao,* Ser. 2, April 1936, p. 329–340.

210) Noiah Mishkovsky, *Ethiope, Yiden in Afrika un Asie,* 1936, Chicago, in Yiddish, p. 131–160.

211) Walter Fuchs, "The Chinese Jews of Kaifengfu," in the *T'ien Hsia Monthly,* Aug. 1937, p. 27–40.

212) James A. Muller, *Apostle of China: Samuel Isaac Joseph Schereschewsky, 1831–1906,* 1937.

213) Thomas Torrence, *China's First Missionaries—Ancient Israelites,* 1937, London.

214) Rudolf Lowenthal, *The Jewish Press in China,* 1937, Tientsin and Peiping.*

215) Hans E. Krueger, "Kaifoeng, die alte Chinesische Judenstadt," in *Ostasiatischer Lloyd,* Feb. 19, 1938, Shanghai, p. 4.

*The capital of China was established in Beijing in 1368 and has remained there ever since, except between 1928 and 1949, when Chiang Kai-shek moved his Nationalist government to Nanking. During the interregnum, Beijing was called Peiping. But some use the terms inter-changeably when referring to this period.

216) Leo Hirsch, "Die Juden von Kai-Fung-Fu," in —*Zeitung*, June 30, 1938, Berlin, p. 8.
217) Bruno Kroker, "the Chinese Jews of Kai-fung," in *The China Journal*, September, 1938, Shanghai, p. 141–146.
218) R. Lowenthal, "The Jews in China: A Bibliography," in *The Yenching Journal of Social Studies*, January, 1939, Peiping, p. 256–291.
219) R. Lowenthal, "The Jews in China: An Annotated Bibliography," in *Chinese Social and Political Science Review*, Feb. 1940, Peiping.
220) W. C. White, *Chinese Jews*, 1942, Toronto. See (169), (177).
221) Nathan Ausubel, *A Treasury of Jewish Folklore*, 1948, New York, p. 550–557.
222) Crawford, an article in the *Journal of the Ethnological Society*, No. 3, p. 106.

SUPPLEMENTARY

223) Antoine Gaubil, *Letters* sent from Beijing on Sept. 4, 1725, later published in collections (58) and (74).
224) Terrien de Lacouperie, article regarding the time of entry of the Jews into China, in the *Babylonian and Oriental Record*, June, 1891, p. 132–133.
225) Cordier, an article in *L'Anthropologie*, Sept/Oct., 1890, p. 549.
226) Lemirault, "Chine" in the *French Encyclopedia*, Vol. XI, p. 92.
227) Feng Chengjun, *Jing Jiao Bei Kao (A Study of the Nestorian Tablets)*, 1931, Shanghai, Commercial Press, p. 40–43.
228) (Editor's pen name) Tian Xia Di Yi Shang Xin Ren (The Most Broken-Hearted Man Under Heaven), *Pixie Jishi (A Faithful Record of Suppressing Evil)*, 1861, Beijing, Vol. I, p. 7.
229) Same editor, same collection (228), "Tianzhu Xie Jiao Ru Zhong Guo Kao Lue" ("A Brief Study of the Entry into China of the Evil Religion of Catholicism").
230) "Yangwu Zaji," ("Miscellaneous Notes on Self-Cultivation"), quoted in (229).
231) Kato Shinkichi (ed.), "The Jewish Religionists of Kaifeng, a Personal Portrait," in collection entitled "The Land and People of North China," in the periodical *North China*, February, 1942, Tokyo (in Japanese).
232) Shioten Nobunaka, "Jewish Thought and Movements," 1941, Tokyo, p. 373–383. Appendix entitled "The Tragedy of the Jewish People in China"—said to be a translation from *The American Jew* (?), issue unknown (in Japanese).
233) Bai Meichu, *Zhong Guo Renwen Dili (Human Geology of China)*, 1928, Peiping, Vol. V, p. 150–151.

Jiang Qingxiang and Xiao Guoliang

GLIMPSES OF THE URBAN ECONOMY OF BIANJING, CAPITAL OF THE NORTHERN SONG DYNASTY, 1981

Jiang, born in 1915, is a professor and research fellow at the Institute of Economics in the Shanghai Academy of Social Sciences. Xiao, born in 1947, is a research intern at the same Institute. Their joint article called "Cong Qin Ming Shang He Tu, He Dong Jing Meng Hua Lu, Kan Bei Song Bianjing de Chengshi Jingji." The full title in English can be found in the Bibliography at the end of this volume. I have shortened it somewhat to read: "Glimpses of the Urban Economy in Bianjing, Capital of the Northern Song Dynasty." Published in *Zhong Guo Shehui Kexue (Social Sciences in China)*, Vol. 4, 1981, the article says not a word about Israelites, but it does provide ample reason why the Jews should have chosen to settle in Kaifeng, or Bianjing as it was then called. In addition to Song dynasty writings, Jiang and Xiao cleverly utilize a famous Song painting to bring Bianjing colorfully to life.

The writers draw heavily on *Dongjing Meng Hua Lu (Reminiscences of Dreamland Glories of the Eastern Capital)*, a book by Meng Yuanlao which appeared in 1147 in Linan (Hangzhou) twenty years after the Song court fled to the south, recalling nostalgically the former capital. It has been a classic source book for later historians.

As to the painting, it is a superb panorama, executed in meticulous detail of virtually every aspect of medieval life in Bianjing, from its suburbs to its teeming streets. Presently in the Palace Museum in Beijing, it measures 525 by 25.5 centimeters. The artist, Zhang Zeduan, though born in Shandong province, was raised in Kaifeng. He developed a painting style of his own which culminated in the early years of the 12th century in the masterly *Qing Ming Shang He Tu (Riverside Scene at Clear and Bright Festival Time)*. A section of it is included here.

The following are extracts from the Jiang and Xiao essay. The remarks in parentheses are mine:

The scroll painting *Riverside Scene* begins at the farms and gardens in the eastern suburbs of the Outer City, extends upstream (westward) along the Bian River, passes the Upper Tu Bridge outside the Tong Jin Bridge and the East Jiao Zi Gate, and ends at Bao Kang Gate Street, covering a length of three or four *li* (over a mile). Depicted are more than 770 people, 90 animals, 100 houses, public buildings and pavilions, and 20 river vessels. We see people rowing or towing boats, toting sedan chairs, driving carts, setting up market stalls, hawking their wares along the streets or simply loafing. *Riverside Scene* is an animated reflection of a prosperous market economy, busy land and water transportation, and the close urban-rural relationships in Northern Song nearly 1,000 years ago. This artistic creation is more realistic than any photograph could be, a gem of pictorial history enabling a close study of the urban economy of the Northern Song Dynasty as epitomized by its capital, Bianjing.

Reminiscences is about 30,000 words long. It describes the economic and cultural life of the inhabitants of the capital, and goes into detail about such things as city walls, rivers, imperial palaces, government buildings, market places, scenic spots, merchandise on display, shops in streets and lanes, local customs, and living conditions.

Zhao Kuangyin, the first emperor of the Song Dynasty, ordered the capital reconstructed and enlarged to make it the "center of the realm," the "hub of the world" and a "strategic metropolis overlooking the four seas." What made this new emperor so enthusiastic about the old city? The reason can be found in an article by the poet Qin Guan (1049–1100):

> Kaifeng, surrounded by level land in all directions, is a convergence of roads which connect it with Chu to the south, Han to the west, Zhao to the north, and Qi to the east. Neither great mountain ranges nor big rivers isolate it from the surrounding regions; in fact its communication with them is aided by the Bian and Cai and other rivers. These waterways teem with boats, the bow of one touching the stern of another, while men, carts and animals jam the roads in an endless flow from every corner of the country . . . Correcting the strategic error of past dynasties of stationing troops at remote points, the present regime garrisons the capital with a heavy concentration of armed forces over one million strong. Supplying these troops is the government's responsibility, in contrast to the practice of the Tang Dynasty of making the peasantry shoulder the burden. But this could not be done if the capital was situated in a place without good communications. A

regime that relies on its armed forces cannot afford to locate its capital in remote mountainous terrain, or on an open (riverless) plain.

Qin Guan put his finger on the secret of why the new emperor kept Bianjing as his capital and rebuilt it. Zhao Kuangyin had been commander of the Imperial Guards during the previous dynasty, and seized the throne by a coup known as the Chenqiao Mutiny. He knew all too well that the army was the foundation of power, and so he concentrated an overwhelming proportion of his armed forces in the capital, thus "strengthening the trunk of the Tree of State while weakening its branches." (That is, not allowing generals of troops in other parts of the country to become so strong that they might be tempted to try coups of their own.) Bianjing suited the emperor's purposes perfectly, its network of land and water communications easily supplying his huge army with food and other provisions from neighboring areas.

According to historical records, the volume of goods flowing into the capital via the Bian River was beyond calculation. For instance, a passage in a report published in the "Economic Gazette" section of the *History of the Song Dynasty,* and submitted to the court by Censor Liang Tao in the fourth year of the Yuanyou period (1089), reads: "After dredging, the Bian River was connected with the Yangtze and the Huai, thus permitting direct transportation of huge volumes of merchandise on boats of every size from all points of the compass . . . The Bian River carries every year several million piculs of tribute rice, shipped from Hunan, Hubei and Zhejiang provinces via the Yangtze and the Huai rivers. And the products transported in from the southeastern area and other places are incalculable."

The river served both official and commercial shipping. . . . Although not as important as the Bian, the Huimin and Wuzhang rivers were also arteries for the transport of grain and merchandise.

With waterways serving as the main lines of communication with the provinces, boats and vessels occupied a prominent place in life in the capital, and even caught the attention of poets. Zhou Bangyan (1057–1121) describes a river spectacle in his "Ode to Biandu" (another term for Kaifeng, along with Bianliang and Bianjing) thus:

> One thousand *li,* stern crowding bow,
> A hundred types of vessels flow,
>   Sails a-bulge when winds are fair,
>   In rain punt poles thrust everywhere.
> Boatmen chanting, accents broad,
> In twos and threes the craft sweep for'd,
>   As trumpets blare,
>   Drums pound,

And bells ring out
In clamorous sound.

No wonder Zhang Zeduan devoted almost one-third of his *Riverside Scene* to the vessels and men afloat. Through them, he shows us how the needs of the population and the armed forces were met and the prosperity of the capital was built.

(The authors estimate that during Northern Song, the population of Kaifeng Prefecture, which embraced the capital and sixteen surrounding counties, was about one and a third million, with roughly 100,000 troops garrisoning the city itself. They go on to detail who were the inhabitants and how they lived.)

Bianjing was a rendezvous for the power elite, the nobles, the wealthy merchants. Wang Mingqing wrote at the time in his *Yu Zhao Xin Zhi (A New Record of Illustrious Portraits):* "Much in evidence are mansions of imperial concubines, members of the royalty, princes and dukes, and high-ranking officials." The Forbidden City occupied one-tenth of the total area of the Inner City, which contained whole "blocks of palaces" with "resplendently painted beams and carved pillars."

What's more ". . . everywhere were premises of the various departments of the central government, private homes of nobles and high officials, such as Minister of the Privy Council Deng, High Justice Liu, Imperial Son-in-Law Zhang, Queen Ming Jie, Grand Tutor Cai, and so on," wrote Meng Yuanlao in his *Reminiscences.* There were simply too many official residences for him to list them all, to say nothing of the big officials who over-ran the city.

Apart from these were minor officials and their families. Lu Mengzheng of the Song Dynasty said: "The city being the site of the Imperial Court, the common people gather here to offer various services. That is why the place is so prosperous." Also present were those hoping to become minor functionaries—people who came to sit for the civil service examinations, and those seeking appointments to lesser posts . . . *Reminiscences* mentions that the inns along the city wall on the east of the Zhouqiao Bridge close by the Imperial Palace provided accommodations for small officials from the south on their visits to the capital.

The third category included big and medium-sized landlords and former officials of the previous regime. In the fourth year of the Jing-you period (1037), Emperor Ren Zong issued a mandate which noted: "Of late many upper-class families have moved from other parts of the country to Henan province and to the capital in order to avoid paying taxes and providing men for labor service."

In *Ode to the Imperial Capital,* Yang Kan tells about the former officials:

Muslim services in the White Crane Mosque, in Yangzhou, October, 1982. The only one with a blue hat is Zhang Zixiang, whose ancestors have worn them for generations. Kaifeng Jews were called "Blue Hat Hui Hui" to distinguish them from the Muslim "White Hat Hui Hui." Could the Yangzhou customs have been the same? *Photo by Zhu Jiang.*

Two foreigners from the Western Regions. Tri-color
Tang figurines recently unearthed near Sian.

Foreign pedlar, figurine, 9th century, monochrome, Luoyang. According to the
Luoyang Museum, he came via the Silk Road. One of the many Semitic types
in Chinese sculpture and painting between Northern Wei and the Song dynasty
(4th–13th centuries). While the country or the religion of the persons depicted
was never specifically designated, several are quite Jewish in appearance.
Chinese cities hosted thousands of people from the Middle East, some of
whom were Jews. A few may have had their likenesses recorded by Chinese
artists.

The Luoyang Museum says this 7th-century foreigner was a confectionery baker. He holds a sweat-rag over his right shoulder. Tang (618-907) tri-color.

A Kaifeng Jew, in 1906. *National Geographic Magazine,* photo by Oliver Bainbridge.

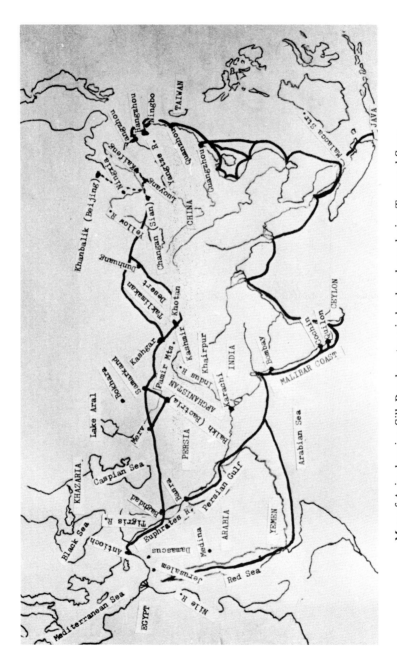

Map of Asia showing Silk Road routes via land and sea during Tang and Song.

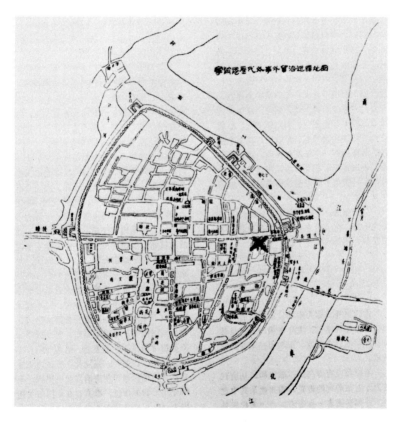

Ancient map of the seaport Ningbo during the Song and Yuan dynasties.
"X" marks the location of the "Persian Hotel" which provided
accommodations for foreigners.

Visitors from Western Asia wait deferentially for an interview with busy Tang dynasty officials. A mural in the tomb of Prince Zhang Huai, outside Sian.

Foreigners from various countries of the Western Regions paying their respects at a Buddhist shrine, Tang dynasty. This is a copy of part of a mural in Dunhuang, once a major post on the Silk Road. The Dunhuang Grottoes preserve over 2,000 beautiful colored sculptured figures, frescoes and ceilings created between Northern Wei and Tang. Although primarily religious in nature, they provide a wealth of detail regarding the features and dress of foreigners in China at that time, as well as of the Chinese themselves.

Kaifeng street scene, Northern Song. The elaborate building is a large restaurant. Seen also are shops, merchandise stalls, ladies in sedan chairs, a camel caravan leaving for the Silk Road. Also from *Riverside Scene.*

Boats on the Bian River passing under a bridge in Kaifeng during Northern Song (960-1127). Kaifeng, then called Bianjing or Bianliang, was China's capital, and a very active commercial center. From an embroidered reproduction of the famous scroll painting, *Riverside Scene at Clear and Bright Festival Time,* by Zhang Zeduan, Southern Song, 12th century.

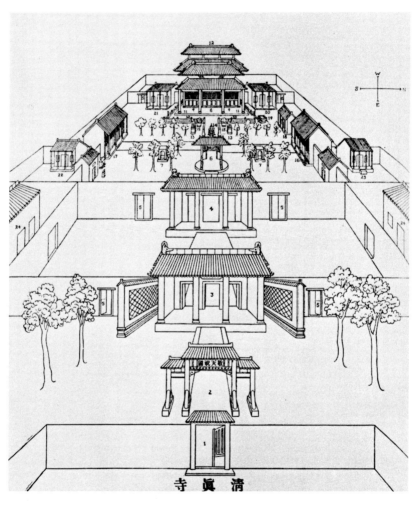

Copy of drawing of Kaifeng synagogue compound by French Jesuit Jean Domenge, 1722.

Copy of drawing of Kaifeng synagogue interior by Domenge, 1722.

Groom about to bathe the piebald "Satin Shoulders," of the Imperial Stable. Part of the scroll painting, *Five Horses* by Li Gonglin, Northern Song (960-1127). The inscription says "Satin Shoulders" was eight years old and stood four feet six inches high. Unfortunately, we are not told anything about the groom. The present whereabouts of the painting is unknown.

The 1489 inscription commemorating the rebuilding of the Kaifeng synagogue. A rubbing reproduction.

The 1512 Kaifeng inscription commemorating the rebuilding of the synagogue. A rubbing reproduction.

Section of a 15th-century Torah scroll, Kaifeng.
London Jews Society.

וְצָבָ֣א עָלָ֔יו הַשָּׁמַ֖יִם כִּ֣י נִחָ֑מְתִּי
כִּ֣י עֲשִׂיתִ֑ם וְלֹ֣א מָצָ֣א חֵ֖ן בְּעֵינֵ֣
זָהֹ֖ה׃ קְמ֖וּ
קֹ֣דֶשׁ לַיהֹוָ֣ה

מריע רביע רבי יעקב כי אבש השל־
שׁליה רבי שׁאדי כר יעקב בי אבש׳ השל׳
כעשׁית רבי עקיבה כר אהן נ עזרא ל׳ ל׳
׳ל׳ נדר אברם כר אהרן בו
׳ל׳ גין פצ׳י חשה בר אהר׳

במדינת באול כין ליגן שהר
עישת אול בסמו צלי אלף תשׁעה
לאה שלשים אחר מאני מרחשׁין
ארבעה בשׁבא דהו רודי שׁלשׁה

עישת כודאי אזמר אסׁמאן תורה
מגאה סי פרשׁה כחג צלי אלף
ישׁעה מאה שלשׁים שׁע מאהי טבת
עשׁרים אב ארבעה רודי חדק

First page of *Genesis,* Kaifeng
"Square Scriptures," 1621. Chinese
Library, Royal Ontario Museum.

בְּרֵאשִׁ֖ית בָּרָ֣א אֱלֹהִ֑ים אֵ֣ת
הַשָּׁמַ֖יִם וְאֵ֣ת הָאָ֑רֶץ׃ וְהָאָ֗רֶץ
הָיְתָ֥ה תֹ֨הוּ֙ וָבֹ֔הוּ וְחֹ֖שֶׁךְ עַל־פְּנֵ֣
תְה֑וֹם וְר֣וּחַ אֱלֹהִ֔ים מְרַחֶ֖פֶת עַל־
פְּנֵ֣ הַמָּ֑יִם׃ וַיֹּ֣אמֶר אֱלֹהִ֖ים יְהִ֣י א֑וֹר
וַיְהִי־א֑וֹר׃ וַיַּ֣רְא אֱלֹהִ֖ים אֶת־הָא֑וֹר
כִּי־ט֑וֹב וַיַּבְדֵּ֣ל אֱלֹהִ֔ים בֵּ֣ין הָא֑וֹר
וּבֵ֣ין הַחֹ֑שֶׁךְ׃ וַיִּקְרָ֣א אֱלֹהִ֖ים לָא֑וֹר
י֑וֹם וְלַחֹ֖שֶׁךְ קָ֣רָא לָ֑יְלָה וַיְהִ֣

A page of *Genesis,* Kaifeng "Square
Scriptures," 1620–1621. Hebrew
Union College, Cincinnati, Ohio.

Persian letter in Hebrew script, written by a Jewish merchant in the 8th century. Discovered near Hotan (Khotan) by Aurel Stein in 1901. British Museum, London.

Hebrew prayer, late 8th century. Found by Pelliot in 1908 at Dunhuang, Gansu province. Bibliothèque Nationale, Paris.

Gravestone, 12th or 13th century, written in Arabic and Chinese, of a Persian named Ibn (son of) Gaus Dagog. The Chinese inscription renders the surname as "Guo," and says he was the first of his family to settle in China. Since the stone has neither Nestorian nor Catholic crosses, nor the cross and lotus combination of the Manicheans, nor Muslim references to Allah, nor quotations from the Koran, and is simple and unadorned in the Jewish tradition, it is possible that Ibn Gaus Dagog was a Persian Jew. *Museum of Overseas Communications History, Quanzhou, Fujian.*

Stone fragments claimed by Prevost, a French Lazariste, to be written in Palmyrian Hebrew, dating from Eastern Han (25-220). *Museum of History, Beijing.*

Manasseh ben Israel. An illustration from his *Hope of Israel,* Latin edition, 1650.

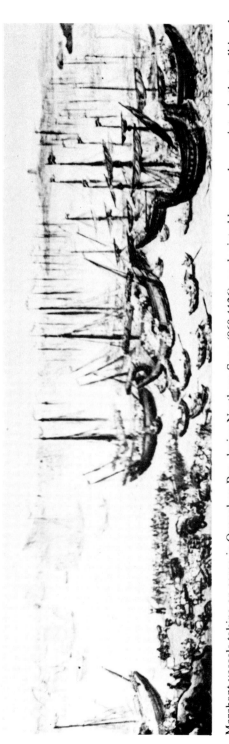

Merchant vessels taking on cargo in Quanzhou Bay during Northern Song (960-1126), as depicted by a modern painter in the traditional style. *Museum of Overseas Communications History, Quanzhou, Fujian.*

Emperor Tai Zu, by virtue of his military genius, and Emperor Tai Zong, thanks to his political and cultural accomplishments, conquered in succession the lands of Jiangbiao, Sudu, Nanyue, Dong Wu, Bing, Fen, Jing and Hu. The defeated kings were ordered into the capital, together with their disarmed soldiers, ministers and retainers.

Although these former monarchs and elite had lost their political power, they retained their wealth. They were quite content with idle, comfortable lives in the capital, parasitically battening on the labors of the common folk.

The fourth category was composed of rich traders and merchants. In the *Records of Jing Kang,* Ting Teqi said: "The capital is a rendezvous for rich traders and merchants from all parts of the country." During the Zhen Zong period (998–1022) Wang Dan said:

> The long period of peace in the country has made it possible for landlords to enlarge their holdings by annexing farmlands. Free from taxation and the duty to provide unpaid laborers, they have made enormous profits. Many people in the capital have assets up to a million strings of cash. (Each string usually contained 1,000 copper coins, and varied in purchasing power from dynasty to dynasty. A rough estimation would be around one pre-World War II U.S. dollar per string.) Those possessing over 100,000 strings are to be met almost everywhere.

(A passage in the *Reminiscences* offers a glimpse of the shops that dealt in luxuries for the rich, and the affluent merchants who owned them).

> To the east was Panlou Street, on the southern side of which was "Eagles' Inn," which accommodated only traders in hawks and falcons. Here also were shops selling pearls, silks, joss-sticks, medicinal herbs and mats. The street turns south into Jie Shen Lane, where trade in gold, silver and colored silks was transacted. The buildings, with broad open fronts, were awesome to the common people. A single deal could run into the astonishing sum of ten million strings of cash. These traders and merchants were doubtless multi-millionaires.

The greatest portion of the population embraced the countless middle and small merchants, handicraftsmen, pedlars, laborers, porters, servants, slaves, singers, story-tellers, prostitutes, vagabonds, beggars, and the like. These people of the lowest social strata are strikingly represented in *Riverside Scene.* Among the 770-odd figures spread over the length of the picture are boatmen, small merchants, artisans,

Buddhist monks and nuns, Taoist priests, quacks, fortune tellers, and stall-keepers of every sort. Among the hurrying pedestrians are people toting loads on their backs and across their shoulders, sedan-chair carriers, cart haulers, horsecart drivers, men hawking wares on wheelbarrows, and ragged figures begging along the street. There is a multifarious humanity for you!

A passage in *Reminiscences* goes into even greater detail about the many different kinds of laborers—carpenters, wall-painters and white-washers, street-sweepers, scavengers, and odd-job men. We get some idea of the tremendous number of people engaged in small businesses and service trades.

Now let us look at the consumption in this thriving city. The affluent were the greatest consumers of both necessities and luxuries. Take grain for instance. In 1008 tribute rice from various parts of the country amounted to seven million piculs. (One picul equals 133.3 lbs.) The devouring of porkers and other animals was also stupendous. *Reminiscences* notes: "Herds of swine to be slaughtered by private owners passed through Scarlet Sparrow Gate from dawn to dusk in streams each numbering tens of thousands." The well-off inhabitants of Bianjing were obviously big eaters.

If the quantity consumed was staggering, the quality was dazzling. Rich men, nobles, high officials, landlords, and wealthy merchants had practically unlimited purchasing power and could afford to be finicky in their tastes, always demanding the best. Extravagance prevailed. Apart from monthly gratuitous allowances of rice, officials received seasonal gifts of damask, spun silk, silk floss and piece goods. They had high monthly salaries, ranging from three hundred strings of cash to four hundred thousand, corresponding to their different official ranks—from petty functionary to prime minister—41 grades in all. Toward the end of Northern Song during the Cong Ning period (1102–1106) when Cai Jing was premier, his favorite ministers, like Wu Juhou and Zhang Kangguou, received subsidies for food which, in effect, doubled their salaries. They further supplemented their official incomes by embezzlement, bribe-taking, blackmail and extortion, with the ordinary people as their victims. Not only could they and their families live in luxury, but they had enormous amounts of cash left over to spend in unbridled extravagance and the pursuit of pleasure.

Meng Yuanlao, in his preface to *Reminiscences,* writes:

> Wherever you went in the fashionable streets, brothels met the eye—pavilions draped with embroidered and pearl-studded curtains. Ornately carved carriages vied for parking space before them, while dandies on horseback raced across the imperial high-

way. You caught glimpses of women resplendent in gold and jade ornaments, their silk perfumed apparel filling the air with fragrance. Through their windows floated pleasing melodies and cajoling laughter.

Teahouses and wineshops were gay with instrumental music. The metropolis was the mart for all things precious and expensive and the venue of those who sought them. Its shops were spread with rare goods from every corner of the country, its restaurants offered sumptuous dishes famed at home and abroad...

With the capital, a political and economic center, setting an example of profligacy and waste, inevitably other cities followed suit. As Chen Sunyu remarked:

> The provincials imitate the capital's style of living, and what is the capital? A nest of oddities, a hotbed of falsities. Bizarre garments and weird utensils displayed in the Court in the morning, by evening appear in imitation in the marketplace and on the streets. Within a month they are in great demand all over the land.

In the last years of Northern Song, with Emperor Hui Zong personally taking the lead, upper class' indulgences reached inordinate proportions. According to Yuan Jiang of the Song Dynasty, ladies in the capital constantly changed their fashions in dresses and hair adornments. No price was too high for gold and jade ornaments, and a pair of stockings or a collar might cost a thousand coppers. Lovely and expensive garments were put on for only a few days, then cast aside. Though hardly worn, they were already out of style.

Consumption in Bianjing was enormous in quantity, luxurious in quality and costly in price. To satisfy such human appetites and vanities, it was necessary to bring in commodities from distant parts of the country and even from abroad. This gave great impetus to the market and to the development of the economy.

There were wholesale and retail markets. . . . They fell into several categories: morning, daytime, evening, seasonal, and periodic. Most shops mentioned in *Reminiscences* were daytime shops, such as Tang's Gold and Silver Smithery, the Wenzhou Laquerware Store, the Bai Zhong Yuan Drugstore, Liang's Pearl Mart. . .

Night markets had been prohibited by feudal governments until Northern Song, when they became so popular and prosperous that the first emperor of that dynasty, Zhao Kuangyin, felt obliged to issue an edict in 965, reading: "Night markets may stay open in the capital, but only until the third watch" (midnight). Business was brisk, especially during the reign of Emperor Hui Zong in the Zhenghe and Xuanhe periods (1111–1126). As *Reminiscences* described it:

> The night market in and around Scarlet Sparrow Gate Street was so crowded with horses and carts that people could not get through or even stop anywhere . . . The streets overflowed with stalls and shops selling rice gruel, and stewed and preserved meats. On the square below the King Tower were stalls with tables where you could sit down to a meal of badger or fox meat, or chicken if you preferred. If you still were not satisfied, you could stroll over to Mei or Lu's cafe where you could have delicious goose, duck, chicken or rabbit, pork entrails or lungs, buns with eel stuffing, chicken skin, kidneys, or any sort of hodgepodge. Delicacies were cheap, too, costing only 15 coppers each . . .

> The brilliant lights in the wineshops were dazzling. Even more so were the beautifully dressed prostitutes, some in the wineshops drinking with the revelers and others sauntering outside. Charming minxes, all . . .

> Truly these booming markets turned Bianjing night into day. It is said, with only slight exaggeration, that when mosquitoes were at their worst, they never bothered you in the market places. The oily vapors rising from innumerable frying pans drove them away!

Clothes, articles for daily use and luxuries were for sale also in the "ghost market." In front of the Panlou Wineshop at the southeastern corner of the Inner City ". . . sellers of clothing, calligraphy scrolls and paintings, curios and jades, arrived at the marketplace before daylight. . . . At sunrise they vanished as quickly as they appeared, and for this reason the place was called the 'ghost market.' For instance, near the Panlou Wineshop while the night was deep and dark, the teahouses were brightly lit for the ghost market trade in clothes, paintings and garlands. All disappeared at the peep of dawn."

(Such markets existed for centuries all over China in the old days. Here stolen goods were disposed of, or people from formerly well-to-do families down on their luck came surreptitiously to sell their valuables.)

The seasonal markets, which catered to the various festivals, were a merry scene. For example, the Drum and Fan Market opened just before the Dragon Boat Festival, when drums were needed to spur on the paddlers and fans to cool the heated spectators. Trinkets, gadgets and toys were displayed at the Skillful Handicraftsmen's Mart, for the festival called the Seventh Night of the Seventh Month. According to legend, only then could the Cowherd and the Weaving Girl (actually two constellations) meet and exchange small gifts to pledge their undying love.

A typical example of the periodic markets was the temple fair held in the Xiangguo Monastery in the Inner City. *Reminiscences* brings this fair to life:

> The Monastery threw open all its gates five times a month to admit streams of shoppers. From the broad grounds inside the Front Gate rose a cacophonous chorus of rare birds in cages, cats in baskets, dogs straining at the leash, and other animals chained for sale. In the courtyard inside the Second and Third Gates were tents and sheds and awning-covered stalls where traders sold rush-cushions, bamboo-mats, screens, curtains, basins, spittoons, saddles, bows, swords, fruits, salted meats . . .
>
> In the square next to the Hall of Buddhas, Taoist Priest Meng sold his special recipe honey-preserved fruits, Zhao Wenxiu displayed writing brushes of his own handiwork, and Pan Gu offered special ink sticks. Along the corridor on either side, nuns, standing behind stalls, sold embroideries, stockings, collars, embroidery patterns, bridal headgear, hats, false haircoils, silk threads, etc., in every color and shade.
>
> In front of the Zhisheng Gate, behind the Hall of Buddhas, scholars browsed among books, paintings, calligraphy scrolls and curios. Retired and dismissed officials timidly beseeched onlookers to buy the scented herbs and native products brought from their home towns. Superstitious folk in the backyard of the monastery sought charms, incantations and talismans, or to have their fortunes told.

Here all humanity met—the hoi polloi, merchants big and small, handicraftsmen, important and petty officials, monks, priests and nuns. They filled the temple to overflowing, even though the main court with its two corridors alone was reportedly spacious enough for 10,000 persons.

Of all the trades in the capital, wineshops, restaurants, amusement houses, and brothels were the most prosperous. According to *Reminiscences*, wineshops and eating places accounted for more than fifty percent of the 100-odd trades. Inside the city there were 72 first-rate restaurants with enticing names such as Plenty, High Sun, Cool Breeze, Celebration, Kindness and Harmony, Fairies Rendezvous . . . There is a passage in *Reminiscences* about Plenty, the most popular of these first-class restaurants:

> During the Xuanhe period (1119–25) Plenty was expanded into five 3-storied buildings facing one another, all connected by railed

bridges spanning the top floors. The gate of the front building facing the street was hung with a horizontal embroidered banner, bearing the name Plenty. The doorway of the gate was draped with a pearl-studded silk screen. All the halls and rooms were flooded with light.

Second-class restaurants, known as *jiaodian,* were everywhere in Bianjing. They catered to upper and middle class patrons, selling tasty dishes to go with wine. In 1027 Emperor Ren Zong issued a mandate which read: "If the Bai Fan Lou Wineshop will undertake to collect and pay the tax into the Imperial Treasury on behalf of the others, it shall be designated as the sole wine distributor for 3,000 selected *jiaodian* wineshops in the capital." This affords us some idea of the vast number of wineshops operating in Bianjing.

The back streets and lanes were proud of their third-class teashops and eateries. *Reminiscences* mentions only a few—Cao's Eating House, Shi's Squash Soup Kitchen, Wang's Steamed Buns, Ting's Teahouse, Li's Northern-Style Eating House, Jin's Southern-Style Food Shop, Zheng's Deep-Fried Dough-Cakes, Haizhou Zhang's Sesame Seed Buns, Ma Dang's Soup Shop . . . Families engaged in business did not usually cook, but bought their meals at these wineshops and teahouses which lined the back lanes.

Bianjing had a large number of amusement grounds and brothels. In *Riverside Scene,* on the corner of the crossroads in the Old City, sitting in a shed below a large awning, is a crowd of elderly people listening to an old man telling an ancient tale, probably some heroic legend or folklore anecdote. Professional story-tellers were very popular.

Theatres drew capacity audiences. According to *Reminiscences:*

> At the southern end of the street, Sang's Amusement Center stood. Near the north end were over 50 theatres. Among the larger ones were the Lotus Flower, Peony Stage, and Elephant Garden. This last seated several thousand.

Most theaters gave variety shows, including story telling, acrobatics, short skits, shadow plays, dancing, singing, instrumental music, poetry recitals, and obscene comedies. Around the theatres, says *Reminiscences,* was a motley assortment of "medicine pedlars, fortune tellers, second-hand clothing vendors, gamblers, food sellers, barbers, and ballad singers. So entrancing were they that persons wandering among them didn't even notice the approach of evening . . . Rain or shine, day after day, the lively Amusement Center swarmed with common humanity."

Next in degree of activity came depots and warehouses, which were run either privately or by the government. *Reminiscences* notes that

there were about 50 storehouses for rice and wheat in the capital, and
about 20 hay yards near the New City. Some government-run warehouses were available for private merchandise as well as government
provisions.

There were also many private warehouses, an example being Shisan-
jan Lou, the largest warehouse in the city. Goods and merchandise
were piled up inside it mountain high, and the owner netted an average
annual profit of tens of thousands of strings of cash. These warehouses
and depots provided storage facilities for traders from the provinces,
and reflected Bianjing's prosperity.

As the main commercial center of China during Song, Bianjing attracted merchants and traders from all over the country and from
abroad. In *Riverside Scene* we see leaving the Eastern Corner Gate a
caravan of camels with traders from Central Asia trudging behind.
Having completed their transactions in the capital, the men are now
going home. It was through these merchants and their "ships of the
desert" that Northern Song was able to establish close trade relations
with such (Central Asian) kingdoms as Western Xia and Western Liao.
A passage in *Reminiscences* describes some of these outlanders as they
appeared at an imperial morning audience, one New Year's day:

> The emissary from Great Liao wore a golden hat with a broad
> rim curling upwards like a lotus leaf, a fitted purple robe, and
> gold-thread-plaited boots. The deputy emissary was clad in Han
> style in a robe bound at the waist with a gold-threaded belt. Both
> the emissary and the deputy emissary of the Xia State wore
> golden hats, short and close-fitting scarlet robes and gold-thread-
> plaited boots. They bowed with crossed hands . . . The Huihes
> (Uygurs) had long beards and high noses, and wore turbans and
> caps. The Khotans wore flower-patterned gold-threaded felt hats
> and gold-threaded robes with belts around their waists. They
> brought their wives and children with them, all riding camels with
> jingling bronze bells, to pay tribute to the Song Court.

Nominally, these emissaries came to present tribute to the Song
emperor. In fact, they engaged in a busy trade. Along their routes, they
picked up merchandise which they sold in the capital for a substantial
profit, collaborating secretly with Han interpreters and courtiers.
Though politically there was only hostility between the Hans and Liaos
and Xia, the commercial relations channelled through the emissaries
were smooth enough. It may therefore be said that as early as the
Northern Song Dynasty the Hans and the northern ethnic minorities
already belonged to a common economic community.

Traders from the south in Bianjing outnumbered those from the
north, as the commodity economy was more developed in the south of

China. These included, according to *Reminiscences,* traders from Korea, Kampuchea and other countries in southeast Asia, and from Dashi (Arabia). It is recorded in history that Dashi envoys travelled to China twenty-four times during the Song Dynasty, and "of them, many were merchants coming as emissaries."

Traders of all categories had their respective guilds, organized by the government to facilitate the collection of taxes and dues. Chinese guilds were very different from those in Western Europe, which were formed by the merchants and handicraftsmen themselves, and were, from the very start, an antithesis to the feudal economy.

Ironically, once organized, even these feudalistic Chinese guilds joined together with the trades and professions to protect their own interests and oppose arbitrary fleecing by the feudal government. During the Northern Song, the guilds in Bianjing registered a strong protest against extra levies forced upon them by local officials in addition to the taxes authorized by the Court.

The formation of the guilds also raised the social status of merchants, especially those of the elite among them. The traditional contempt for merchants began to give way to respect. Some officials even resigned their posts and went into business.

Prosperity in Bianjing's market trade stimulated the growth of the economy and brought about new types of commodity exchange— renting and hiring, and selling on credit.

According to *Reminiscences* sedan-chairs were no longer used exclusively by the Empress. They were rented also by the elite and commoners for going to the Court, or for weddings and other occasions. The chairs with their entourage, and even apparel for the carriers, could all be rented. There were also carriages for six, hired both by commoners and high-born ladies alike.

All the paraphernalia for a funeral could also be hired, including the guide, a "Fan Xiang" (image of an ugly god whose four fearful eyes searched out evil spirits and drove them away from the grave), the hearse, crepe garments, ribbons and pennants.

Those who had to travel long distances on business, found horses for hire on street corners and in front of the market. There were even places where one could rent furniture and utensils, such as tables, chairs, bowls, plates, dishes, chopsticks, spoons and drinking vessels, for large banquets or funeral dinners. Cooks, too, could be hired at a reasonable price for special feasts in gardens, pavilions or monasteries. Boats were available for outings on the lake.

The hire and rental system put expensive services and commodities within reach of ordinary people. Needless to say, this stimulated the production and consumption of commodities.

Business on credit was an important aspect of the development of commodity exchange. In 1022 Emperor Zhen Zong issued an edict:

> The Commercial Tax Bureau of the capital shall see to it that all travelling merchants be notified that hereafter ordinary goods shall be bought or sold for cash only. For high priced goods, or goods in large quantity, necessitating deferred payment, the buyer shall get three to five persons of property to guarantee payment by signing with him a bond fixing a date of payment. They shall be required to make payment if the buyer fails to do so on the date agreed. If only the buyer signs the bond, without guarantors, the government will not hear the case in the event of default. If the guarantors actually have no property, and are collaborating with the middleman to deceive the seller, both the guarantors and the middleman shall be prosecuted according to law.

This imperial edict was, in substance, a law regulating purchase and sales on credit. The bond was a prototype of the modern promissory note. The credit system acknowledged assets and liabilities in the relations between buyer and seller. Money now was not only a measure of values, a means of circulation and accumulation. It had also become a means of payment within a credit system. This last function, in China, had its origins in Bianjing when it was the capital of Northern Song.

Throughout the 220 years from when Bianjing became the capital of the Later Liang of the Five Dynasties in 907 till the collapse of the Northern Song in 1127, each dynasty, especially the Northern Song, made successive efforts to improve the city. Bianjing flourished primarily because it was the capital. Its decline and desolation likewise resulted from the collapse of the imperial dynasty.

The Song government through heavy taxes, forced labor and rents, extorted tremendous wealth, as well as grain and goods, from the people of the villages and towns throughout the country. It was this which created the huge purchasing power of the royalty and the elite. Bianjing had little independent urban production, and relied on supplies shipped in from the outside on the Bian and other rivers. Its economic boom was built on shifting sands and would collapse the moment any social or political change occurred.

This change came in the form of a military defeat suffered by the Song in the second year of the Jingkang period (1127).

According to historical records, beginning in the eleventh month of the previous year, Jin (Golden Tartar) troops besieged the capital for the second time, cutting the city off from the outside and depriving it of supplies of tribute and commercial grain. By the 19th of the twelfth month ". . . the price of rice in the city rose to 3,000 coppers per *dou* (peck), and the streets and lanes were littered with the corpses of the starved." By the fourth month of 1127 the Jin army sacked the city, looting public and private property, and kidnapping Emperor Qin Zong and his father Hui Zong, as well as many other members of the royal family. The Jins appointed Zhang Bangchang, as leader of the surrender advocates, as puppet emperor. Another son of Hui Zong fled south, leaving the old capital in ruins, and established a Southern Song capital in Linan (Hangzhou), where he assumed sovereignty as Emperor Gao Zong. The end of the Northern Song was complete. Zhuang Jiyu, an eyewitness, wrote:

> From Xuchang to Bianjing for thousands of *li* not even a chicken or dog remains. Wells are filled with corpses and the water is undrinkable. Once busy crossroads are now covered with weeds and underbrush. No one is left to gather the beans and millet in the fields, and the pears and dates on the trees.

This passage gives us an idea of the extent of the devastation of the Huang and Huai River valleys, the two main economic regions of the time.

During the early years of Southern Song, Fan Chengda (1126–93), a noted poet, was dispatched as an emissary to the Jins. After passing Bianjing, he noted:

> The New (Outer) City was mostly in ruins. Some places had been converted into fields and put to the plough. In the Old (Inner) City a few markets lingered on. Here and there were tall edifices—the empty hulks of devastated palaces, pavilions and temples.

With the decline and fall of Bianjing, the Bian River, once the main artery of the Northern Song, silted and dried up, turning eventually into a stinking ditch. The Bianjing depicted so minutely by Zhang Zeduan in *Riverside Scene,* and recalled so vividly by Meng Yuanlao in his *Reminiscences,* was no more.

But its heyday left indelible impressions on the minds of many. The publication of *Reminiscences* had an important influence on the people of the time, spurring their efforts to oppose the invaders and recover their land. Today it facilitates our study of the socio-economic history of the Northern Song Dynasty. For the same reason, *Riverside Scene* is also much valued by scholars at home and abroad.

(From the foregoing one can readily see why Israelites of the 12th century should have chosen Kaifeng, or Bianjing, as a place of permanent abode. Its bustling commerce and prosperity offered many opportunities to earn a livelihood. As the cosmopolitan capital, as a center of learning and the arts, it was attractive to the intellectuals. Foreigners were no novelty; in fact there was considerable trade with non-Chinese. Indeed, Kaifeng proved to be an ideal site for a long-term community of Jews. Not only in Northern Song, but during all the succeeding dynasties, they lived relatively unmolested, even flourishing for a time, until they gradually forgot their own traditions and were culturally and physically assimilated into the overwhelming mass of Chinese society.)

Gao Wangzhi

CONCERNING CHINESE JEWS, 1983

Gao Wangzhi was born in Shanghai in 1927. He is a graduate of Tsing Hua (Qinghua) University, Beijing, where he specialized in Western Languages and Literature. Gao is Secretary General and Director of Christian Studies in the Institute for Research on World Religions, and member of the Academic Council of World Religions, both of the Chinese Academy of Social Sciences. He is the author of a number of articles on Judaism and Chinese religions, and is presently working on a book entitled *Comparative Studies of Chinese Religions.*

Gao disagrees with Chinese and foreign scholars on several controversial questions and offers original arguments to support his views.

I. THE FIRST PERMANENT SETTLEMENTS IN CHINA

There is no specific reliable record regarding this in Chinese or foreign historical material, says Gao. The three Kaifeng inscriptions all give different dates. He quotes Chen Yuan: "The Hong Zhi (1489) inscription says Song (960–1279), the Zheng De (1512) inscription says Han (206 B.C.–220 A.D.) the Kang Xi (1663) tablet says Zhou (1066–256 B.C.)."[1]

Gao notes that Chen Yuan culled through a huge amount of historical data and reached the conclusion that the Kaifeng Jews "could not have come prior to Song."[2] Yet Arab traveller Abu Zaid Hassan wrote that when Huang Chao sacked Guangzhou at the end of Tang, he killed a large number of foreign merchants, including Jews.[3] Gao points out that another Arab, Mas'ud, who came to China somewhat later, made a similar statement.[4]

This indicates, says Gao, that there were many Jewish merchants living in Guangzhou at the end of Tang, a fact which neither Chinese nor foreign historians doubt. While Chen Yuan agrees with this, he asserts: "They were only temporary, not long term, residents. These are two different matters."⁵ Gao disputes Chen Yuan's view. He queries:

> Could it be possible that among these "temporary" residents were some who decided to remain permanently? Who settled in Kaifeng or some other city? If so, we cannot say positively the Jews "could not have come prior to Song." In my opinion a more reasonable premise would be that there already were permanent settlements of Jews in Kaifeng and Yangzhou at the end of Tang. My reasons are this:
>
> Large-scale Diaspora began after the Bar Cochba revolt against the Romans was crushed in 135. The Romans expelled the Jews from the city of Jerusalem, and they were compelled to leave Palestine. At first they migrated to two main areas—Alexandria and Babylon.
>
> The Jews in Alexandria gradually accepted the cultural influences of the Greek conquerors. They spoke Greek. The *Torah* was translated into Greek and became the edition known as the *Septuagint*. But the Babylonian Jews were able to continue their ethnic traditions, and established a very large Jewish community. After Babylon was conquered by the Muslims in 637, the Jews to some extent were influenced by Arab culture, but they retained their religion and their language right up to the 11th century, when the Jewish community finally disintegrated.

In 750 the Arabs established the Abbasid Dynasty and in 762 built their capital in Baghdad, slightly north of Babylon. Before long, their empire extended over Europe, Asia and Africa.

They were known in China as the *Black Robed Dashi*—Black Robed because that was the color Arabs in the eastern portion of Arabia favored, and Dashi because that was the Chinese term for Arabia. Starting in 752 the Black Robed Dashi engaged in active trade with the Tang empire, says Gao, especially by sea. They resided in Guangzhou and Yangzhou in large numbers. During an insurrection in Yangzhou in 757 and 758, "Arab" and "Persian" merchants were slain by the thousands.⁶ Nor were these only "temporary" residents, Gao maintains. Many had taken Chinese wives and settled permanently. According to Chinese history, in 8th century Guangzhou, "Foreigners and Chinese lived side by side and inter-married. Many bought land and built homes."⁷

Since there was still a large Jewish community in Babylon in the 8th and 9th centuries, says Gao, it is conceivable that the Dashi merchants who came to China included Jews who settled in cities like Guangzhou and Yangzhou. Kaifeng and Yangzhou are connected by rivers and the Grand Canal, and it was easy to travel by boat. It is entirely possible that some of the Jews living in Yangzhou in the Tang dynasty moved to Kaifeng, Gao maintains. He explains the lack of historical records regarding them:

> At that time the Jews in Babylon were subordinate to the Black Robed rulers of Dashi. And so when they came to China they naturally presented themselves as Dashi merchants. In outward features they were no different from the Arabs. They spoke Arabic. During Tang, Abu Zaid and Mas'ud, who were themselves Arabs, could spot them as Jews, but the Chinese people could not. No wonder Tang and Song historians make no specific mention of them, and refer only to Dashi merchants and foreign traders generally.

Another question requires an answer, says Gao. According to the 1489 inscription, the Jews brought ". . . entry tributes of Western cloth. The Emperor said: 'You have come to our Central Plain. Preserve your ancestral customs and settle in Bianliang (Kaifeng).'" Does this prove the Jews did not take up permanent residence in Kaifeng until the Song dynasty? Gao contends the reliability of the inscription is questionable. Chen Yuan had also noted that there was no historical record confirming the statement[8]. Surely, an important directive by an emperor would be written down. Gao thinks the Kaifeng Jews inserted an unidentified emperor into their story to lend prestige to their original settlement. Gao concludes this section with:

> I cannot positively claim there was a Jewish settlement in Kaifeng during Tang, because to date there are no historical records to substantiate it. But the existence of a Jewish community in Babylon at that time and the active trade between East and West lead me to doubt the assertion that the Kaifeng Jews "could not have come prior to Song."

Compare the contention that an official record identifies the emperor and shows that the Jews arrived in Kaifeng in 998 during Northern Song. See Chen Changqi, p. 142.

II. THE JEWISH COMMUNITY IN KAIFENG

To conjecture that in Tang Kaifeng had a Jewish settlement, says Gao, does not mean we can go further and allege there was a Jewish community, for the settlement then lacked the synagogue which is the main pillar of a Jewish community wherever it may be. From the time of King Solomon, who ruled from 973–933 B.C. and built the first temple, the tradition of maintaining a place of worship has passed down from generation to generation. Gao elaborates:

After the destruction of the Second Temple and the commencement of the Diaspora, the Jews attached great importance to the
construction of synagogues, both as religious sanctuaries and as
centers of social activities. All three Kaifeng inscriptions agree
that the first synagogue was erected in that city in 1163. This,
therefore, should be considered the date of the establishment of
Kaifeng's Jewish community.

It lasted for approximately 700 years. When American missionary W. A. P. Martin visited Kaifeng in 1867 he found the synagogue in ruins. It was never restored. And so we can say the
Jewish community in Kaifeng existed from the middle of the 12th
century to the middle of the 19th.

From the three inscriptions it is apparent that while the Kaifeng
Jews made some superficial changes from time to time during this
period, in actuality they exerted every effort to keep their folk
and religious ways. Jews scattered all over the globe struggled to
retain their identity, and those in Kaifeng were no exception.

First and foremost, says Gao, was by means of the synagogue. He
notes that according to Chen Yuan's calculations the synagogue was
repaired ten times in the 500 years between 1163 and 1688[9], and the
inscriptions tell us the Jews did this at their own expense, clear evidence of the importance they attached to the maintenance of a religious
center.

When it was restored in 1511, they called it "The Synagogue Which
Respects the Scriptures of the Way" (the *Torah*), says Gao, but on
every other occasion they referred to it either as the "Ancient Temple
Synagogue of Purity and Truth," or simply the "Purity and Truth Synagogue." This shows, on the one hand, the close relationship between
the Chinese Jews and the Muslims—who called their mosques, in Chinese, "Temples of Purity and Truth." On the other hand, Gao asserts, it
demonstrates the Jews felt because they were not of much significance
in Chinese society they had to use Islamic names to bolster themselves
and their religion.

Secondly, Gao avers, the Jews sought to maintain their identity
through their Scriptures. The holiest of these was the *Five Books of
Moses,* or the *Torah*. The Kaifeng Jews spared no effort to preserve
them. The 1512 inscription movingly recounts how they labored to
restore 13 *Torah* scrolls damaged by the flood. Yet in 1851 a member of
the London Missionary Society was able to purchase six of the precious scrolls, which shows to what a sorry state Judaism in Kaifeng
had been reduced.

Lastly, were the rites and customs, says Gao. The 1663 inscription
notes that the Jews prayed three times daily, an evidence of how
strictly they observed their religious rules. Gao tells us what Italian

Jesuit Gozani wrote of his observations in Kaifeng in the early 18th century.

> Two or three thousand Jews venerate Jehovah, calling Him "Tian" (God), "Shang Di" (the Lord), or "Shang Tian" (the Supreme Being). They pray every sabbath in their synagogue, and observe Passover and the Feast of the Tabernacles[10].

Gao continues with his own comments:

> For many years they observed the custom of removing the sinews from the cattle and sheep they slaughtered, because of the injury their ancestor Jacob sustained. As it says in *Genesis* 32: "Even today the descendants of Israel do not eat the muscle which is on the hip-joint . . ." Only the Jews had this custom. It became the main feature by which the Chinese identified them, so much so that they labelled Judaism the "Sinew Plucking Religion."
>
> Yet of circumcision, to which Judaism attaches much importance, the three inscriptions say not a word. This is understandable. Circumcision is in direct contravention of the Confucian injunction against "harming the body bestowed by one's parents." It would have been unwise for the Kaifeng Jews to publicly proclaim it. But they did in fact observe the ceremony for many years. In 1867 when Martin went to Kaifeng, he was told they no longer practised circumcision. This was strong evidence that Kaifeng Judaism was nearly at an end.

III. THE *ZHUHU* AND THE *WOTUO* OF THE YUAN DYNASTY

The Jews who came to China during Tang and Song were mainly merchants, Gao says. There was another large influx in the 13th century, because of the westward expansion of the Mongols. If there were no records of the Jews in Chinese history prior to Yuan, there was a plethora of documents about them once that dynasty was established, Gao alleges.

During Yuan they were called *Wotuo* and *Zhuhu,* and various other transliterations of the latter. In Chinese Islamic texts they were described as *Zhuhu* and *Zhuhude* and the like[11]. Gao tells us of the derivations of these terms:

> The Arab word for Judah was *Jahuda,* and for Jews, in the plural, *Jahud.* The same terms were also used in Persian and Turkic, and were adopted from these three languages by the Mongols. In the Yuan dynasty and thereafter, *Zhuhu* became the derivative of *Jahud,* and *Wotuo* the derivative of *Jahuda*—the *Jahu*

combining into *Hu,* which in Han Chinese was represented by the character *Wo,* and *da* becoming *ta* or *tuo.*

Hong Jun, in Section 29, "A Survey of the Various Religious Sects During the Yuan Dynasty" of his *Annotations To the Chinese Translation of the Yuan Annals,* correctly identifies *Wotuo* as Judaism, or Jews. Pelliot thought *Wotuo* came from the Mongol *ortoq,* which he believed meant a Muslim commercial organization.

Gao says this is not convincing, and quotes Zhang Xinglang to show that while the *Wotuo* engaged in commerce, they were not a commercial organization of the Muslims[12]. But he disagrees with Zhang's contention that *Wotuo* is derived from European appellations for Jews[13], rather than the Arabic/Persian source stated above.

The concept of *Zhuhu* for Jews in Yuan documents is clear, Gao maintains. He quotes a 1330 passage in the *History of the Yuan Dynasty,* requiring *Zhuhu*—as well as Buddhists, Taoists, Christians and *Dashiman* (Muslim Imams)—to pay the usual taxes[14]. These were all "semu ren," that is, "people with colored eyes," the general term for foreigners from the Western Regions. But they were also all members of religious orders.

He admits that the question of *Wotuo* is more complicated.

> *Wotuo* appears over ten times in the *Laws and Regulations* of the Yuan dynasty. Although in some places they are mentioned in conjunction with Tartars, Uygurs, and other races[15], in others they are indicated as a special kind of merchant, that is, "*Wotuo* shanggu," or *Wotuo* traders.[16] These traders, openly or privately, invested or loaned monies on behalf of the Mongol aristocracy[17], or used these funds in foreign sea trade[18]. The Yuan *Laws and Regulations* mention the names of some of the *Wotuo* traders: Ala-eddin, Mahmud, Yussuf . . . typical Arabic names.[19] In addition, "*Wotuo* loans" are also mentioned. While historical records do not reveal their numbers, the *Wotuo* obviously were many, and they operated all over China.

But were they Jews? Gao is convinced they were. His reasons:

> In the 13th century, Jews were dispersed in Europe, Asia, and Central Asia. Many of them engaged in lending money at high interest rates. In some parts of Europe "usurer" was synonymous with the word Jew. After they migrated to China, they naturally continued in this profession.* From the nature of the transactions

---

*Nothing in Chinese history or records suggests that Jews ever engaged in money lending in China, usurious or otherwise. Usury was practised mainly by rural landlords, who charged tenants exorbitant rates for loans of seed or food grain. The *Wotuo,* if they were Jews, served only as investment brokers for wealthy Mongol nobles.

we can deduce that the practitioners were Jews. Their main function was to act as agents in the placement of loans for the Mongol aristocracy. The *Wotuo* were certainly not a Muslim commercial organization, as claimed by Pelliot. That some had Arabic names is not surprising. Jews often adopt names commonly used in the land in which they reside—and they had lived in Arab-ruled countries for centuries before coming to China.

IV. THE ASSIMILATION OF THE CHINESE JEWS

As noted above, says Gao, there were two large migrations of Jews to China. The first occurred in the Tang and Song periods, the second during the Mongol westward expansion. Although the two situations were not the same, historically speaking both were stages in the gradual dissolution of the ethnic characteristics of the Chinese Jews and their ultimate assimilation.

Worldwide, the Jews fought persistently to retain their characteristics, notes Gao, and during the 1,800 and more years since the start of the Diaspora, in spite of severe oppression, they generally succeeded. Their global population today exceeds 14 million, and their synagogues stand wherever they have settled.

But China is the exception. Why were the Chinese Jews assimilated? asks Gao. This is a question well worth examining. He gives us his analysis.

> The "people with colored eyes" who came to China as a result of the Mongols' westward expansion, intermarried with the Han Chinese and proliferated. By Ming, they had become a new race, known as "Hui." Living in small settlements all over China, they spoke Han Chinese, but believed in Islam and preserved their own rites and customs.

> During Yuan, the Jews, known as *Zhuhu* and *Wotuo,* were also part of the "people with colored eyes." Although before coming to China they had long been under the influence of Islamic Arabs, Persians and Turks, they managed to retain their ethnic characteristics. And so the Yuan Mongols had special appellations for the Jews, and Marco Polo was able to recognize them. He wrote of Jews then living in Peking and Hangzhou. Fourteenth century Arab traveller Ibn Batuta also noted in a district of Hangzhou a Jewish settlement whose entry was called the "Gate of the Jews."

> Yet there is no record, either Chinese or foreign, of any Jewish synagogue being built in China during Yuan. This is not simply an oversight. It is because the newly arrived Jews, dispersed in various cities, had not yet formed solid communities—such as the one in Kaifeng created by the Jewish settlers earlier in Song—capable of establishing central places of worship.

The Yuan dynasty lasted less than a hundred years. After the Mongol rulers the Jews had served were overthrown, had they not, along with other "people with colored eyes," blended in with the Hui, it would have been difficult for them to continue to exist in China. When Zhu Yuanzhang took the throne as the first Ming emperor in 1368, he tried to turn all Mongols and "people with colored eyes" into Han Chinese. The attempt proved futile, and he changed to a more liberal policy. Because this was advantageous to the Hui and strengthened their position, it also speeded the conversion of the Jews into Hui.

This does not mean that during the Ming dynasty all of the Jews became Hui. As stated above, Islamic scholars in Qing were still referring to Jews as *Zhuhu* and *Zhuhude*.[20] But by the end of Qing descendants of the Yuan dynasty Jews were, beyond doubt, for the most part assimilated.

With regard to the Kaifeng Jews, says Gao, the question was not so simple. They had existed as a community for 700 years. Their history was unique. And so their decline and assimilation was necessarily different.

From Ming on, their political status was weak and unprotected, Gao explains. In 1642, during the peasant uprisings led by Li Zicheng, the dykes of the Yellow River were breached and Kaifeng flooded. As the 1663 inscription put it: "The synagogue was destroyed and the Scriptures were sunk beneath the waves. Only two hundred some-odd families of the congregation managed to get across to the north side of the river." Says Gao:

> This was a terrible blow to the Kaifeng Jews. But not once in the three centuries of the Qing dynasty were they able to obtain any assistance from the imperial court. On the contrary, because it was Qing policy to suppress the Hui harshly, and because the Jews lived in close proximity to the Hui, they were often looked down upon. Some felt impelled to conceal their identity, and went so far as to obliterate their family names from those listed in the 1489 inscription[21]. Racial oppression by the Qing government was the political cause of the disintegration of the Kaifeng Jewish community.

But, Gao points out, the political cause alone is not the answer. The Jews were scorned and oppressed in other countries as well. They were even victims of large-scale pogroms, yet their communities were not destroyed. It was the feudal Confucian traditions which the Kaifeng Jews found themselves unable to withstand. If they wished to attain a reasonably good social status, they had to, from childhood, study the Confucian classics. A knowledge of these was indispensable to anyone who sought to become an official by taking the government examinations. But this was so time-consuming that it meant an abandonment of the study of Hebrew and any prospects of becoming learned in Judaism.

An example was the Kaifeng Jew Ai Tian, who visited Matteo Ricci in Beijing at the end of Ming. He had always studied Han Chinese, and had no knowledge of Hebrew.[22] There were many such Jewish scholars in Kaifeng. Although the rabbis were opposed to members of the community becoming officials, they were powerless to prevent it. The weak and isolated Jewish community, crushed by China's powerful feudal traditions, eroded daily. By the middle of the 19th century no one understood Hebrew. All of the scholars in Judaism were gone.

The continued existence of a Jewish religion has been an extremely important factor in the maintenance of the many Jewish communities throughout the world, Gao alleges. Today, Judaism has vanished from Kaifeng, and the Jewish community is breathing its last. As Chen Yuan says: "Some of the Jews have joined Islam, some have integrated with the Hans."[23]

Like the Jews in other Chinese cities who in Yuan were known as *Zhuhu* and *Wotuo,* the overwhelming majority of Kaifeng Jews have gradually been assimilated, Gao concludes, swallowed in the surging waters of China's torrential history.

NOTES

1. Chen Yuan "A Study of the Israelite Religion In Kaifeng" in *The Academic Theses of Chen Yuan,* Vol. I., 1980, Zhonghua Shuju, p. 275
2. Ibid., p. 276
3. M. Reinaud *Relation des voyages faits par les Arabs et les Persans dans l'Inde et à la Chine"* 1845, Paris, Chap. I., p. 64. See also Zhang Xinglang *A Survey of Historical Material Regarding Contacts Between China and the West,* Vol. II., 1977, Zhonghua Shuju, p. 207–208
4. Meynard et Comteille *Les prairies d'Or de Macond,* translated from the Arabic, 1861–1867, Paris, Chap. I., p. 64
5. Chen Yuan, ibid, p. 276
6. *Old Tang History,* Sec. 110, and *New Tang History,* Sec. 141 "Biography of Deng Jingshen"
7. *New Tang History,* Sec. 182, "Biography of Lu Jun"
8. Chen Yuan, ibid. p. 276
9. Chen Yuan, ibid. p. 284
10. Louis Pfister *Notices Biographiques et Bibliographiques sur les Jesuites de l'Ancienne Mission de Chine,* 1932, Shanghai, p. 469–470. Also Chen Yuan, ibid, p. 284–285, quoting Gozani and Domenge
11. Liu Zhi *Islamic Rites,* Sec. 14 "Residences," and Lan Xi *Islamic Othodoxy,* Sec. 7, "Inscription Inside the Tomb of Holy Muhammud"

12. Zhang Xinglang, ibid, Vol. III, p. 51

13. Ibid, p. 37

14. *History of the Yuan Dynasty,* Chap. 33, "Emperor Wen Zong"

15. *Yuan Laws and Regulations,* Sec. 35, and Zhang Xinglang, Vol. III., p. 45

16. Ibid, *Yuan,* sec. 51, and ibid, Zhang, p. 49

17. Ibid, *Yuan,* sec. 20, and ibid, Zhang, p. 41

18. Ibid, *Yuan,* sec. 35, and ibid, Zhang, p. 46

19. Ibid, *Yuan,* sec. 22, and ibid, Zhang, p. 42

20. Liu Zhi, ibid, regarding "*Zhuhu* yuan." ("Jewish residences"?)

21. Chen Yuan, ibid, p. 269

22. Pelliot *Ngai Tien (Ai Tian),* translated into Chinese by Feng Chengjun in his *History of the Western Regions and the South Seas,* 1956, Zhonghua Shuju, Part 6, p. 244

23. Chen Yuan, ibid, p. 300

Li Jixian

AN SAN AND AN CHENG, 1983

Born in 1926 in Beijing, Li Jixian studied history at Yenching University. He is presently a Research Fellow in the Ming Dynasty Division of the History Institute of the Chinese Academy of Social Sciences. What led me to him was this:

In his treatise, *A Study of the Israelite Religion in Kaifeng,* Chen Yuan sets forth and analyzes the text of the Hong Zhi (1489) tablet which the Israelites erected to commemorate a rebuilding of their synagogue. This tablet, in outlining the history of the community, relates that Israelite physician An Cheng had been encouraged by the Prince of Zhou, whose fiefdom embraced Kaifeng prefecture, to supervise an earlier rebuilding of the synagogue in 1421, and had received from him a donation of incense (money). Chen Yuan says An Cheng had probably won the prince's favor by helping edit two massive medical texts which the prince was compiling.

The tablet notes that in 1423 An Cheng was rewarded by the Emperor for meritorious conduct, which had been reported to the throne, by permission to change his surname to Zhao, and by appointing him to two official military posts.

The text of the tablet and Chen Yuan's explanation seemed straightforward enough, but in the April–June, 1965 issue of the *Journal of the American Oriental Society,* in an article entitled "Notes on the Chinese Jews of Kaifeng," Fang Chao-ying alleged that An Cheng the physician was in fact An San, a soldier in the Henan Central Guards, also a Jew, who earned the gratitude of the Emperor by exposing the intention of the Prince to commit treason. Fang supported his allegations by quotations from *Ming Tai Zong Shi Lu,* that is, *Records of Ming Emperor Tai Zong.* Tai Zong was the posthumous title of Cheng Zu, who ruled during the Yong Le period when the events in question took place.

The *Records* do indeed state that a certain An San was so rewarded, but they give the date as 1421 rather than 1423. Fang says this was because the "writer of the (tablet) inscription cleverly camouflaged An's unsavory conduct by placing it two years later . . ." He asserts that An Cheng the physician never existed, that the very name was invented by "a stroke of genius on the part of the writer of the inscription . . . to form . . . a name . . . to suit the status of a physician of non-Chinese ancestry about to be honored with a Chinese surname by imperial order."

Why such a deception? According to Fang it was to conceal An's relationship to the Prince he "betrayed," namely, that of "a slave to the master," since "to inform on one's master, however justified, was always an unworthy act."

The *Records* state that the Prince was forced to admit his plot to the Emperor, and disband his armed forces. After this "humiliation," says Fang, he had no choice but to "humble himself" before An San—"a former bondservant and a turncoat who had put him in danger of sentence of death"—by supporting the rebuilding of the synagogue.

"Whatever the reason," Fang insists, "it could not have been a voluntary act of friendship the writer of the inscription would like the reader to construe. But to An and to the Jewish community it was certainly a cause for elation and an event to be proudly celebrated. So the writer of the inscription cleverly camouflaged An's unsavory conduct by placing it two years later, in 1423 instead of 1421, and worded it so vaguely that no one could detect the truth by reading the document alone."

In other words, a deliberate fraud was perpetrated, not only by Jin Zhong, the respected Kaifeng Israelite intellectual who composed the inscription, but also by the leading members of the Jewish community—who would certainly have known whether or not An Cheng the physician existed only a few decades before.

It seemed incredible to me that such people would endanger their tenuous social position, to say nothing of risking stringent legal penalties, and have carved in stone and erected in public statements which, if untrue, could easily be recognized as falsifications.

I wondered, too, how a scholar of Chen Yuan's attainments and painstaking research abilities, a man who examined even minor county gazettes, could have missed the entries in the imperial Ming *Records* concerning the activities of An San the soldier. Surely Chen Yuan had seen them. Why didn't he also consider them a negation of the existence of An Cheng the physician?

Another thing which troubled me was Fang's antipathy to the Kaifeng Jews. He says:

Concerning the synagogue the inscription records how it was first erected in 1163, rebuilt in 1279, restored in 1421, and enlarged in the years 1461 and 1489. The years 1163 and 1279 happen to be two milestones marking low points in the history of the Chinese people. In the former year the Jurchen (Nuzhen) Chin (Jin or Golden Tartar) dynasty moved its capital to Kaifeng and in the latter the last Sung (Song) emperor was drowned, ending the Chinese resistance to the Mongols.

To this, Fang appends the pious note:

That the Jews showed their prosperity by building or rebuilding their synagogue in precisely these two years may be coincidental, and to read any significance into the matter is entirely speculative . . .

So strong were Fang's passions that he even found An San's exposure of the Prince's treason reprehensible. Didn't a citizen's loyalty to his sovereign emperor place a far higher moral demand upon him than his duty to his local prince? How could An San's revelation have been both "justified" and "unworthy"? Why revile him as a "slave," a "bondservant," a "turncoat"?

Whether by the standards of today, or of 15th century feudal China, An San behaved righteously and with courage. As a Chinese scholar Fang certainly knew this. Could it be that his emotional responses where Jews are concerned had beclouded his judgment?

Yet, that still left the other questions Fang had raised: Was there an An Cheng the physician? Was he actually An San? Were they the same, or two different persons?

I sought out the History Institute of the Chinese Academy of Social Sciences for the answers. Li Jixian, Research Fellow of the Ming Dynasty Division, was kind enough to examine the records and do considerable additional research. His analysis, which follows, I believe disposes effectively of Fang Chao-ying's contentions.

According to historical records, during the Yong Le period (1403–1425) of the Ming dynasty (under Emperor Cheng Zu, posthumously titled Tai Zong), an Israelite called An San was granted permission by imperial edict to change his family and given names to Zhao Cheng, and Israelite An Cheng was allowed by imperial edict to change his surname to Zhao.

Were these the same person or two different persons? asks Li Jixian. He says this is a question of concern to both Chinese and Western scholars. He offers an analysis on the basis of the material he has examined. It is necessary to look first at the historical records, he says.

Ming Tai Zong Shi Lu, or *Records of Ming Emperor* (posthumously called) *Tai Zong,* section 27: "On the fifth day of the tenth (lunar) month of the eighteenth year of the Yong Le period (Nov. 10, 1420), Su the Prince of Zhou was ordered to appear at the capital (Beijing) in the second month of the following year. This was because An San, a soldier of the Henan Central Guards, and others, had repeatedly accused Su of treasonably plotting. The Emperor could not believe this, and ordered an investigation which proved the charges to be true. As a result there was an edict."

Ming Tai Zong Shi Lu, section 27: "On the 14th day of the 12th month of the 18th year of the Yong Le period (Jan. 18, 1421) An San, soldier of the Henan Central Guards, was appointed a Jin Yi Wei Zhihui Qianshi (Lt. Colonel of the Brocaded Robe Security Corps), and was granted the name Zhao Cheng. (The Brocaded Robe Security Corps was a national organization with broad police and prison powers). This was because his charges of misconduct against Su the Prince of Zhou proved to be correct."

Ming Tai Zong Shi Lu, section 28: "On the 12th day of the second month of the 19th year of the Yong Le period (Mar. 16, 1421) Su the Prince of Zhou arrived at the capital. The Emperor showed him the charges of misconduct levelled against him by An San and others. Su knocked his head on the ground and said: 'I deserve to die. I deserve to die.' Because they were relatives, the Emperor was lenient and did not pursue the matter further."

The Prince was Emperor Cheng Zu's younger brother, born of the same mother. Their father had been Tai Zu, the first Ming emperor.

Zhu Mouwei, a historian in the late years of the Ming Dynasty, in his book *Fan Xian Ji,* says the following in Section One entitled "Zhou Fan": "In the spring of the 19th year of the Yong Le period (1421), because An San accused the Prince of misconduct, the Prince was summoned to the capital. He submitted a written promise to disband his three guards divisions, and returned to Kaifeng."

Or, the last sentence may mean "He submitted a report that he had already disbanded his three guards divisions." This is not clear, says Li. In any event, either before or shortly after his visit to Beijing, he dismantled his entire military force.

In the second year of the Hong Zhi period (1489), midsummer, in the prefecture of Kaifeng, Confucian scholar Jin Zhong and others erected a memorial tablet entitled "A Record of Rebuilding the Qing Zhen Si (Purity and Truth Synagogue)", Li continues. It said:

"The founder of the Israelite religion was Abraham, 19th generation descendant of Pangu/Adam . . . Physician An Cheng, in the 19th year of the Yong Le period (1421) of Emperor Cheng Zu, was presented with ceremonial incense (money) and authorized by the Prince of Zhou, whose posthumous name was Ding, to rebuild the synagogue. An erected therein a plaque wishing 'Long Life to the Emperor of the Great Ming Dynasty.' In the 21st year of the Yong Le period (1423) his merits were reported to the throne, and he was rewarded with permission to change his surname to Zhao and was designated a Jin Yi Wei Zhihui, that is, a Major in the Brocaded Robe Security Corps, and was subsequently raised to the rank of Zhejiang Du Zhihui Qianshi, that is, Lt. Governor of the Military Area of Zhejiang Province."

The pertinent written historical records regarding An San and An Cheng consist essentially of the above, says Li. How accurate are they? How reliable? He sees it thus:

1) The *Shi Lu* were records of events during the reign of the previous emperor, compiled soon after his death by the government of the new emperor. Compilation of the *Ming Tai Zong Shi Lu* began in the first year of Emperor Ren Zong, whose brief reign (1425–1426) was known by the period title Hong Xi. The task was entrusted to three high officials—Zhang Pu, Yang Shiqi, and Yang Rong. Emperor Cheng Zu (Yong Le) had died shortly before. His dockets were readily available. Generally speaking, therefore, the material regarding his reign was reliable.

Of course the officials making the compilations were not the persons originally reporting the events. The reports tended to be long, and sometimes included things the officials chose not to repeat. These, they changed or abridged, with the result that the *Shi Lu* occasionally deviated from the original. For example, reports of An San becoming Zhao Cheng in a few places write Cheng without the speech radical. The officials were not familiar with the matter, and accepted the shorter form of the word since the sound of both is the same.

Chinese written characters are usually composed of a "radical" and a "phonetic." Originally, the first indicated the general nature of the word—water, earth, wood, speech, etc., the second the sound. Over the centuries, in many instances both of these elements have come to have little relationship to their early symbolism.

2) Commemorative tablets were written as a rule by local persons and concerned contemporary events. The construction or repair of a temple was usually recorded on a commemorative tablet. Unfortunately, the text of the tablet commemorating the

rebuilding of the Purity and Truth Synagogue in the 19th year of the Yong Le period (1421) has not come down to us. But it was only sixty years or so from that date to the second year of Hong Zhi period (1489). People from the Yong Le period were still alive, and could testify to the happenings of that time. Moreover, Jin Ying and Jin Li, who joined with Jin Zhong in the 1489 reconstruction of the synagogue, were also "descendants of the Purity and Truth Faith" (Jews)—as stated in the 1489 tablet. Jin was one of the Chinese surnames adopted by the Israelites.

This means that not only was the text of the Hong Zhi tablet written by a local person about a recent event, but that it was written by a Jewish person about a Jewish event. Its veracity and reliability, therefore, surpasses that of other records, including even the *Shi Lu,* Li maintains.

Rubbings of the tablet show that it was composed by Jin Zhong, is rectangular in shape, with thirty-six lines of vertical text containing 56 characters each, and is 147 cm. high and 79 cm. wide. It clearly sets forth the material about An Cheng as stated.

Namely, that he was a physician who rebuilt the synagogue in 1421, and who was rewarded for merit in 1423 with a new surname and official appointments.

Since the *Shi Lu* and the commemorative tablet are both reliable, says Li, and since An San and An Cheng were both subsequently called Zhao Cheng, were An San and An Cheng the same person or two different persons? It would help if we examined the reasons for the change of names, the dates when the two Ans became officials, the grades conferred upon them, their differences in status, and their respective helps and harms to the Prince of Zhou. Li proceeds to do so:

1) The reasons for the change of names.

An San was granted permission to change his name because his accusation of "treasonous plotting" by the Prince of Zhou "proved to be correct." According to the section regarding "Wu Gao" ("False Accusations") in Chapter Five of "Xing Lu" ("Criminal Law"), Book 22 of *Da Ming Lu (Legal Code of the Great Ming Dynasty),* anyone lodging a false accusation was held criminally responsible. Su was a prince of royal blood, a brother of Ming Emperor Cheng Zu. He was of extremely high rank and very powerful. That An San, an ordinary soldier, should dare to level repeated accusations against such a person was a demonstration of his absolute loyalty to the emperor. It was entirely logical that he should, therefore, have been permitted to change his name to Zhao Cheng.

An was not a Chinese name, whereas Zhao is the first on the list of the Hundred Chinese Surnames. Cheng means honest. The change was both an honor and a mark of social acceptance.

An Cheng the physician already had the given name of Cheng. When he supervised the rebuilding of the synagogue in 1421 he set up a plaque wishing "Long Life to the Emperor of the Great Ming Dynasty." This demonstration of fidelity naturally pleased the Emperor, and so he was already favorably inclined toward An Cheng when other meritorious conduct was reported two years later in a bid for imperial reward. It was then that he granted the new surname.

If An Cheng was actually An San, and had already received the name Zhao in the 18th year of the Yong Le period, that is, January, 1421, why give him the same surname again in the 21st year of the same period (1423), asks Li?

2) The dates when the two Ans became officials.

An San was made a Jin Yi Wei Zhihui Qianshi (Lt. Colonel of the Brocaded Robe Security Corps) on the 14th day of the 12th month of the 18th year of the Yong Le period (Jan. 18, 1421).

An Cheng was appointed a Jin Yi Wei Zhihui (without the Qianshi) of the same Corps in the 21st year of the Yong Le period (1423). (The suffix Qianshi means Lieutenant or Deputy.)

The titles are not the same, and there is a time difference of more than two years between them. How could this be, if they were the same man?

3) The grades conferred upon them.

Subsequent to the above appointments, An Cheng was raised to the rank of Zhejiang Du Zhihui Qianshi (Lt. Governor of the Military Area of Zhejiang Province).

According to the "Provisions Regarding Military Officials" in Chapter One of *Leaders of Various Departments,* a Du Zhihui Qianshi (Lt. Governor of a military area) was Grade Three. The lowest grade was Eight, the highest was One. Wei Zhihui Shi (General of a defense or security corps) was also Grade Three.

A Lt. Colonel was Grade Four. This would include Lieutenant Colonels in the Brocaded Robe Security Corps. A Lt. Governor of the Military Area of Zhejiang Province was Grade Three.

But the List of Eight Official Grades contains no such title as Jin Yi Wei Zhihui (without either the suffix qianshi or the suffix shi), nor does history offer any clear explanation of its meaning. It seems to me, says Li, there are two possibilities: (A) It indicated a low rank, or, (B) it was an abbreviation for Zhihui Shi, or General, a relatively high grade. Let us examine both possibilities:

(A) A low rank. The *Ming Shi (History of the Ming Dynasty)* Chapter 89, in Bing Zhi (Military Ranks) section one, states the sequence in which officials could enter the Palace to attend the Emperor's morning audiences. Zhihui is listed immediately before qianhu (a major of 1,000 troops). Wang Shidian in his *Jin Yi Zhi (Grades in the Brocaded Robe Corps)* says: "All qian hu are Fifth Grade." If Zhihui is deemed to include the zhihui of the Brocaded Robe Security Corps, and was only slightly in advance of Fifth Grade qian hu, then it probably was itself Fifth Grade, or slightly higher. In that case An Cheng going from Zhihui of the Brocaded Robe Security Corps to Lt. Governor of the Military Area of Zhejiang Province would be a rise from Grade Five or Four to Grade Three, which would correspond to the order of official promotions.

(B) If Jin Yi Wei Zhihui was an abbreviation for Jin Yi Wei Zhihui Shi, then it meant General and was a Grade Three post. But how could An Cheng subsequently "rise" to Lt. Governor of the Military Area of Zhejiang Province, which was also Grade Three? Clearly, Jin Yi Wei Zhihui could only have been of lower grade.

We have, therefore, says Li, An San being appointed a Lt. Colonel of the Brocaded Robe Security Corps in 1421, a Grade Four post, and remaining in that rank. An Cheng, on the other hand, was made a major, or some such equivalent, in the same Corps in 1423, a Grade Five or Four post, and subsequently promoted to the Grade Three post of Lt. Governor of the Military Area of Zhejiang Province. His ultimate grade was higher than that of An San.

4) Differences in status.

To strengthen their dictatorial feudal control, Ming Dynasty rulers kept meticulous registers of their citizens, especially those with military rank. No confusion of civil and military status was permitted.

In *Leaders of Various Departments,* a provision regarding "False Registration" states that if a local official erroneously registers a civilian as a military person, "he must correct it and restore the civilian status in the register."

Section 131 of the *Ming Tai Zu* (1368–1399) *Shi Lu (Records of Ming Emperor Tai Zu)* notes an imperial edict on the 5th day of the 5th month of the 13th year of the Hong Wu period (1380). It said: "Military and civilian persons all have their definite status. It is absolutely prohibited for any civilian to pose as a military person and upset the status categories among the people."

Legal Code of the Great Ming Dynasty, Book Four, "Citizens Regulations" section one, puts it even more plainly: "All military and civilian personnel, such as cooks, doctors, fortune-tellers, or people in the amusement field, shall register according to status. Whosoever registers falsely to lessen his obligations (such as to pay taxes, or give labor) shall receive 80 strokes of the staff. Any official who abets such falsification shall be equally culpable."

Thus it can be seen how strict the Ming authorities were about registration and records of status. Differences were clearly delineated. An San was a soldier. An Cheng originally was a doctor. Each had his own status. With penalties so severe in the Ming Dynasty, no one would have dared to falsify records regarding status, whether in an official registry or on a commemorative tablet, Li insists.

5) The helps and harms to Su the Prince of Zhou.

By the early years of the Yong Le period (1403–1425) the Prince compiled a medical treatise entitled *Prescriptions for Common Ailments.* It defined 2,175 types of illness, outlined 778 forms of treatment, and contained 1,960 diagnoses, 239 illustrations, and 61,739 prescriptions, including those of famous pre-Ming doctors, folk remedies, and special treatments. Of very broad coverage, the book today is still an important reference work.

Later, the Prince compiled a *Materia Medica for Epidemic Diseases,* which listed 414 kinds of medicinal grasses and wild herbs. Unfortunately, the wood blocks from which the original printing was made have been lost, but new blocks were carved in the 4th year of the Jia Qing period (1525). Its preface, by Li Liu, states: "This book has illustrations and text, the first to show their (the grasses and herbs) appearance, the second to relate their use . . . It tells where they are found, their various names, and whether they are cold or hot in nature, sweet or bitter to the taste. And finally, how to wash, steep, steam, sun-dry and prepare them . . . Even in times of drought you can find them with the aid of the illustrations. They are everywhere, and not difficult to obtain. If taken according to prescription, they can save lives."

Books such as these—large works of much public benefit for many generations—could never have been prepared by Su the Prince of Zhou alone, says Li. He had to have a body of medical experts participating as editors. An Cheng was a prominent physician of that day, and it is reasonable to believe he took part. He and the Prince had this interest in common. They had no cause whatsoever for conflict. It was only natural, after the medical treatises were completed, that the Prince should have supported An Cheng in rebuilding the synagogue, and later requested a reward from the Emperor for the physician's meritorious aid in the production of the two important medical treatises.

With An San the Prince's relationship was quite different, Li maintains. An San was a soldier in the Henan Central Guards Division. Because he reported that the Prince of Zhou was "intending misconduct," he aroused the suspicion of Ming Emperor Cheng Zu. The sovereign feared that "once he (the Prince) sets forth, there will be no holding him." He therefore "directed Marshal Qiu to march with 10,000 troops" and "crush him . . . before he can move." This was reported in the chapter entitled "Wang Zhang Zhuan" ("The Biography of Wang Zhang") in the book *Shou Qi Bi Ji (Notes on Defending the Stream)* by Wang Ao, a historian in the middle years of Ming.

> According to the *History of the Ming Dynasty,* Chapter 90, entitled "Military Ranks," a decree promulgated in the fifth year of the Hong Wu period (1372) set forth "Rules Regarding Guards Divisions of Royal Princes." These provided that each such prince "shall have three guards divisions."
>
> But when An San's accusations were confirmed, Emperor Cheng Zu ordered that unless the Prince of Zhou "disbands his Guards Divisions within three days, he will be decapitated." This, too, was reported in the chapter entitled "The Biography of Wang Zhang" in Wang Ao's *Notes on Defending the Stream.* Only after the Prince disbanded his Guards Divisions did the Emperor turn "lenient and . . . not pursue the matter further."

Accounts seem to differ as to whether the Prince dispersed his army before or after his visit to Beijing, says Li. In any event, there is no doubt that he presented a real threat of an armed uprising, and that he was compelled to divest himself of all military power.

> If An San had not exposed the Prince he would not have risen so swiftly from an ordinary soldier to a Grade Four Lt. Colonel of the Brocaded Robe Security Corps. Nor would new names have been bestowed upon him. Nor would the Prince have been put in danger of losing his head.
>
> Plainly, the positions of An San and the Prince of Zhou were incompatible.

In summation, Li says that considering the times An San and An Cheng received their official appointments, and comparing their respective Grades, legal status, and helps and harms to the Prince of

Zhou, the likelihood of them being the same person is very slight, whereas the likelihood of them being two different persons is extremely strong. He notes:

> Since ancient days there have been many people with identical names. Reliable material is needed in such matters before one can reach a positive conclusion. When data is insufficient a cautious attitude is advisable. To build up a case on the basis of an identity of names is to risk the absurdity of mistaking a mule for a horse.

Chen Changqi

BUDDHIST MONK OR JEWISH RABBI? 1983

The youngest of our scholars, Chen Changqi was born in Wuhan, Hubei, in 1954. He has made a special study of the Kaifeng Jews and is presently at Henan Teachers College preparing for a Master's degree in ancient history. Chen claims to have discovered evidence of the exact date of the arrival in Kaifeng of the Jews, and the name of the emperor who invited them to settle in the nation's capital. The following is from an article by Chen called "Some Questions Regarding the History of the Kaifeng Jews." For convenience sake I have arbitrarily chosen a title for the material here introduced.

Describing the arrival of the Jews in Kaifeng, the tablet the Jews erected in 1489 to commemorate the rebuilding of their synagogue says:

> Our Religion was transmitted to China from Tianzhu (India). We settled in Kaifeng by imperial command. More than seventy clans . . . arrived during the Song dynasty bringing entry tribute of Western cloth. The emperor said: "You have come to our Central Plain. Preserve your ancestral customs and settle in Bian-liang (Kaifeng)." . . . In the first year of the Long Xing period (1163) of Emperor Xiao Zong, when *Wusida* Liewei (Rabbi Levi) was the leader of our faithful, the *andula* commenced the building of our synagogue.

A number of Chinese historians have noted the absence of details regarding the Jewish arrival, and the lack of a specific date. Chen Yuan (p. 29 of this volume) refers to an 18th century treatise by Zhou Cheng on Kaifeng during Northern Song, in twenty-nine volumes, and based on over 390 items of information culled from Song dynasty sources. He says:

Not one of them mentions the Israelites. Nor is there any record confirming the statement in the 1489 inscription that the Israelites brought tribute of Western cloth in Song times, and that the emperor directed them to respect their ancestral customs and settle in Kaifeng.

Gao Wangzhi (p. 120 of this volume) contests the reliability of the inscription, since any such imperial decree would surely have been recorded. He suspects the Kaifeng Jews of inserting an unidentified emperor into their story to lend prestige to their original settlement, which Gao himself believes more likely was in Tang.

Pan Guangdan says (p. 55 this volume): "We don't know which emperor he was," but is of the opinion that the Jews probably reached Kaifeng 50 or 60 years prior to 1126, when the Song dynasty abandoned Kaifeng to the Golden Tartars and fled south to Hangzhou (p. 56 this volume).

Was there, in fact, no record of an arrival date, no identification of the Song emperor? Chen Changqi insists there was. His article tells us what led him to this conclusion.

Chen had several interviews with descendants of the Kaifeng Jews. Many of them repeated the story that their forebears came to Kaifeng during the Song dynasty, bearing tribute of "white Western cloth." A few fixed the time specifically as during the reign of Emperor Zhen Zong (998–1023). With this as a lead, Chen checked Volume Six, entitled "Concerning Emperor Zhen Zong," of *Song Shi (History of the Song Dynasty)*. There, under the "inaugural year of Emperor Zhen Zong," Chen found the following notation:

> "In spring of the first month . . . a seng named Ni Wei-ne and others arrived at our Court from Xitian (India). They said the journey had taken seven years."

Ordinarily "seng" meant Buddhist monk. How do we know that "Ni Wei-ne" was not a monk from India? Chen explains:

> *Song Shi* was compiled by the succeeding Yuan dynasty, based on original Song records. These listed foreign arrivals according to a fixed set of entries—date of arrival, nationality, name, purpose of visit, and tribute brought. If the person was a Buddhist monk only his religious appellation, not his personal name, was listed. In the case of "Ni," the reverse was true.

Could this have been some accidental error on the part of the record clerk? Most unlikely, says Chen. Indian monks were a familiar sight in the capital during Song. They were often hired to translate Indian documents for the Chinese Foreign Office, and many spent months translating Buddhist sutras for Chinese monasteries. If "Ni" was an Indian monk, the record keeper would have known it.

But doesn't the record show that he was an Indian? No, Chen replies. In Song ledgers under "nationality" the practice was to write the name of the country—"India," "Persia" . . . But for "Ni" we have merely the entry: "he *came* from India." In other words, India was where he set out from; his nationality was unknown.

Perhaps he was a Buddhist monk from some other country? Not necessarily, Chen asserts. While it is true that "seng" commonly signifies Buddhist monk, in Chinese historical records it may also denote leaders of other religious persuasions. Chen cites Volume 49 of *Tang Hui Yao (Important Tang Events)*, in which Olopen, a Persian who in 635 was the first Nestorian Christian to come to China, is described as a "seng."

If "Ni" was not a Buddhist monk, and not an Indian, what was he? Chen contends he was a Jew, that "Ni Wei-ne" was "Levi," which later Chinese writings rendered either as "Lie Wei" or "Li Wei," and that he was a religious leader heading a contingent of Jews who reached Kaifeng in 998.

Chen takes it for granted that everyone knows, and so doesn't bother to explain, that all southern Chinese, and some fairly far north, cannot hear the difference between an initial "l" and an initial "n." Many pronounce all such "l" sounds as "n." Kaifeng, the national capital, had civil servants from every part of the land. The record clerk might have been a southerner. Or he might have had difficulty catching the pronunciation of "Levi" by a Jew with an Indian, Persian or Arabian accent. Witness the experience of Jewish immigrants to America in the nineties on Ellis Island, where record clerks wildly mis-rendered their family names!

As to the "ne" sound at the end of "Ni Wei" or "Li Wei," Chen says it is simply an emphatic particle, often used in common Chinese parlance.

Obviously, the Levi who arrived with a band of Israelites in 998 was not the Rabbi Levi who presided over the building of the first synagogue a century and a half later in 1163. But Chen maintains that since the earlier "Ni Wei" or "Li Wei" was a "seng," or religious leader, and since the Levi clan traditionally had always served as High Priests and Chief Rabbis, he too must have been a "Rabbi Levi."

Chen Changqi deals neatly with the question of what made the 998 arrivals say their journey from India took "seven years." A sea voyage in those days at most lasted several months. Even by land, a traveller could reach China in a year or so. Chen explains that among Jews the number "seven" is frequently used to indicate a large number, or a long time. He cites the statement in *Genesis* that God stopped work on the seventh day, after creating heaven and earth. To which I may add the Yiddish phrase *Ziben iss a ligen,* that is, "seven is a lie," or an exaggeration. The time the voyage allegedly required is not to be taken literally.

Emperor Zhen Zong was a warm advocate of religious freedom, Chen declares. Himself a Taoist, the monarch also wrote essays in support of Buddhism and Confucianism, and encouraged the preaching and development of all religions. This created favorable conditions for the entry of the Jews into China. Chen Changqi concludes:

> For the foregoing reasons I believe that the "seng named Ni Wei-ne and others" who "arrived at our Court from Xitian . . . in spring of the first month of the inaugural year of Emperor Zhen Zong," as stated in the *History of the Song Dynasty,* were none other than a rabbi named Levi and a large group of Jews. Moreover, that the unnamed emperor in the 1489 inscription was in fact Emperor Zhen Zong, and 998 was the unspecified time. The notation in the *History of the Song Dynasty* is, therefore, an official record of the entry of the Jews into Kaifeng.

Zhu Jiang

JEWISH TRACES IN YANGZHOU, 1983

Born in Yangzhou, Jiangsu, in 1929, Zhu Jiang took his graduate studies in the history department of Beijing University. He is Curator of the Yangzhou Museum, Vice Director of the Archeology Institute of Jiangsu, and a member of the Overseas Traffic History Institute of China, the Yuan History Institute of China, and the Chinese Archeology Institute.

Zhu Jiang has done much research on the Muslims of Yangzhou and their history. From this, and his knowledge of the history of West Asia, he has been able to make some highly original deductions concerning the presence of Jews in that ancient city in days gone by.

YANGZHOU'S ROLE AS A PORT CITY

Originally, Yangzhou was a sea port, says Zhu, but in Sui and Tang (7th–9th centuries) the course of the Yangtze River changed and its delta extended further into the ocean, and Yangzhou became a river port, though still fairly close to the coast. Meanwhile the Sui emperors had organized the construction of the Grand Canal, running from Kaifeng in the north, through Yangzhou, to Hangzhou in the south, and linking the Huai River with the Yangtze. Yangzhou became a major traffic hub from which one could travel not only south to Fujian and Guangzhou, and north to the Eastern Capital (Kaifeng) and the Western Capital (Henanfu), but also west into Hubei and east to the sea, and from there to Japan and the countries of southern and western Asia. Zhu Jiang quotes Shen Gua, an 11th century writer in Northern Song:

> Seventy percent of the merchants, whether they go by boat or cart west along the Huai or east along the Yangtze, or travel to the Five Mountain Ranges or Sichuan or Hankow, or anywhere within the eleven provinces and the hundred prefectures, all start from Yangzhou. (*Yu Di Ji Sheng,* Vol. 37)

Zhu notes that according to the *Old Tang History* "Guang Ling (Yangzhou) was the richest city between the Yangtze and the Huai." And because it had every attribute needed for a port engaged in foreign trade, "It was only within reason that Arab merchants bringing goods for the Imperial Court, with left-overs to be sold to the common people, should store them first in Yangzhou." (*A Study of Commercial Ports During Tang*, Vol. 4, by Japanese historian Jitsuzo Kuwabara)

WHY THE JEWS CAME TO YANGZHOU

Zhu quotes Pan Guangdan to the effect that the Kaifeng Jews left their native land in the 2nd century B.C. and settled in the Bombay district of India, sailing for China eleven hundred years later, in the 11th century. He feels that while Pan does not say they came to Yangzhou, his indication that they travelled by sea is important. Zhu explains:

> We know that in ancient times there were two routes between China and the West—a Silk Road by land and a so-called Silk Road by Sea. Although the land route started earlier, it was not used as long as the sea route. This was because the countries through which the land road passed were often at war, and transport was disrupted. And so, in the Middle Ages, a sea route was opened, gradually developing into the great traffic artery which exists to this day.
>
> As the northern terminus of the Silk Road by Sea, and the southeastern spur of the overland Silk Road, Yangzhou became famous as a port. It provided a route between north and south China for the transport of merchandise, with resultant economic prosperity and cultural expansion. It vastly expedited trade between China and Japan, Southeast and West Asia, North Africa, and the countries along the Mediterranean.

Ships from China to West Asia, says Zhu, set sail generally from ports along the southeast coast, and travelled through the Gulf of Tonkin and the Straits of Malacca to the Bay of Bengal, on past Sri Lanka into the Persian Gulf, and ending at the port of Basra at the mouth of the Tigris and the Euphrates. From there, the cargo was carried by land to Baghdad, capital of the Arabian Abbasid dynasty. From West Asia to South Asia and the Far East the same route was more or less followed in reverse, and was known as the Spice Road by Sea. In addition to promoting trade, these sea routes brought the teachings of Islam to China, and conveyed Chinese Muslims on pilgrimages to Mecca. Zhu is convinced that the Jews in India travelled by this route. He says:

> By Northern Song interference by countries like the Xi Xia along China's western borders cut all travel via the land road,

leaving West Asian nations no links with China except by sea. It was the only route Jews coming from Bombay could have used.

But why should Jews heading for Kaifeng land first in Yangzhou? Says Zhu:

> Yangzhou was directly connected with the capital in Kaifeng by the Grand Canal, which greatly facilitated travel and the transport of goods, a fact well known to the West Asians. Korean emissaries and merchants, whose country was much nearer, preferred sailing down to Yangzhou and then up the Grand Canal to the overland road across the Shantong Peninsula. Traders and emissaries from West Asia had even more reason to consider this the quickest, safest and cheapest way to travel and transport merchandise to and from Kaifeng. Jews sailing to China from Bombay would, of necessity, first have to land in Yangzhou before they could go up the Grand Canal to the nation's capital. This is what brought so many Jews to Yangzhou.

Zhu says the reason for the eastward migration of the Israelites was that people felt insecure under the unsettled internal conditions of the caliphate nations in West and Central Asia. At the same time the emperors of Northern Song were maintaining an open door policy toward foreigners. The result was that thousands of Arabs, Persians and Jews came to China and settled down. The Jews in India were affected by this flow of migrants, most of whom called at Indian ports en route, as well as by the fact that the Song court was extending preferential treatment to Jews. And so, many of them moved to China, and a large number made homes in Yangzhou.

Actually, Jewish migration to China began well before Northern Song. Some arrived as early as Sui and Tang (late 6th to early 10th centuries), on board the merchant ships which plied China's southeast coast. Zhu elaborates:

> Japanese historian Toyohachi Fujita, in his article regarding foreign traders in north China during Tang, after quoting from *Tang Yu Lin (Tang Commentaries)* by Song dynasty author Wang Dang, draws this conclusion: "Since there were Arabs and Persians in Youzhou and Yingzhou, no doubt there was a considerable number of Jews as well." (*Shigaku Zasshi*, p. 57). In Yangzhou, which had a population of thousands of Persians and Arabs, the presence of Jews was even more inevitable, either as permanent residents or on their way north. Naturally, during the large influx of Jews during Northern Song, many settled in Yangzhou.

THE DESTRUCTION OF JEWISH RELICS

A great quantity of Jewish cultural artifacts in China were destroyed between the final years of Yuan and early Ming. The fundamental cause, says Zhu Jiang, was that the "se mu ren" ("people with colored eyes"), and the Jews among them, had served the ruling Mongols in oppressing the Han Chinese. Therefore, says Zhu:

> When Zhu Yuanzhang, the future first emperor of Ming, was winning victory after victory against the Yuan in the mid-14th century, the Han population, thirsting for vengeance, wrecked whatever cultural relics of the "people with colored eyes" they could lay their hands on in every conquered city and town. Not until 1368 was an imperial Ming decree promulgated against the ". . . killing, pillaging, destruction of buildings, or desecration of graves, of the vanquished." By the time the emperor issued this prohibition and ruled that ". . . talented Mongols and people with colored eyes may be given employment . . ." (*Imperial Ming History,* Vol. I), their cultural relics had long since been demolished.

In the winter of 1357, eleven years before the 1368 edict, Yangzhou was conquered by a Ming army under General Liao Daheng, Zhu notes. Most of the people had fled. Destruction was so extensive that the city could not have been defended against future aggressors. To remedy this the Ming forces built a fortified walled area—in later years known as the "Old City"—in what had been the southwest corner of Yangzhou in Song and Yuan days, and erected a "Defence Tower" outside the South Gate. Zhu adds:

> Monuments inscribed with "Imperial Edicts" of Yuan dynasty rulers were broken and used as foundation stones for the east wall of the city under construction. Gravestones and tomb slabs torn from the cemeteries of Arabs, Persians and Italians, were laid as bricks in the bases of the newly rising city walls. Since throughout Chinese history the Jews were constantly mistaken for Muslims, the "Arabs" and "Persians" mentioned above included the Jews, whose cultural relics met the same fate.

This pattern was repeated all over China, says Zhu. The worst damage was done in the Fujian port of Quanzhou. During the Yuan dynasty Pu Shougeng, an Arab believed to have come from southern Annam (Vietnam), had been appointed a high provincial official. In that capacity he had severely oppressed the Han Chinese. They rose in fury when the Ming forces conquered the city, and smashed every "Arab" and "Persian" relic, tablet and monument—many of which were in fact

Jewish. Present figures reveal that of all the gravestones and tomb slabs of the "people with the colored eyes" unearthed to date, eighty percent were found in the bases of the city walls of Quanzhou. Zhu Jiang quotes from Professor Zhuang Weiji of Xiamen (Amoy) University:

> Between 1946 and 1948 in the ruins of the foundations of Quanzhou's South Gate Tower and southern wall we excavated more then twenty large white gravestones, inscribed in Arabic on both sides. They obviously had been taken from a demolished Islamic mosque. The area overlooked the Jin River and was known as South Quanzhou, or the "Foreign District." It was here that merchants from overseas and their families had lived during Song and Yuan.

Other gravestones and tomb slabs written in Arabic were discovered subsequently, Zhu observes. He quotes from a report by an investigating committee of Quanzhou's History Museum of Overseas Traffic, which reads: "In 1952 in the base of the southern corner of the city wall we found a gravestone engraved in Arabic on both sides." Zhu adds: "Both this report and the comments by Professor Zhuang appear on pages 70 and 210 of *Yicilan Jiao Zai Zhong Guo (Islam in China)*." He offers these conclusions:

> The destruction in Quanzhou of the Yuan dynasty relics of the "people with colored eyes" spared none of the relics of the Jews, who also came within this category. The same thing happened in Yangzhou. A few Arab and Persian relics have survived. But the Jews, who were much smaller in number, had less cultural artifacts, and so the annihilation of these was more complete. That is why no Israelite relics remain testifying to a Jewish presence in China prior to Ming.
> The problem is further complicated by the fact that the Chinese Jews lived always among the Muslims, making it difficult to distinguish their relics from those of the Arab and Persian believers in Islam. Since they inter-married with other Chinese ethnics, particularly the Muslims, it is among these people that Jewish traces must be sought.

Zhu then sets forth the results of his studies and investigations in this regard.

JEWISH TRACES IN YANGZHOU

Zhu Jiang quotes from a letter written to him in April, 1982, by Zhu Zhuanyi, a Research Fellow in the American Institute of the Chinese

Academy of Social Sciences, concerning the question of a Jewish community in Yangzhou, commonly called Weiyang in ancient times.

> Only a few scattered references exist. No systematic treatise on the subject has ever been written. This is quite different from the Kaifeng Jews, about whom there are many records, materials, and books. The story of the Yangzhou Jews is virgin territory, difficult to explore.

But Zhu Jiang is more optimistic. There is, he maintains, some written material, and perhaps something can be found in a study of folk customs. Here he examines both of these aspects.

WRITTEN EVIDENCE

The earliest written reference to Yangzhou Jews known to date appears on a Kaifeng stone tablet, says Zhu, dated 1512 during the Great Ming Dynasty, and entitled "Zun Chong Dao Jing Si Ji" ("A Record of the Synagogue Which Respects the Scriptures of the Way"). It reads:

> An, Li, Gao and Jin Pu of Weiyang contributed a scroll of the Scriptures (Torah) and constructed a Second Gateway to the temple . . .

Professor Pan Guangdan in his "Jews in Ancient China—A Historical Survey" (*Social Sciences in China* 1980, vol. 3), says, Zhu notes:

> There is ample evidence of the presence of Israelites in Yangzhou.

Zhu Zhuanyi in his letter, (ibid), Zhu Jiang continues, says the following:

> A man named Jin Pu brought a parchment scroll of the Hebrew Scriptures, which had been deposited in Yangzhou, to Kaifeng and presented it in celebration of the reconstruction of the Kaifeng Jewish temple, known as the "Qing Zhen Si" ("Purity and Truth Synagogue").

Where had these Jews originated? queries Zhu Jiang. According to Professor Pan:

> The Kaifeng Jews left their homeland in the seventh decade of the second century B.C. and migrated to the Bombay region of India, where they remained for 1100 years. In the middle or the end of the 11th century they travelled east by sea to China and settled in Kaifeng.

Zhu Zhuanyi believes that some of these Jews later migrated from Kaifeng and established another community in Yangzhou.

Recent writings also note the presence of Jews in Yangzhou in ancient times, says Zhu: Jin Xiaojing's "I Am a Chinese Jew," Wang Yisha's "The Descendants of the Kaifeng Jews and Relics of the Sinew Plucking Religion," and Chinese-American Song Nai Rhee's "Jewish Assimilation: The Case of the Chinese Jews."

Are there any indications in Yangzhou life today of early Jews? In the course of my research into the culture and history of the Islam religion and ethnic Muslims in Yangzhou, says Zhu, I have come across several traces of a Jewish past.

SOCIAL PROOFS

After the Jews came to China they lived in a manner very similar to the Muslims, Zhu explains. And so, to seek Yangzhou Jews one must start by examining Muslim outer manifestations.

> Most of the Muslims scattered throughout the country are of Hui nationality. Those in Yangzhou traditionally fall into two categories—the Hui Hui and the Han Hui. Hui Hui means those Muslims whose ancestors migrated from the Western Regions, as Central and Western Asia were called.
>
> For example, Yangzhou Muslims popularly refer to the tomb inscribed with the words "Buha-ud-din, Progenitor From the Western Regions" as the "Hui Hui Tomb," or the "Baba Tomb." (In the language of the Islamic religion "Baba" is a term of respect. Elderly and virtuous *Imams* [religious scholars] among Chinese Muslims are hailed as "Venerable Baba." It also means grandfather.)

At a seminar in Ningxia in October, 1983, scholars discussed the origins of the Hui Hui. Some said they developed mainly from centuries of intermingling of Persian and Arab merchants, who came to China by sea in Tang and Song, with the various peoples of Central Asia north of the Pamirs and the Hindu Kush, but part of them are descendants of Arabs and Persians who moved eastward during the 13th century and intermarried with Mongols, Uygurs and Hans.

Others believe most of the ancestors of the Hui Hui were the Turkic-speaking people of Central Asia, including the Huihe of the Kashgar region who converted to Islam in the 10th century.

But all agree that the Hui Hui race and the Hui Jiao religion are two different concepts, although Islam had a great influence on the formation of the race.

Numbering around seven million, the Hui Hui today live all over China. Their heaviest concentrations are in the northwest in Ningxia, Gansu, Xinjiang and Qinghai, as well as in the provinces of Henan, Hebei and Yunnan.

Han Hui indicates Muslims of native Han Chinese ancestry. But, since the Jews lived among the Hui Hui, says Zhu Jiang, it is in their society, rather than that of the Han Hui, where Jewish traces must be sought.

Yangzhou has a Muslim population of 3,575. Within this number are five large clans generally believed to be Hui Hui from the Western Regions. They bear the Chinese surnames Ha, Ma, La, Da, and Sa (or Sha). According to *Min Shu, Xiyu Ji (Fujian Chronicles, Western Region Notes)* the Islamic religion was first transmitted to Yangzhou thirteen centuries ago, in 622. But there was no large influx of Hui Hui from the Western Regions until the eighth century.

In the succeeding years descendants of the five large clans were, for the most part, assimilated. Very few of the original race remain, or know the country of their ancestors. They know only that they were "Arabs." But, says Zhu:

Fortunately, a branch of the Ha clan has retained its jia pu (family genealogy). It is in the possession of Dr. Ha Yuzhi, a practitioner of traditional Chinese medicine in Yangzhou's People's Hospital. Dr. Ha quotes from the genealogy as follows:

"The Ha clan are Hui people from the Western Regions. They entered China at the inception of the Sui dynasty. The given name of the progenitor in China was Shen. He came from the Western Regions country called *Lumi*."

The first syllable of a foreign name usually becomes the Chinese family name, and the second syllable becomes the Chinese given name. Thus Shen of the Ha family is plainly derived from the Arabic Hassan or Hasan ("Ha Shen"), says Zhu. *Lumi* in English is the ancient land of Rum, Zhu explains. In Chinese Rum is transliterated in various approximations.

Three different places have been put forward in Chinese writings for its location. The first, according to *Ming Shi, Xiyu Lie Zhuan (Ming History, Western Regions Section)* is what is today broadly called Asia Minor.

The second is near present-day Istanbul in Turkey, and was part of the 13th century Osman Emirate, precursor of the great Ottoman Empire. The *Ming History* notes that on five occasions between 1524 and 1554 envoys from the Ottoman Empire paid friendly visits to the Chinese court.

The third place is the Byzantine Empire. Some believe *Lumi* meant Eastern Rome, referred to in the Chinese Koran as *Lumu*, that is, the Byzantine Empire, which conquered Palestine and Arabia. Many of the subject people became naturalized Romans. Zhu Zhuanyi in his letter (ibid) points out that Paul, in the New Testament, calls himself a "Jewish Roman."

From the foregoing we can conclude that Rum was an ancient country in Asia Minor, and the ancestral land of the Ha clan, Zhu Jiang asserts. It proves that the Ha family is from the Western Regions, and that probably all five of Yangzhou's large Muslim clans originated there. Aside from these five, there are a number of other smaller Hui Hui clans from the Western Regions. They too have become Sinified.

> According to the *Min Guo Jiangdu Xianzhi (The County Gazette of Jiangdu Under the Republic)*, in Chapter 13 of the *Ming Ji (Famous Relics)* section—Jiangdu was another term for Yangzhou—during the Song dynasty an Arab named Kutb-ud-din, who had been living in Yangzhou, died and was buried northeast of the Muslim mosque east of the Dongguan River. The place became known as the Gu Family Cemetery.

> An old stone tablet noted that because "several times during the Jia Qing period (1796–1821) of the Qing dynasty, people dug earth from the cemetery to repair the dyke," Gu Yaoting petitioned the emperor for an order "forever prohibiting" the removal of the cemetery's soil. Kutb-ud-din was an original Arabic name. Gu Yaoting was the Sinified name of one of his descendants.

Another Muslim family in Yangzhou bears the surname Zhang, says Zhu Jiang. It is noted both on a stone tablet erected in 1551 during the Ming dynasty, dedicated to "the illustrious General Zhang," and in the *County Gazette of Jiangdu Under the Republic* (ibid), that General Zhang Xing was a Muslim. Also that he was "the grandson of *Damuchi* (Tamudj), a captain of the cavalry who, because of his skill in archery, had been given the surname Zhang by imperial decree and raised to the post of Commander of the Yangzhou Guards."

> Tamudj is a family name. It is similar to the name *Damuding* (Tamudj-din) in the song by the Yuan dynasty composer, Wang Yi, entitled "Lao Hu Mai Yao Ge" ("The Old Foreign Medicine Seller"). According to the song Tamudj-din was a "merchant from the Western Regions" who sold medicine on "frequent trips south of the River." That is, he was an Arab doctor who practised in the towns and villages south of the Yangtze. "Din" in Arabic is simply a suffix meaning a religious believer. That is the only real difference in the names Tamudj and Tamudj-din. Both men were probably members of the same Tamudj religious clan, and both were descendants of people from the Western Regions.

Thus we see beyond doubt that the Hui Hui of Yangzhou are direct descendants of Arabs from the Western Regions, namely, the Middle East, says Zhu.

In Kaifeng, the Jews were known as the Blue Hat Hui Hui, to distinguish them from the Muslims of Arab ancestry, who were called the White Hat Hui Hui. Yangzhou also has Blue Hat Hui Hui. Zhu Jiang offers two examples.

> On the north side of the western end of Jiangdu Road, next to the ironmonger's shop, live Zhang Zixiang and his family. They have two blue hats handed down from their ancestors—a round one of cloth, and a dark blue soft satin hat of six panels coming to a point at the top. Zhang Zixiang received them from his father, Zhang Guocheng, now deceased. They were made during the Qing dynasty (1644–1911).
>
> Mi Xialin and his family live at the east end of Dong Ying Tou Lane. They also have a six panelled blue satin hat handed down from the Qing dynasty, only this one has insets of strips of black satin.

Do these blue hats prove that their owners are of Jewish ancestry? Zhu Jiang queries. He proposes to submit the question to a few tests.

VERIFICATION

Zhu Jiang first goes into the history of how the Arab Muslims of Yangzhou got their Chinese surnames. He recalls that many of them, after becoming Chinese citizens, converted the first syllable of their names into Chinese family names. The descendants of Kutb-ud-din became "Gu." The Arabic name Muhammad is usually transliterated in Chinese as *Mahamade,* or *Muhamude.* And so, the surname of those named Muhammad became "Ma."

> There are also those upon whom Han Chinese names were bestowed. We have already mentioned Illustrious General Zhang Xing, whose family name originally had been Tamudj, and whose grandfather the emperor rewarded with the surname Zhang. This was similar to the case of Ma He, a eunuch in the imperial palace. His father's name had been Mahaj, and so the family name became Ma. But as a mark of distinction, Ming Emperor Yong Le (1403–1425) bestowed on the eunuch the surname Zheng, and he became Zheng He.
>
> Zheng and Zhang were descendants of Hui Hui from the Western Regions. Zhang, appointed Commander of the Yangzhou Guards, settled permanently in the city. It therefore follows that among those with the surname Zhang in Yangzhou some are de-

scendants of Tamudj. While observing the Muslim religious service at the Xian He Si (White Crane Mosque) on October 15, 1982, I had occasion to notice Zhang Zixiang, mentioned above. He was wearing his ancestral blue cloth hat, as usual, typical of the blue hats still found in Yangzhou.

The Chinese, says Zhu Jiang, have customarily loosely called all persons from Western Asia and North Africa "Dashi Guo ren," meaning people from the country of Dashi (Arabia), or, simply, "Alabo ren" (Arabs). In these categories they included Jews, many of whom had Arabic names, and dressed and looked like Arabs, among whom they had lived for centuries. Therefore, in seeking Jewish traces, we must examine the descendants of those who were called "Arabs."

Moreover, since large numbers of Chinese Jews intermarried with Chinese Muslims, and adopted Islam, says Zhu, we must take a look at the members of the various Muslim sects, including those not of Arab ancestry.

And since the Chinese Jews in places like Kaifeng were distinguished by blue hats as a symbol of their religious faith, he continues, we can also seek traces of Jews among the blue-hatted Hui Hui of Yangzhou.

(See also Chen Yuan, Chap. V.)

THE "ARABS"

Of those Yangzhou Muslim families possessing a jia pu (family genealogy), only one—the family of Chinese traditional medicine doctor Ha Yuzhi—lays claim to ancestry in the Western Regions' country of *Lumi* (Rum), Zhu notes. Dr. Ha has copied out the relevant passage. It reads as follows:

> The Ha family are Huis (Muslims) from the Western Regions. We entered China at the inception of the Sui dynasty. Our progenitor's given name was Shen (Ha Shen, that is, Hasan). He came from the Western Regions' country of *Lumi*. At the request of the Sui Emperor, the King of *Lumi* sent scholars who were skilled in astronomy, calendar calculation, and mathematics to join Chinese scholars in research. Our progenitor (Hasan) was among them.
>
> He settled in Taiyuan in the province of Shaanxi. He had four sons, all of whom knew calendar calculation, medicine and technology, very useful at that time. Later, they were officials in several places. Their progeny flourished, and settled in Sichuan, Hebei, Jiangsu and Anhui. The Hebei branch lived in Hejian, which is where our (Yangzhou) branch of the clan originated.

Zhu Jiang asserts that the genealogy is inconsistent with history. It claims that the Ha family are Hui people, that is, believers in Islam, who came to China from the Western Regions at the beginning of the Sui dynasty.

We know that Muhammad, the creator of the Islamic religion was born in 570, and was nearly forty when he made his first journey to Mecca in 609 and established the monotheistic religion of Islam. Thirteen years later, in 623, he went secretly to Medina where, in the course of constant debate with the disciples of Judaism and the Guraish nobility, he established a politically unified Islamic state.

The Ha Family Genealogy says there were already Muslims when they came to China from Rum at the start of the Sui dynasty. But the first Sui emperor took the throne in 581, nearly thirty years before Islam was created in 609. Obviously, they could not have been Muslims at that time.

Another distinguished Muslim from Rum is noted in Chinese records, says Zhu Jiang. The *Ci Hai* Encyclopedia in its entry on the Jing Jue Si (Mosque of Pure Awareness) states:

Jing Jue Si, one of China's most ancient mosques, is on Jian Kang Road in Nanjing. It was built between 1388 and 1405 by order of Ming Emperor Tai Zu to honor Jamal-ud-din, and others, then living in China, who had come from *Lumi* (Rum, transliterated also as *Lumei,* that is, the Ottoman Empire).

We know, therefore, that by the 14th century there were indeed Muslims from Rum living in China. But these came much later than Hasan. Their presence in no way confirms the arrival of Hui Muslims at the inception of Sui, Zhu alleges.

The allegation that Hui Muslims came from the Western Regions in early Sui is repeated in the *Ming Shi (Ming History)* in the section entitled "Lie Zhuan, Xiyu, *Modena*" ("Biographies, Western Regions, Medina"), notes Zhu. It says that a certain Sahab Saad ben Abu-Waggas left Medina, described as the "ancestral land of the Hui Hui (Muslims) . . . at the beginning of Sui and . . . came to China to start the transmission of their religion." Medina today is in Saudi Arabia.

This is, of course, also an error. Abu-Waggis could not have been a Hui (Muslim) at the inception of Sui any more than Hasan, Zhu Jiang maintains, and for the same reason—the Islamic religion had not yet been created. But if they were not Muslims, he asks, what were they?

I believe they were Jews. Twelve centuries before Muhammad created Islam the Jews had already established a homeland in what was later called Palestine. Judaism had spread to Egypt, Mecca, and Asia Minor. Many Jews had moved to nearby Asia Minor two centuries before Christ. During the lifetime of Jesus, says the *Gospel According to John,* Jews in seven cities in Asia Minor were preaching about a "Saviour" and laying the ground-work for Christianity. Six centuries later, there were still many Jews in Asia Minor in the country called Rum, and many of them had become citizens. We cannot say that the eastward migration to China of Hasan, the Ha family ancestor, bears no relation to the Jewish citizens of Rum.

It is true that most of Asia Minor in the late 13th and early 14th centuries became part of the Turkish Ottoman Empire. But there is no record in Chinese histories of any substantial travel of Turks to China. This strengthens our conviction that the Ha family an-cestors from Rum were Jews.

BLUE HATS

The presence of blue hats among Yangzhou's Hui population is a complicated matter, says Zhu Jiang. Ordinarily, soft white hats, flat on top, predominate in Muslim communities in China. Pointed blue hats are in the minority. But, he relates, in Yangzhou we not only have blue hat Hui Hui, we also have black hat Hui Hui. We even have hats with panels of both black and blue. In an investigation I made among fifteen Yangzhou Muslim families, reports Zhu Jiang, I found only twenty percent with white hats.

Does that mean the wearers of the blue or black hats are all descend-ants of Jews? Obviously, no. In Chinese history it was the Jews who integrated with the Muslims, not the other way around. The Jews were always a small minority. That being so, why were there so many blue hat Hui Hui?

When the People's Republic was founded in 1949, most of Yangzhou's Muslims wore soft white hats, flat on top, Blue hats were rare. According to Suo Guolang, vice-director of the Islamic Association of Jiangsu Province and Islamic delegate from Yangzhou, this was because Muslims in other parts of China mostly wore white hats. Yangzhou believers therefore bought them too. They tended to go with the prevailing fashion. Earlier, some of them may have worn blue hats, or black. This did not necessarily signify a particular ancestral religious origin.

But in certain families, the color of the hat clearly does just that, Zhu Jiang insists. He says his investigations show beyond doubt that some families were indeed White Hat Hui Hui (Muslims), while others were Blue Hat Hui Hui (Jews). He cites examples.

> Gu Peiyu, a woman of 76, told me her paternal family considers the tomb of Song dynasty Arab Kutb-ud-din, located east of the river outside the city's Fengdong Gate, to be their "ancestral tomb." The family has worn pointed white hats for generations, and has always been fairly numerous. The family of her husband Gu Sifa, from another branch of the Gu clan, also wears white hats. Whenever the husband's family conducts prayer services, according to Gu Peiyu, it invariably invites "a dozen or so white-hatted *Imams*."
>
> Does the Gu family have any blue hats? Some, says Gu Peiyu, but these have been presented to them by travelling *Imams*.

It is a tradition for orthodox Muslims to wear white hats, says Zhu. An entry in the *Ming Shi, Lie Zhuan, Xiyu, Modena Zhuan (Ming History, Biography, Western Regions, Medina)* reads: "They are strict about ritual animal slaughter, and do not eat pork. They always wear white hats. Even when they go to other countries, they do not readily change their customs."

> We therefore have reason to believe that the Gu family are descended from Medina Arabs, and that their faith is orthodox Islam.

For a contrary example, Zhu Jiang introduces the Zhang family. Zhang Zixiang, 45, told Zhu Jiang that his family has an old blue cloth hat, an old satin hat of deep blue, and an old black satin hat. The hats are soft, made in six panels. He himself has several new violet-blue hats. He was the only one wearing a blue hat of all the Muslims attending the prayer service in Yangzhou's White Crane Mosque in October, 1982.

Zhu Jiang visited his home and spoke with his brother, Zhang Ziji, and saw the family's blue hats—both the new and the ones handed down. Zhang Ziji had no idea where the old hats came from, nor could he say which was the country of his family's origin. But one or two of the blue hats go back well over a hundred years, to a time when nearly all Muslims wore only white. Says Zhu:

> In my opinion the Zhangs are probably a branch of the descendants of Ming dynasty Illustrious General Zhang Xing, whose grandfather was Tamudj, a foreign Muslim cavalry captain upon whom the surname Zhang was bestowed by the emperor for meritorious service in battle. For a Hui Hui to be granted a Han name was an honor. Another instance of this was bestowal of the

name Zheng on the imperial eunuch Ma He by Ming emperor Cheng Zu.

One may speculate as to why Tamudj the cavalry captain was given the name Zhang, rather than some other Han name. Cleanliness is one of the main tenets of the Muslim faith, and Zhang in south China is pronounced "zang," meaning "unclean." Scholars in ancient China were fond of punning. Could this have been their way of jestingly calling Tamudj a heretic for accepting a non-Muslim name?

In any event, the Zhangs became a famous Hui Hui clan, entered as citizens in the Yangzhou records. Zhang Xing was entitled the Illustrious General, his son was named the Honest General. In Ming dynasty Yangzhou the Zhangs were a very prominent family. One of the streets in the old city—Zhang Hui Zi Xiang (Lane of the Zhang Muslims)—was probably named after them.

It is my opinion that Ming dynasty cavalry captain Tamudj, as well as Yuan dynasty Tamudj-din, the doctor from the Western Regions who sold medicine south of the Yangtze, were both descended from the Persian and Arabian Jews who came to China via Bombay in the 11th century. By Ming times, because of their long standing in the Yangzhou community, the Jews had such a high social position that "Jin Pu of Weiyang" (Yangzhou) was able to support his fellow Israelites in Kaifeng on the occasion of the rebuilding of their synagogue.

If this surmise is correct, it would explain why the Muslim family named Zhang, although now believers in Islam, have been wearing blue hats for centuries.

Zhu Jiang also investigated three different families named Jin. While not directly related, he says, they had one characteristic in common— all possess hats either black or blue-black in color. The Jins are a large and ancient clan. The Jin Zhiliang branch, for example, can trace its ancestry back twenty generations.

Many families named Jin in Yangzhou are Muslims, says Zhu Jiang. But except for the *Imam* Jin Mingbiao, now deceased, who sometimes wore a white hat, nearly all of Muslim Jins wear hats which are either black or blue-black, carefully handed down from generation to generation.

What is this, Zhu Jiang asks, if not a symbol of former religious affiliation? Wasn't one of the most prominent Jewish families in Yangzhou during the Ming dynasty headed by a man named Jin Pu? Have we any reason to doubt that there are descendants of Jews among those Muslims who wear blue-black hats in Yangzhou today?

And so, from the record regarding the Israelite "Jin Pu of Wei-yang," from historical evidence that Chinese Jews were known as "Blue Hat Hui Hui," from the tradition of wearing of white hats of China's followers of orthodox Islam, we may reach this conclusion: That all descendants of blue-hatted Hui Hui from the Western Regions found today among Yangzhou's Islamic population probably stem from Jewish ancestors who were culturally assimilated.

Xu Zongzhe

SOME OBSERVATIONS ON THE JEWS OF KAIFENG, 1943

During the early twentieth century a number of Chinese priests and ministers of foreign religious denominations took an interest in Chinese Judaism. Generally, their writings recapitulated the observations of earlier commentators. A few, like Xu Zongzhe, reflected the influence of European anti-Semitism.

I have not been able to discover anything of Xu's personal background, but have only the article which he wrote, in Chinese, for the *Revue Catholique* (April, 1943, Shanghai). Entitled "Some Observations on the Jews of Kaifeng," it concludes with the following:

> Alas, the Jewish tablets are of use today only to the archeologists. The (Kaifeng) Jews no longer know their own religious ceremonies. The Israelite religion has lost its reason for being.
>
> I say this is no cause for regret. The Messiah for whom the Jews are waiting has already come and a new faith, namely Roman Catholicism, has been established. The Israelite religion will soon vanish. That remains of it can still be found in China is truly miraculous.

Such attitudes, fortunately, were the exception rather than the rule among Chinese Christians.

Wu Zelin

AN ETHNIC HISTORIAN LOOKS AT CHINA'S JEWS, 1983

Wu Zelin was born in 1898 in the province of Jiangsu. A lifelong friend and colleague of Pan Guangdan, he served for many years as a professor of social anthropology in Qinghua University in Beijing. Although well into his eighties, he is still active. Today he is a professor of ethnic history in Zhongnan (South-central) Nationalities Institute in Wuhan.

Here he examines the question of how it was that, while Jews the world over have generally managed to survive as cultural and religious entities despite the severest oppression, in China they were so thoroughly absorbed and assimilated that they have vanished almost without a trace.

Professor Wu's reasoning is of course his own. But it also expresses views with which several Chinese scholars are in accord.

This article written in June, 1982, originally appeared as a Preface to Pan Guangdan's book, contained herein, and had no title of its own. For convenience sake I have taken the liberty to call it "An Ethnic Historian Looks at China's Jews."

Wu recalls that he and Pan Guangdan studied together for nine years, a number of them in America, and were colleagues for twenty-two. As children both had read the Bible, including the Old Testament, considered by some to be the early history of the Jews. Part of this, says Wu, are myths which are simply laughable.

Later they read Shakespeare's *Merchant of Venice*. The merciless image of Shylock the usurer led them to feel the Jews were despicable.

When they read world history, they learned how the homeland the Jews had so painstakingly built in ancient times was destroyed and the people driven far and wide—east into Babylonia, west into Byzantium, eastern Europe, Africa, even the vast areas of western Europe. In these alien lands, says Wu, they were cruelly oppressed by the Arabs, the Catholics, the Protestants and the Crusaders. Thousands were slaughtered or sold into slavery. Their religion was prohibited, their property plundered. Wu concluded that the Jews were pitiable.

Yet when countless numbers of them were humiliated and threatened with annihilation by Muslims and Christians unless they renounced their faith, they stubbornly resisted, and chose death rather than surrender. Their splendid courage struck Wu as admirable.

They produced great figures—Moses, Jesus Christ, Heine, Hertz, Mendelssohn, Zamenhof, Freud, Marx, Spinoza, Disraeli, Einstein . . . men who made enormous contributions to civilization. It seemed to Wu the Jews were indeed enviable.

While in America Wu observed that Jewish tycoons, like other big capitalists, used their wealth and power to drive smaller businesses into bankruptcy and throw their employees onto the street. He angrily concluded the Jews were hateful. But he says:

> . . . These impressions of mine, shared today by many, gradually changed as, over the years, I studied the matter more deeply. I came to understand that to appraise a race subjectively, with a prejudiced and superficial knowledge of their history, can only result in an inaccurate and distorted picture. My earlier reactions—that the Jews were laughable, despicable, pitiable, admirable, enviable, hateful—were all one-sided, without any depth.
>
> Admittedly, the Jews in general believe that God created mankind, and that they, the Jews, are His Chosen People. But in the long history of man's primeval ignorance, the myth that one's own kind are the center of human existence is by no means restricted to the Jews. Even among the most enlightened races today there are millions who cherish this illusion. The belief in one god is a big step forward from polytheism, and the Jews were among the first to take this stand when they affirmed Jehovah as the sole deity. It was a qualitative advance and should not be dismissed as "laughable."
>
> Everywhere the Jews were small traders, dealers in second-hand merchandise, high-interest money lenders. These occupations were said to be second nature to them. Moreover, they were considered persons devoid of feeling, callous, rapacious.
>
> Actually, these activities were imposed upon them by objective circumstances. As they wandered from country to country, they were mainly segregated in cities and had no opportunity to engage in farming. The Muslim, Catholic, or Protestant rulers deprived them of the right to participate in many respectable professions. Money lending was against the religious principles of the rulers. It

was unclean, prohibited to members of the prevailing religions. But the Jews were allowed, nay compelled, to engage in this dirty practice as one of the few means available to rise above their poverty. With their lives and property in a state of constant insecurity, the interest they required for loans was naturally a bit high.* Over the years, the profession was handed down from generation to generation. This is how some of the Jews became usurers and were labelled despicable.

While no one can deny the numerous and great contributions to world culture the Jews have made, says Wu, these do not prove an innate genius or an intelligence superior to that of other races. Only in those countries where they, along with the rest of the population, are allowed to receive education and training, do their talents flourish. Backward countries with low scientific and cultural levels rarely produce outstanding people, whether they be Jewish or native inhabitants.

Wu maintains that all races are entities whose development contains both biological and historical elements. The first, which he calls the warp, determines a race's characteristics in common with other races. The second, which he likens to the woof, are the aspects of a race which are different from those of other races.

Wu elaborates: The Jews on today's political stage play a variety of roles. In addition to their political aspect, the Jews have also an economic aspect, a cultural aspect. Whether it be the Zionist movement and Israel's incursions into Arab countries, or activities in international finance by Jewish banking tycoons, or the splendid contributions to mankind by Jewish scholars—all are only the behavior of a portion of the Jewish race. They cannot be taken to represent the Jewish people as a whole, nor can they be offered in either categorical blame or praise. On this, says Wu, Professor Pan Guangdan and he are in complete accord.

After a review of the history of the Jews, from their origins to the Diaspora, to their present situation in the various countries in which they settled, Wu notes that everywhere they tended to congregate in the cities, and that this was true of the Jews who came to China. He comments too on the many changes which have occurred in them over the centuries.

> Physically, it has been inevitable that the Jews should become a blend of many races. It is no longer possible to distinguish them by their traditional features, such as hooked noses. Other races also have hooked noses, and millions of Jews have none. The change in them is particularly marked in Kaifeng, where it is difficult to distinguish them from the other residents. If you gathered Jews from northern Europe, the Middle East, New York

*See footnote, p. 123.

City, and Kaifeng in a single room, you would have a hard time convincing the average person that they were all members of the same race.

Jews no longer have a common language. They speak either Hebrew, Yiddish, English, French, German, Slavic, Arabic . . . whatever is the language of the country in which they live. In China, not long after they arrived they began forgetting their original tongue and speaking Han Chinese.

Today, in many parts of the world the Jews speak a patois which springs from German but is written in Hebrew letters. It is called Yiddish, and contains vocabulary of Hebrew, Russian and Polish origin. Because its use is so widespread, while not a true common language, it may perhaps be considered a manifestation of ethnic consciousness.

Many Jews in many countries have been middle class merchants, Wu says, but in recent years, in America particularly, a polarization of classes among them has become marked. Although class contradictions to a certain extent have weakened their ethnic entity, the still existing discrimination against them, however subtle, tends to strengthen a racial consciousness and a feeling of kinship. At the same time, the religious faith which most of them retain serves as a common tie and a reminder that they are different from other races. The Kaifeng Jews had their own distinctive characteristics. Wu explains:

> As we all know, the more a religious faith is discriminated against, the more it resists and refuses to change. But in a generous, free environment, there is often mutual influence, mutual permeation, among religions. That is how it was with the Kaifeng Jews. Over a long period of time they gradually blended their own faith with that of Islam—a religion similar in many ways to their own.

Contradictions between races vary in intensity, says Wu, and at times end in reciprocal slaughter. This is historical fact. In their years of wandering, the Jews endured the cruelest persecution. This can be divided into two main periods—religious persecution before the 19th century, and racial oppression thereafter. Religions clash on the question of faith. Races vie over a comparison between types of people. Religions may change, Wu asserts, but contentions over racial superiority can only result in battles to the death.

The Jews were able to cope with religious persecution, says Wu. He cites the example of the Middle Ages, when the major religions vied for converts. At times in medieval Spain the Jews were expelled, slain, or sold into bondage. But the moment they were willing to give up their faith and accept baptism, all was well.

They became known to the Spaniards as *Conversos*—the "converted ones," and to the steadfast Jews as *Marranos,* or "pigs." Not a few continued to practise their religion in secret, while preserving their lives and their property.

Racial conflict, Wu indicates, is quite a different matter.

> Its main objective is to wipe out the opposition. There is no question of reform or conversion. In the 19th century theories of racial inequality and Nordic superiority spread throughout Europe. Members of the self-professed superior races viewed all other races with scorn and, out of fear of "contamination," advocated their isolation, expulsion or, best of all, extermination.
>
> By the 20th century, this evil, fanned by Nazism, brought the Jews under the knife. As we know, both religious and racial conflict are loaded with violence. Extreme action is the fuse. Once it explodes it is beyond the control of reason.
>
> And so, in the forties of the 20th century, the respectable government of Germany, a leader in the fields of science and culture, blatantly announced to the world that the Jews could no longer hold public office. They were forbidden to be lawyers, doctors, teachers or editors. They were denied the most elementary citizens' rights. Month after month, Nazi Death Squads electrocuted Jews, gassed them, shot them down. In Nazi-controlled Europe during World War Two, a total of six million Jews were put to death, one of the most frightful tragedies in history.

Wu recalls that philosopher Kant in the 1790s postulated that when a body of people holding one faith enter a vast sea of another, its own religion gradually diminishes until it is completely absorbed in the religion of the surrounding host. At the same time, Kant felt the Jews were an exception. Although isolated among alien religions all over the globe, they managed to retain their faith intact. He thought this was because they had long possessed relatively complete written scriptures. But the Jews of Kaifeng did not fit in with Kant's explanation, says Wu.

> They had their scriptures, religious teachers, a temple, and were in the midst of people whose religion was very different from their own. Under those circumstances, according to Kant, they should have been able to retain their faith and ethnic characteristics, like Jews in other parts of the world. But exactly the opposite happened. In a fairly short time they were assimilated. To find the reason we must examine not only their internal factors, but also their external environment.
>
> Throughout history the Chinese people have always had a

broad magnanimity. Except when subjected to alien political pressures, every dynasty advocated a policy of unity with the outside world. Foreign races and religions were welcome, the Jews included.

This is obvious from the words of the 1489 Kaifeng inscription, relating how when the Jews arrived during the Song dynasty the emperor said: "You have come to our Central Plain. Preserve your ancestral customs and settle in Bianliang (Kaifeng)." Clearly, the Song dynasty rulers were permitting them to retain their religious faith and preserve their own customs and traditions.

Moreover, in referring to the erection of the first synagogue in 1163, the inscription states the time in terms of the Song dynastic period, although Kaifeng was then occupied by the Jin Golden Tartars and Song had moved its capital to Hangzhou. To thus stress the sovereignty of the Han Chinese several hundred years after the event demonstrates the friendly relations the Jews enjoyed with their hosts, and the gratitude they still felt for the freedom of religion which had been granted to them. This warmth and generosity on the part of the Chinese no doubt enabled the Jews, through their religious practices, to preserve their ethnic characteristics. But it also avoided or dissolved any doubts or psychological obstacles which may have existed between the Chinese and the Jews, and thereby created the conditions for a natural absorption.

Another factor, Wu explains, is that the Kaifeng Jews had an equal opportunity to take part in qualifying examinations for official posts. Starting in the 14th century increasing numbers of Jewish merchants and intellectuals were appointed to office, a few to quite high positions. They came under the sway of traditional Chinese thought and Confucian teachings. In an environment of feudal officialdom and frequent contact with bureaucrats of China's various races, they gradually changed their philosophic concepts. Ethnic consciousness dimmed, particularly among those Jews who had become powerful and prominent, and this in turn influenced the entire Jewish community. Subsequently, the Jews of Kaifeng adopted the feudal Three Duty Relationships and Five Cardinal Virtues, even using the vocabulary of Confucian theory to describe their own spiritual ideals.

There was also inter-marriage, something much deplored by master racists and racial segregationists. Whenever a race migrates, the men always outnumber the women, says Wu. They are of course eager to marry local women when they arrive in an alien land. In old China with its rigid feudal social structure much attention was paid to matching those of similar family status. Under such circumstances it was very difficult for men of different race, language and customs to find a marriage partner. Yet the Jews were able to do so, Wu asserts. He does not tell us why, but only goes on to describe the change:

> Before they were in China very long, in physical appearance, speech and way of life they were virtually indistinguishable from the local Chinese, proving that for them inter-marriage was not an isolated phenomenon but a common practice. This breakthrough was obviously a pivotal point in their absorption. Inter-marriage not only gradually eliminated religious traces from their family lives, but as these marriages increased they of necessity weakened the cohesiveness of Jewish society and culture, and eradicated their unique characteristics as a race.

Wu sees the assimilation of the Chinese Jews as primarily the result of economics. As middle class merchants, doctors and artisans living amidst a vast native population, they could not possibly maintain their original styles of economic existence. Although they had to compete with the Chinese, they were also reliant upon them. Inevitably, they came to emulate them—in methods of production, in culture, in speech . . . they even adopted Han Chinese names.

By the middle of the 19th century, Wu says, in physical appearance and dress they were identical with the local Han and Muslim populations. This was also true of their religious ceremonies, such as sacrifices to ancestors, mourning for parents, marriages and funerals. Their written language had vanished, their very names had been changed. In every sense they had become Chinese.

The integration of the Kaifeng Jews illustrates a very important principle, Wu alleges:

> Neither individuals nor groups exist in isolation. They are mutually used and influenced by other groups and individuals. Although one side may exercise the initiative, to a very large extent it is reacting to the behavior of others. In the metamorphosis of the Kaifeng Jews, they themselves did indeed play the leading role. But the religion, culture and social system of the peoples around them gave powerful impetus.

> The traditional magnanimity of the Chinese people has remained constant, not only toward the Jews, but toward every race with which they have come in contact. For this reason China has been able to live in harmony with all individuals and all races within its borders, and ultimately absorb them.

> Generosity, open-mindedness, recognition and reward of merit, fair and equal treatment—these are traditions we must continue to foster and develop, for in world history they are all too rare.

Wang Yisha

THE DESCENDANTS OF THE KAIFENG JEWS

Wang Yisha, Curator of the Kaifeng Museum, probably knows more about the Kaifeng Jews and their descendants of the past century than any scholar in the world today. Living and working among them for many years, he has gathered some remarkable, previously unknown information.

The following is based on his unpublished survey, made at the end of 1980, and several hours of conversation I had with him in Kaifeng and Beijing in 1983.

INTRODUCTION

Noting the three different times of arrival in China set forth in the three different stone inscriptions—commemorating the rebuilding of the Kaifeng synagogue in 1489, 1512, and 1663, respectively, Wang thinks it possible that Jews first came to China during the first and second centuries. They may have been fleeing racial oppression, he speculates, and travelled via the Silk Road, which ran from the Roman Empire to China, across Central Asia.

But he thinks they settled in Kaifeng later, probably during Northern Song (960–1127). Since the 1489 tablet states they brought "entry tribute of Western cloth," Wang says they most likely were cotton cloth merchants. And the reference in the tablet to "more than seventy clans" convinces Wang that these Jewish migrants came as a group including family, relatives and friends. Says Wang:

> From then on, the Jews of Kaifeng lived in harmony with the Han and Hui (Muslim) Chinese, sharing the bitter with the sweet, learning and progressing together. They made positive contributions to the arduous development of Kaifeng City. In the silk trade, in the manufacture of gold and silver ornaments, as merchants, in the scientific and cultural fields, they made considerable achievements.

167

Local people called their faith the Sinew Plucking Religion. Wang states three explanations offered by various persons for the derivation of this term: First, to commemorate the injury their forebear Jacob sustained to his sciatic nerve while wrestling with an angel, Jews remove this nerve when they slaughter their animals. Second, they remove the sinews of the cattle or sheep which they prepare to cook. Third, when the Jews arrived in Kaifeng they were toting their Scriptures on carrying poles, and so their religion was named the "Tiao Jing Jiao," meaning "Scripture toting religion," and this title was subsequently corrupted and mispronounced as "Tiao Jin Jiao," meaning "Sinew Plucking Religion," which is written with different characters but sounds almost the same. Wang favors the second explanation.

In any event, the Kaifeng Jews maintained a synagogue for more than seven hundred years—from the third year of the Da Ding period (1163) of the Jin (Golden Tartars) to the thirtieth year (1850) of the Dao Guang period of the Qing dynasty, Wang points out. It was the center of their religious life, and the place to which Jews from cities such as Yangzhou, Ningxia and Ningbo constantly gravitated, and there in the course of some seven centuries, the so-called Sinew Plucking Religion emerged, developed, and finally declined. Wang observes:

> For many years Chinese and Western scholars have been intrigued by the remarkable history of the Kaifeng Jews and their Sinew Plucking Religion. Scores of books have been published about them. The stream of visitors to Kaifeng, especially foreigners, never ends.
>
> Several things puzzle them. "The history of the Jews in China is long," they say, "but they never suffered oppression. How was that? And why did they intermingle with the Han and Hui Chinese? . . . What is their situation today? . . . Do any of their ruins or relics remain? . . ."

Wang agrees that deeper studies need to be made of the Kaifeng Jews and the Sinew Plucking Religion, and notes that some are under way. Word of mouth stories about them, for example, are being set down in writing. Wang says modestly that what he offers here is only a rough review, based on recent interviews and investigations, of the present circumstances of the descendants of the Kaifeng Jews, and of the ruins and relics which still exist.

THE "EIGHT CLANS WITH SEVEN SURNAMES" CONTROVERSY

Why did the Kaifeng residents commonly refer to the Jewish community by this appellation? How many clans and families were there when the Jews first arrived? Five claims are current, each with its own vigorous exponents. Wang lists them:

One, those who point out that the 1489 inscription states that the Jews who came to Kaifeng consisted of over seventy surnames, although only seventeen are actually listed, three of which appear twice. These were different names in Hebrew (or Persian or Arabic) but were rendered by closely approximate sounds in Chinese speech and writing. This tablet is now in the Kaifeng Museum.

Two, those who quote from the 1679 ancestral tablet of the Zhao clan, which puts the arrival figure at "73 surnames and over 500 families." This tablet is also in the Kaifeng Museum.

Three, those who claim that the "seventy" figure in the 1489 tablet is careless error for "seventeen" ("qi-shi" and "shi-qi" respectively in Chinese). Chen Yuan in his "Kaifeng Yicileye Jiaokao" ("A Study of the Israelite Religion in Kaifeng") seems to give some credence to this story.

Four, those who insist that among the Jews "seven" is a mystic, and rather vague, number, as in the statement in *Exodus* that seven tens of Jews entered Egypt, (Jacob and his family). And so, the argument goes, the "seventy" clans referred to in the 1489 tablet means only a large, indefinite number.

Five, those who allege that when the Jews first came to Kaifeng nine centuries ago they consisted of eight clans. That the emperor bestowed Chinese surnames upon seven of them, namely Li, Zhao, Ai, Zhang, Gao, Jin and Shi. That the eighth clan, who were servants to the Zhangs, adopted the same surname, and became known, therefore, as the "trickled down Zhangs." And that is how Kaifeng got its "Eight Clans with Seven Surnames."

Wang Yisha favors the first two claims. He says:

> I believe there were seventy clans, and they later were joined by another three. In *Shou Bian Ri Ji (Diary of the Defence of Bian)* it is revealed that the ancestors of Li Guangtian, the hero of the siege of Kaifeng in 1642, had moved to that city from Beijing during the early years of the Hong Wu period (1368 to 1399) of the Ming dynasty. That was certainly one additional clan.
>
> Moreover, Jin Zhong, the composer of the 1489 tablet, was a scholar, and Zhao Yinggun, the composer of the 1679 tablet, was a prominent figure. Both were not only Jews, but men of learning who were well known in their day. Since both speak of seventy-odd clans, there must be some foundation for the figure.
>
> Further, both the 1512 and the 1663 inscriptions also list several names not included in the "Eight Clans and Seven Surnames." The claim that the Jews, when they arrived in Kaifeng consisted

only of "Eight Clans With Seven Surnames" clearly does not conform to historical fact.

However, Wang feels there is a reason for the persistence of the phrase in Kaifeng over the past few hundred years. From the start of the Qing dynasty (17th century) to the early fifties of this century, Wang notes the Kaifeng Jews indeed had only seven surnames. Today, these have been reduced to six—Li, Zhao, Ai, Gao, Jin and Shi. What happened to the others? Wang looks back to find an answer.

He points out that the 1679 tablet indicates that by the 16th century Kaifeng Jewry had expanded to more than five hundred families. Calculating at eight persons to the average household in those days, that would be over 4,000 people. Even at only five to a family, says Wang, it would still come to around 3,000.

But the great flood of the Yellow River in 1642 reduced the city's population from 378,000 to less than 100,000. Only about 200 Jewish families managed to escape to the northern side of the river, according to the 1663 tablet. Not until twenty years after the flood, namely, in 1662, were the Jews able to return to Kaifeng, along with their Han and Hui neighbors, and rebuild their synagogue. Wang says:

> One of the main organizers of the reconstruction of the temple was Zhao Chengji, a Defence Commandant of the Kaifeng Area, himself a Jew. Thirteen Scripture scrolls were restored. The main financial contributors were clans with seven surnames—Li, Zhao, Ai, Zhang, Gao, Jin and Shi. They also undertook responsibility for the repair of the thirteen scrolls.
>
> These seven were prominent Kaifeng clans in early Qing (17th century), and their social status was relatively high. In the community of the Sinew Plucking Religion they were the controlling authorities. From Ming to early Qing members of the Li clan served as temple leaders and rabbis. In the Shun Zhi period (1644–1662) of Qing a Zhao qualified as Jin Shi in the Imperial Examinations, another Zhao was a country magistrate, Zhao Yingcheng was Investigating Judge of Fujian Province, Zhao Chengji was Defence Commandant of the Kaifeng Area . . .
>
> The Ai clan produced two rabbis. Shi Zijun and Zhang Wenrui also became rabbis. The Gao clan had an Academy Graduate; in addition to contributing to and participating in the general repairs of the synagogue, they financed the restoration of the Ancestral Halls and the compound's walls and gateways. Nearly all the ancestors of the Jin clan were local officials, and all contributed to the restoration of the synagogue.

Wang concludes that the popular usage of the term Seven Surnames probably arises from the active leading roles played by clans bearing the surnames described above. As to the others listed in the 1489 inscription, they either died or were scattered in the flood of 1642, says Wang. Or perhaps they were so impoverished they simply abandoned their religion.

With regard to the so-called Eight clans, Wang adds, there are also various theories. Some say it was because there were two different clans each transliterated as Li in the 1489 tablet, and each separately listed, which later became known as one. Others say the same thing about the two Zhang clans. But there was even more duplication of clan designation, leading to still more confusion. Wang enumerates:

> During the Yong Le period (1403–1425) of the Ming dynasty, Jewish physician An Cheng was rewarded by the emperor with the surname Zhao. This created a second Zhao clan in addition to the one which already existed.
>
> And not only are the names Li and Zhao listed twice in the 1489 inscription, so is the name Jin. Each of these is an instance of two different clans with the same surname in Han Chinese—although their clan appellations were quite different in their original language. And in 1949 a Jewish family was discovered in Bao Ding Lane who called themselves Zhang, but used a different Chinese character to write it . . .

All of these theories have their supporters among the Jews of Kaifeng, and none will concede to any of the others. Our latest investigation shows that both Jewish Zhang clans have gone from Kaifeng, no one knows where, says Wang. There now remain descendants of only six clans: Li, Zhao, Ai, Gao, Jin and Shi.

THE DESCENDANTS OF THE KAIFENG JEWS

Wang Yisha conducted a series of interviews among persons in Kaifeng whose ancestors were Jews, and compiled detailed statistics as of late 1980. While the figures by now must have changed somewhat, the proportions should be roughly the same. The remaining material is reliable and significant.

BASIC STATISTICS

There are still 140 former Jewish Kaifeng families in China, says Wang, with six surnames. Of these, 79 families live in Kaifeng, 61 families have moved to other parts of the country. At last count (1980) the 79 families contained 166 persons, says Wang, including 36 girls who have married non-Jews and left their parents' homes. It does not include Han and Hui girls who have married into Jewish families. Wang gives a breakdown according to surname:

Li	16 families	46 persons
Zhao	9 families	11 persons
Ai	17 families	32 persons
Gao	3 families	3 persons
Jin	2 families	7 persons
Shi	32 families	67 persons

Of these, 88 are men, 78 are women.

RESIDENCES

Wang obtained most of this information from Zhao Pingyu, who is in the Municipal Tax Bureau, and Ai Fengming, a worker who is also a member of the City Council. They said the story handed down in their families is that most of the Jews in the old days lived in the general neighborhood of their Qing Zhen Si (Purity and Truth Synagogue). This put the Jewish community within a roughly square area bounded on the east by Cao Shi Jie (Haymarket Street), on the west by Bei Tu Jie (North Local Products Street), on the south by Li Shi Ting Jie (Administration Office Street), and on the north by Jiu Fang Jie (Old Arch Street), now called Cai Zhen Ting Dong Jie (Finance Office East Street). Says Wang:

> The Zhao clan lived behind the Shun Xin Shop (west of today's Scripture Teaching Religion Southern Lane), the Ai clan lived on Li Si Ting Street, the Shi and Li clans lived in Xian Ren Lane (pronounced the same but written differently today).
>
> The others lived in the general neighborhood mentioned above, but later gradually moved away. The Ai clan left Li Shi Ting Street only after the start of the Republic (1911). But Li Rongxin's family still lives in Cao Shi Street, and Zhao Pingyu's mother and daughter both continue to reside at number 21 Scripture Teaching Religion Northern Lane (the old site of the Sinew Plucking Religion Synagogue).
>
> Today, the six clans are scattered in a number of places, including Scripture Teaching Religion Northern Lane, Cao Shi Street, Xi Peng Ban Street, Bei Men Avenue, Zhong Shan Road North Section, South Taiping Street, Ci Shan Street, Jin Gui Alley, Da Keng Bank, Xi Ban Zai Street, Hui Jia Lane, Da Huang Family Lane, Hou Bao Ding Alley, Bao Fu Keng Street, Xing Hua Garden, Ying Street, East Avenue, Ma Dao Street, Sheng Chan

Street, Wai Ma Hao Street, Bei Dao Gate, South Song Men Guan Street, Yi Yuan Hou Street, Cai River Bend, Yi Dao Lane, East Guai Street, South Wei Xin Street, the Chemical Factory Hostel, the Tile Kiln Hostel, and Wang Hamlet . . .

OCCUPATIONS

Wang compares the social position of the descendants of Kaifeng Jews before and since the establishment of the People's Republic of China in 1949. He first lists the occupations pursued by parents and grandparents of persons today over fifty, that is, within a time frame of roughly the first half of the 20th century:

> 7 proprietors of handicraft and mercantile shops, namely, the Wan Fu Silver Shop on Gu Lou Street, the Ji Feng Silver Shop on the same street, Shi Ziyu's Silk Emporium on North Local Products Street, a Money Exchange Shop, a Preserved Fruits Shop, a Restaurant, and a Wine Shop.
> 4 proprietors of goods and sundries shops
> 5 odds and ends dealers
> 2 independent handicraftsmen (one silversmith, one cotton fluffer)
> 7 workers (3 house painters, 1 carpenter, 1 stevedore, 2 mailmen)
> 4 teachers (2 private school teachers, 1 family tutor, 1 missionary school teacher—female)
> 1 saltmaker and coaldust seller
> 1 vegetable pedlar
> 1 bookkeeper in a foreign goods shop
> 1 Buddhist monk
> 1 unemployed

This shows 20.5% engaged in fairly large handicraft and mercantile occupations as owners, Wang comments, 41.1% serving as workers, handicraftsmen, shop assistants, and teachers. There was only one woman, constituting 2.9% of the total.

After the formation of the government in 1949, says Wang, there was a fundamental improvement in the occupation of Kaifeng Jewish descendants. He lists the present jobs of 104 persons of working age:

> 68 workers, of whom 7 are retired and 4 are women
> 14 civil servants, of whom 1 is retired and 4 are women
> 5 teachers, 4 of whom are women
> 3 in the armed forces

1 farmer
10 young people waiting for jobs, 7 of whom are girls
3 information not yet obtained

Wang adds, it is clear that since the new government was formed the social position of the descendants of Kaifeng's Jews has improved considerably. This is certainly true of the women, he notes, who now comprise 30.7% of those employed, as against only 2.9% previously.

MARITAL STATUS

According to Wang by the 17th century at the latest, Kaifeng Jews had already broken the strictures against marrying persons of other races. They took brides among the Hans and the Huis (Muslims). Zhang Mei (17th century) had six wives, some of who were not Jewish. In the genealogical records of the seven clans during the Qing dynasty we find Jews marrying girls of 36 different non-Jewish surnames. Wang explains:

> Shi Zhongyu, who works in the Bureau of Industry and Commerce in the Shunhe district, and Zhao Pingyu and factory worker Li Shichang, tell me that people of their great-grandparents' generation married pretty much within the Seven Surnames. Li Shichang's great-grandmother was one of the Ai girls. The Shi clan and the Ai clan also intermarried with one another.
>
> But by their parents' and grandparents' generations, almost all married Han and Hui Chinese. This was due both to the small numbers of their own race, and to their division into rich and poor. Brides were no longer chosen on a racial basis. It was rather a question of social status.
>
> One ancestor of the Shi clan had been a Grade Four official, another a famous merchant—Shi Ziyu, who owned the Bian (Kaifeng) Silk Emporium. The clan had lots of property. Its men selected their brides from clans of important scholars or contributors to the Imperial Court. By the time of Shi Qi's father, however, the clan was so down on its luck that he had great difficulty in finding a bride.
>
> Gao Fu's mother starved to death. His younger brother was killed by Japanese soldiers. Before Liberation (1948) Gao Fu lived from hand to mouth. It wasn't until after Liberation that he was able to marry his present wife. She is not of Jewish descent. As Gao puts it: "Among poor people, if the man and woman suit each other, they get married. Who cares about race!"

Since the promulgation of the Marriage Law in the early 50s, says Wang, the attitude of the parents is: "Now young people are free to marry anyone they like. We don't interfere." Even middle-aged people no longer feel obligated to marry only members of their own race.

Wang notes that all 41 of the girls of Jewish descent who have married in recent years have chosen Han husbands, and that of the 42 men of Jewish ancestry who took brides in the same period, 41 married Han girls and one a Hui.

POLITICAL STATUS

A fairly large percentage of the young people and adults of Jewish descent in Kaifeng take part in political activities, reflecting the large extent to which they have been integrated into Chinese society. Wang reports that among them six are Communists, including one woman; 22, including 10 girls, are Youth Leaguers; one is a member of the Democratic League; and two, one of whom is a woman, are members of district People's Congresses. Wang cites examples from two well-known Kaifeng families:

> Before Liberation Shi Qi's father Shi Weixun was the proprietor of Kaifeng's famous Wan Fu Silver Shop. Shi Qi himself worked in the city's big Department Store until recently, but now he is retired. He has four sons and four daughters. All are married, and work outside the city. The wife of the second son, and each of the husbands of the four daughters, are Communists. The second son, the third son and his wife, the fourth son and his wife, and all four daughters are Communist Youth Leaguers. In other words, 87% are members of either the Communist Party or the Communist Youth League. The third daughter is also a Representative in the District People's Congress.
>
> Li Enshou is employed in the office of a wrench factory. His two younger brothers and a younger sister are Communists. They work outside the city. He himself, his oldest son—who is a Youth Leaguer—and the son's wife, as well as his second son, are on the staffs of government enterprises. The wife of his second son, his third son and daughter-in-law, his fourth and fifth sons, and his oldest daughter and her husband, are factory workers.

During past political campaigns a number of descendants of Jewish families came under attack, although none, Wang points out, on racial or religious grounds. One was erroneously classified a "capitalist." Two were mistakenly labelled "Rightists." During the Cultural Revolution (1966–1976) one was accused of being a "traitor," and another of being a "spy." The lives of their relatives were also affected to a greater or lesser extent.

After the downfall of the fanatical Gang of Four in 1976, the madness came to an end, says Wang. Communist Party policy was again implemented, the names of the above persons who had been slandered were cleared, and amends were made. Gao Qi, for example, honorably retired from his job. All of his daughter's pay, which had been docked, was restored to her. She was then promoted two grades and elected a Representative in the District People's Congress.

STANDARD OF LIVING

In early Qing (17th century) the widely known Shi Ziyu's Silk Emporium was already growing weak financially because of the erosion of the Jewish community. By the 1860s, as a result of natural and man-made disasters, the Kaifeng Jews fell into extreme poverty, Wang Yisha says. They weren't even able to maintain their Purity and Truth Synagogue. After more floods during the Dao Guang period (1875–1908), the Zhao clan scattered and disappeared. The once wealthy Jin and Shi clans ruined themselves with extravagance and dissipation. Many of them left Kaifeng for other parts of the country.

The Zhangs also departed at the end of the nineteenth century, Wang reports. The formerly well-to-do Gaos either starved to death or scattered in all directions. Only after Kaifeng was liberated in 1948 were the descendants of the Jews able to regain a secure livelihood and gradually improve it.

Wang's latest investigation, in November, 1980, shows that the Kaifeng Jews have a per capita income of around 30 yuan a month. Some earn as much as forty. Few receive less than twenty. Wang cites some case histories:

> Take Jin Ziru, for example. Before Liberation his clan was very poor. In 1942 his younger brother Jin Ziming was seized by the soldiers of Wang Jingwei, puppet of the Japanese invaders, and carried off. His nephew died of starvation. His younger brother's wife remarried.
>
> When Kaifeng was liberated in 1948 he borrowed five yuan and moved what was left of the family to the Tile Kiln in the northern suburbs. Before he retired he worked himself up to Technician Fourth Grade. Today, his retirement pay is 48.50 yuan a month. He earns another 22 yuan as gatekeeper at the Plastics Factory on Shengli Street, bringing his total income to 70 yuan.

His wife Zheng Yuzhen is a Han. She works in the noodle factory, which is a subsidiary of the Kiln, and draws 34 yuan a month. They have three sons and a daughter. The oldest son is on the staff of the Wrench Factory. He is married and has his own home. The second son is a Second Grade worker in the Kiln. His monthly pay is 42.80. The girl earns 31 yuan per month as a worker in a textile mill. The third son is in the army. The daughter, the second son and a little grand-daughter live with Jin and his wife, making a household of five. Their per capita income is over 35 yuan per month.

People living together as a family in Kaifeng in 1980 could eat not badly on 10 yuan a month each. Rent, water, gas and electricity might be about 50 fen per person. Medicare is virtually free. That would leave them more than enough for clothing, household necessities, and a few luxuries. Wang continues:

Then there is the example of Ai Dianyuan. Ai is a Grade Six worker in the Paint Factory. His wife looks after the house. Both his oldest son and oldest daughter have married and moved away. The second son and second daughter still live with the parents.

Ai earns more than 80 yuan a month. The daughter, a Second Grade worker, brings home 38 yuan. The son, also a worker, has just started, and has a 30 yuan wage. The third son, a high school graduate, has not yet found a job. Since the three wage earners bring in a total of 148 yuan, the family's per capita monthly income is 29 yuan. For Kaifeng, this is about average.

Not all families do as well, says Wang. Some heads of the house haven't as much seniority as Ai, or they have too many children to feed. Or they may be young couples who are new at their jobs and aren't earning much. Wang elucidates:

We mentioned old worker Gao Fu. He's 83 this year (1980), and has long since retired. His wife runs the house and looks after him. Gao's retirement pay is 35 yuan a month. His daughter in Yunnan province sends home 10 yuan every month, giving the old couple a monthly per capita income of 22.50 yuan.

We also have Shi Yanling and her family. Her father, who had worked in the warehouse of the Foreign Trade Company, died in 1972. Her mother remarried, leaving Yanling to raise two younger sisters and two younger brothers. Second Sister has now graduated from senior high school and is looking for a job. Third Sister is still in senior high. First Brother is in junior high. Second Brother is in primary school. Yanling earns 30 yuan a month. An aunt teaching in the Naval Academy sends her another 20, and her mother an additional 15, making a total of 65 yuan, or a per capita monthly income of only 13 yuan. Consequently, this family is living at a bare subsistence level.

CUSTOMS AND HABITS

For many years the Jews of Kaifeng had their own unique teachings, customs and habits, in conformity with their religion. They believed in Jehovah, and worshipped no other gods, says Wang. They would not marry outside their race, or eat pork. They extracted the sinews of cattle and sheep they slaughtered for food. They practised circumcision, rested one day a week (Saturday), prayed three times every day, fasted four times a month, and celebrated seven holy days a year.

The most important of these, Yom Kippur, came in the autumn, Wang notes. It was a day of fasting, and all work stopped. The Jews silently reflected, and beseeched God to forgive their sins.

With the passage of time, these teachings, customs and habits weakened and finally vanished, Wang says. The restriction on marrying non-Jews was ignored. By Ming (14th century) marriage and funeral rites were the same as those of the Hans. Religious services of the Sinew Plucking Religion ceased by the Tong Zhi period (1862–1875) of the Qing dynasty, at the latest. No one could chant the Hebrew in which the Five Books of Moses were written, and infant boys were no longer circumcised.

Kaifeng Jews began eating pork fairly early, although this was considered a serious deviation from their religion. Their descendants say there were several reasons for this breech. Wang Yisha enumerates them:

> First, officials among the Jews, especially high officials like those in the Zhao, Shi, Jin and Li clans, found the restriction very difficult to uphold. Ancestors of the Jin and Shi clans attained posts of Grade Four and above. When such men attended banquets given by the emperor, they either had to break the rule, or content themselves with nothing but vegetables.

Not a very convincing excuse. Surely they could have survived on platters of mutton, beef, chicken, duck and fish!

> Secondly, many intermarried with the Hans. The mothers and grandmothers brought into the Jewish households the Han custom of raising pigs and eating pork. Zhao Pingyu's grandfather, although he had no objection to eating pork, drew the line at his own family raising pigs. But his wife insisted on it.

As Zhao recalls: "Ye Ye (grandpa) tried to scare Nai Nai (grandma). He said a calamity would strike the family if they raised pigs. Nai Nai paid no attention. Ye Ye couldn't do a thing with her. Finally, he let the pigs out, secretly, and drove them away. Jewish families began raising pigs in Kaifeng at that time all much the same way."

By the start of the twentieth century there were still a few individuals who clung to the old customs. Shi Zhongyu's father Shi Taichang at the time of the Chinese Spring Festival would dip a brush in red cinnabar and draw a line on the couplet scrolls flanking the doorway in typical Chinese style. This clearly was a remnant of the Passover custom of smearing the doorposts with the blood of a lamb—to indicate that this was a Hebrew household to be "passed over" by the Lord when slaying the first-born of every Egyptian household to compel Pharaoh to free the captive Jews.

Also at Spring Festival when Shi Zhongyu was a boy, the family cooked what they called "sweet lamb" soup, unsalted. Everyone had to drink the soup, Shi recalls, in the morning. At noon, they would cut and eat the meat. This apparently was also a part of the Passover ceremony, though in violation of the injunction in Exodus 12:9 against boiling. The children found the dish tasteless, and did not continue the custom when they grew up. Shi remembers that when his older sister got married, their father had her sip the soup and eat the lamb before she went off in her bridal sedan chair. But that was the last time. From then on the Shi customs were the same as the Hans.

Wang Yisha tells us of a Kaifeng family which, after abandoning Hebrew customs, learned them again from Jews in Shanghai who had arrived in China much later than their own ancestors:

In 1895 Li Rongxin's father and grandfather moved to Shanghai. The father, Li Shumei, was then only 12. Several years later he started as a bookkeeper in a foreign trade company owned by a British Jew named Abraham. He picked up a number of the old Jewish customs while in Shanghai. He abstained from pork and observed the "Month of Refuge" (Succoth), during which he built and lived in a shed beside the house, fasting on the last day until sunset. He also fasted every Sabbath from sunset of the fifth day of the week until the stars appeared in the evening of the sixth. Li Shumei's father, daughter and son all died in Shanghai. He brought their bodies to the cemetery, where they were "purified" (washed). Before burial, he wrapped them in white shrouds. In the Shanghai synagogue marriages also were performed according to the ancient rites, without the usual drums and pipes of Chinese weddings.

But when Li Shumei returned with his family to Kaifeng in 1946, these old ways were gradually abandoned. By Li Rongxin's generation they all were following local Chinese customs.

In the old days the Jews of Kaifeng had an inflexible rule against the worship of graven images, says Wang, and they paid no homage to Chinese spirits such as the Door Protectors, the Lord of the Hearth and the Earth King. Although some remained firm right up to the time of Liberation in 1948, many had long since adopted the customs of their Han neighbors. A few, like Zhao Pingyu's grandfather and uncle, became Buddhists.

After Liberation, as Shi Qi expressed it: "We did whatever the Hans did, and behaved the same way." Wang notes: In dress, diet, manner of living and conducting business, marriage, funerals, celebrations and holidays, their customs and those of the Han Chinese became identical.

THE RELIGIOUS BELIEFS OF A FEW INDIVIDUALS

Starting with the Dao Guang period (1821–1851) the Sinew Plucking Religion went into a gradual decline, Wang states. Jews who wanted to pray to a single God had to go to a Muslim mosque. Some became Buddhists. Li Rongxin's great-uncle entered the Buddhist monastery in Two Dragons Lane and was ordained a monk. At that time the Catholics and Protestants were actively proselytising in Kaifeng, and some of the Jews became converts. Li Entao's grandmother, who was a Han, and aunt both embraced Christianity, and the aunt taught in the mission school. But many of the Jews were opposed to changing their religion.

Today there are still a few Christian converts among the descendants of the Kaifeng Jews, Wang reports. Eighty-three year old Shi Zhongen, explaining why he converted, says: "Jews are all the sons of Jesus. To believe in Jesus is to remember your origins." He constantly prays, sometimes on the street outside the hospital . . . Shi Gai'en is nearly sixty. She and her husband are devout Christians. Her name originally was Hehua, meaning lotus, a Buddhist symbol. When she became a Christian she changed it to Gai'en, meaning Pervading Grace . . . There are also some who have been influenced by Christianity, although they have not converted.

RELATIONS AMONG THE CLANS TODAY

For many centuries the marriage of a boy of one clan to a girl of another was considered "adding new relatives," says Wang. Thereafter, when people of these two clans met they hailed one another as "lao biao," meaning "kinsman." This custom continued until the previous generation. Those in the same clan always joined together in times of joy or sorrow, paid mutual respects during holidays, and helped out in emergencies.

Wang notes that until the mid-nineteenth century—although some put it at the mid-seventeenth century—there was a Jewish burial ground in the Western suburbs, possibly at Huasheng Hamlet. Relations among the clans had cooled before Liberation, and their common burial ground gave way to separate family cemeteries, but within each clan there were still manifestations of mutual concern. For example, when Shi Qi was leader of the Shi Clan, younger male members would come before him during Spring Festival to burn incense and pay homage to their ancestors, in the Chinese manner.

Since Liberation, however, Wang observes, ties between families of the same clan, as well as between the clans themselves, have been permanently loosened. In recent years only a few people like Shi Yu-lian have troubled to inquire about the welfare of the Six Clans remaining, or to visit any of the other Jewish descendants. Except when one of them is seeking some past record for a legal proceeding, or wants to check a point in his family history, there is no more hailing of "kinsman" as there was in the past.

THE 20TH CENTURY DISPERSAL OF KAIFENG JEWISH DESCENDANTS

Aside from the two Zhang families, mentioned above, whose present whereabouts are unknown, we do have a record of other Jewish descendants of the six clans still in Kaifeng, says Wang. Sixty-one of them left in the past fifty years, including 32 women who married and moved to other towns. Wang offers the following breakdown:

Clan	Total departure	Women who married
Shi	25	13
Ai	4	3
Zhao	5	4
Gao	7	3
Li	15	8
Jin	5	1

Twenty-two left before Liberation. Six of these were unemployed people looking for work. Three were fleeing from the Japanese invaders. Five moved with a change of jobs. Two were women who left to get married. One was running away from a mother-in-law who mistreated her. I don't know the reasons for the other five.

Of the 39 who left after Liberation, 22 were going to new jobs. Thirteen were women who left to get married. One woman went with her husband who had been transferred in his work. Two women were old and went to stay with their children, who lived elsewhere. I don't know the reason for one of the persons who left.

Of the 61 who moved from Kaifeng, 60 settled in 32 different parts of China. One, a man named Jin, went to America.

RUINS AND RELICS

The ruins include the site of the Purity and Truth Synagogue, former dwellings, the common burial ground and family cemeteries. Among the relics are the Ming and Qing dynasty stone commemorative tablets of the Sinew Plucking Religion, family portraits, books, pictures and genealogies.

SITE OF THE PURITY AND TRUTH SYNAGOGUE

The Purity and Truth Synagogue, also called the Scriptures of the Way Synagogue, or the Temple of Worship, was built in the third year of the Da Ding period (1163) of the Jin (Golden Tartar) dynasty. Rebuilt during the Yuan (Mongol) dynasty in 1279, it was named the Ancient Temple Synagogue of Purity and Truth. The compound in which it stood was 40 feet wide and 350 feet deep.

During Ming, Kaifeng was hit by a series of floods, and in Qing the synagogue was repeatedly damaged. With Jews in places like Yangzhou, Ningbo and Ningxia contributing, the Kaifeng Israelites repaired or rebuilt their synagogue six more times, creating edifices of dignity and beauty.

The synagogue was completely rebuilt in 1663, after the big flood of 1642, on the foundations of the former temple. This time an imposing complex was created, 400 feet deep and 150 feet wide, covering an area of over 6000 square yards. The main gate faced east, on the center section of what today is called Scripture Teaching Religion Northern Lane. It was repaired for the last time in 1688.

But in the years which followed the Jewish community, and with it their temple, gradually went into a decline. Wang Yisha elucidates:

> By 1850, although the synagogue was sadly dilapidated, the Seven Clans were financially unable to repair it. The buildings were dismantled, bit by bit, and sold, including even the tiles and timbers. Most of it was bought by the Muslims, who used the

materials to construct their large Dong Da Si (Great Eastern Mosque).

By 1910 all that was left was rubble and pools of stagnant water. In December of 1912, Bishop White bought for the Canadian Church of England the 1489/1512 and the 1679 commemorative tablets and moved them into the Church compound of the Kaifeng Cathedral. In 1914 the Church bought the synagogue land as well. They turned it into a YMCA playground. The Kaifeng munieipal government confiscated the land in 1954 and erected on it a free medical clinic.

Wang sets forth the boundaries of the old synagogue site as west of the northern end of Cao Shi Jie (Haymarket Street), north of Nan Jiao Jing Hutong (Scripture Teaching Religion Southern Lane), east of the Free Clinic, and south of Cai Zheng Dong Jie (Finance Office East Street). He says that during the Guang Xu period (1875–1908) of the Qing Dynasty, what was originally called Nan Bei Tiao Jin Jiao Hutung (Sinew Plucking Religion Northern and Southern Lanes) became Nan Bei Jiao Jing Jiao Hutong (Scripture Teaching Religion Northern and Southern Lanes). Zhao Pingyu and his family live today in No. 21 Northern Lane, Wang adds. Zhao's house is part of the dwellings to which the Zhao clan moved at the time of the synagogue's decline.

THE COMMON BURIAL GROUND AND THE FAMILY CEMETERIES

The common burial ground of the Kaifeng Jews was in the western suburbs, states Wang. Shi Yulin thinks it was on the land presently belonging to Huashan Hamlet of the Xi Jiao (Western Suburbs) Commune. It was very large, running several *li* in each direction (a li is roughly ⅓ of a mile). The big floods of the Dao Guang period (1875–1908)—though some say it was the flood of 1642—levelled the common burial ground and swept away the grave mounds. Severe sandstorms covered new grave mounds as soon as they were built. As a result, the Jews began establishing separate family cemeteries in various other places.

Shi Yulian's family, at the urging of his grandmother, selected ground in the eastern outskirts of the city.

Shi Qi's family chose a site at Zhai Tun, with a special section for burying pre-adolescent girls to the southwest.

Shi Zhongyu's family cemetery originally was outside Cao Men (an old city wall gate) at Li Chang Hamlet. It was 20 mou in size (about seven acres). Some seventy years ago the family bought a new plot on the river side of the dyke and adorned it with stone tables and chairs. They sold this to the Wang family about thirty years ago and moved again to Yang Hamlet in Dong Nan Xiang (Southeast Township). The new plot is called the Shi Family Cemetery.

Shi Yijie's family cemetery is at Bai Ta (White Tower) Village.

Other clans have selected the following family cemeteries: the Gao family, at Zhu Tun, outside Cao Men; Ai Fengming's family, north of Bai Ta Village; Ai Dianming's family, originally at Bai Ta, shifted in 1980 to the area along the dyke in the northern suburbs; Zhao Pingyu's family, northeast of Renhe Tun and San Jiao Tang Village, in the eastern suburbs.

Li Enshou's family cemetery, north of Gao Hamlet, outside Cao Men, has many graves. The foremost is marked "Old Ancestors Grave."

Li Rongxin's family cemetery was originally at Da Hua Yuan (Big Flower Garden). His grandfather, younger brother, and younger sister are all buried in Shanghai. In 1958 the Kaifeng graves were moved to the western suburbs.

Jin Ziru's family cemetery is in Zhai Tun. At the head of the grounds is the "Old Ancestors Grave," followed by burial places marked "Lesser Ancestors Grave." Seven generations of the Jin family are interned in this cemetery.

THE MING AND QING SYNAGOGUE TABLETS

The 1663 tablet has vanished, says Wang. It may be in Rome, or perhaps it is only a rubbing of the stone which is in Rome. In 1912 Bishop White moved the 1489/1512 and 1679 tablets to the Cathedral, intending to ship them to Canada. The protests of the people of Kaifeng prevented him from doing so. He did succeed, however, in removing a number of other things, including stone-carved lotus bowls and a jade chime. These are now in the Royal Ontario Museum in Toronto.

We have the 1489/1512 and the 1679 tablets in our Kaifeng Museum. The first tablet, which had been broken in two, is today bound together with iron hoops. We suspect White split the stone for convenience in shipping.

During the Cultural Revolution (1966–1976) this tablet and 1679 stone inscription were knocked down by the Red Guards in their general attack on antiquities. They were saved by the quick action of the Museum authorities. They are presently in the Museum on display.

We have also a white stone lion, 0.82 meters high, discovered in the rear yard of the old site of the synagogue. But we are not sure whether it actually was once part of the synagogue property, and are still investigating.

WRITTEN MATERIALS REGARDING THE KAIFENG JEWS

Wang lists the written materials today in the possession of the Kaifeng Museum:

The tablet composed in 1489 by Jin Zhong, a Jew from Ningxia, entitled "Chong Jian Qing Zhen Si Ji" ("A Record of Rebuilding the Purity and Truth Synagogue").

The inscription (on the reverse side of the 1489 tablet) composed by Zuo Tang, a Jew from Yangzhou, in 1512, entitled "Zun Chong Dao Jing Si Ji" ("A Record of the Synagogue Which Respects the Scriptures of the Way").

The diary of Li Guangtian, written in late Ming and early Qing, entitled *Shou Bian Ri Ji (The Defence of Bian)*, Bian meaning Kaifeng.

Zun Ji Lu (Respectful Notes) written by a close friend of Li Guanting in early Qing.

Sheng Jing Ji Bian (Annotations to the Scriptures), over two hundred scrolls written by Zhao Yingcheng in the Shun Zhi period (1644–1662) of the Qing dynasty.

Ming Dao Xu (Introduction to the Shining Way) by Zhao Yingdou, also during the Shun Zi period.

The Zhao Clan tablet by Zhao Yinggun in 1679 entitled "Ci Tang Shu Gu Bei Ji" ("A Tablet Record of the Ancient History of Our Ancestral Hall").

Says Wang, the foregoing materials are quite valuable to us in our study of the Kaifeng Jews, their religion and their history, as well as in our research into the Li Zicheng uprising and the general history of the city of Kaifeng.

PERSONAL RELICS OF SHI YULIAN'S FAMILY

Wang lists these as follows:

A portrait of an ancestor.

A painting of orchids for a four section screen done by Jewish painter Shi Xiang, an ancestor of Shi Yulian, in 1876.

Another painting by Shi Xiang, done in 1883, with an inscription by Xu Jinyuan. It hangs in the center of the main wall of the best parlor in Shi Yulian's home.

A set of couplet scrolls written by Li Henian, a Henan Provincial Inspector, during the Qing dynasty.

A portrait of Madame Shi Haichen, Shi Yulian's grandmother.

RELICS KNOWN BUT AS YET UNDISCOVERED

These are, as Wang itemizes them:

Three ancestral portraits of members of the Jin Ziru family, and one "Sacred Instruction."

A *Shi Family Geneaology,* belonging to the family of Shi Qi.

A pair of stone lions formerly in the synagogue courtyard. In the early years of the National Republic (established in 1911), they were sold to a Buddhist temple. Shortly after Liberation they stood before the entranceway of a factory at Shi Fang Yuan, outside Cao Men. But they have been missing since 1958.

The Purity and Truth Synagogue formerly had 13 parchment scrolls of the Scriptures. In the 1850's, ten of them were sold to foreigners. We are still looking for the remaining three.

Epilogue

Much more remains to be done in the study of Chinese Jews—in Kaifeng and many other parts of China. As yet unexplored by Chinese scholars is the great Northwest—Xinjiang, once known as Chinese Turkestan, in Central Asia, through which ran the Silk Road connecting China with the Middle East and Europe, and over which Jews travelled with trade caravans prior to the opening of the sea routes in Tang (618–907) and Song (960–1279). Are there Israelite descendants in Xinjiang's Kashgar and Khotan, for example? Not far on the other side of the Pamirs are Balkh and Samarkand, both with Jewish communities going back hundreds of years. What of the other Xinjiang cities on the old Silk Road, or busy Urumqi?

And what of the thriving port of Guangzhou (Canton) in Tang times and thereafter? And Changan (Sian) when it was capital of Tang and one of the greatest cities in the world? And the ports of Quanzhou, Yangzhou, Ningbo? And Hangzhou, capital of Southern Song, and Khanbalik (Beijing) in Yuan (1279–1368)? All were major political, commercial and cultural centers in their time, sure magnets to every traveller from abroad. Is it possible that no more traces of Jews exist in these cities than the few already discovered?

The common opinion among Chinese historians is that while an occasional Israelite may have reached China earlier, the Jews did not arrive in large groups until Tang and Song, when they came to the southeastern ports with Arab and Persian merchants, in whose countries they had been living for centuries. Though much less numerous, they wore the same dress, spoke the same language, had the same physical features, and even bore the same names, as their fellow traders. Like their Muslim colleagues, they also practised circumcision and would not eat pork. The Chinese could not distinguish them from their Persian and Arab countrymen, or from the devotees of Islam, and tended to lump them together. All foreigners from Central Asia and the Middle East were loosely termed "Arabs," or "Persians," or "Hui

Hui," or simply "se mu ren"—"people with colored eyes." The result was that during the Tang and Song dynasties the Chinese made no separate listing for the Jews in their documents and records.

Jews who may have come pre-Song via the Silk Road were fewer still. Since caravan travel was an arduous and risky business, they were hardly likely to have brought the wife and kiddies. One or two may have stopped for brief periods at one or another of the market towns and way stations—not the kind of event worth noting in the local records. It is possible that scraps of correspondence or Scriptures, similar to those found by Stein and Pelliot early in this century, may still be preserved in the arid sands of the Xinjiang deserts. Or perhaps local folk tales and legends can provide some clues. Or there may have been an influx from the nearer cities of Central Asia.

We have quite a bit of documentation concerning Jews in Yuan and Ming. But there must be more—in histories, records, gazettes, in archeological relics. What of the Jews who were said to have to come to China during Yuan from Western Asia and parts of Europe with the victorious returning Mongol armies? Were they captives, or did they come of their own volition? An absorbing and yet-to-be-explored field.

On all of this we must await the labors of Chinese scholars. I am pleased to say that some have already started. The Society for the Study of the History of Sino-Foreign Relations included my plea to scholars throughout China for research on Jews of the past in its Bulletin No. 3 for 1983. Professor Zhuang Weiji of Xiamen (Amoy) University is searching for Jewish gravestones around Quanzhou, in conjunction with his archeological colleagues. Professor Ai Weisheng advised that in Wuhan the South-Central Nationalities Institute, in which he is a Research Fellow, devoted all of 1983 to a study of Chinese Jews as its sole topic of research for that year. Historians and archeologists engaged in digs around Hangzhou and other cities have promised to keep an eye out for Jewish relics.

Formal organized study by Chinese scholars of the Jews in Chinese history is at last under way. No doubt we shall hear much of interest and of value in the days to come. We offer this book as an introduction to Chinese research to date in this important project.

Sidney Shapiro

August, 1984
Beijing

Jews in Old China
Part Two

Liu Yingsheng

JEWS IN YUAN DYNASTY CHINA

Born in 1947, Liu Yingsheng received his doctorate in history from the Chinese Academy of Social Sciences in 1985. He is presently a professor of history in Nanjing University, and director of the university's Institute of Ethnic Research.

His special expertise includes the fields of Yuan dynasty history, the history of Islamic culture, Sino-foreign relations in the middle ages, and comparative studies of Chinese and Persian history. Lui has done research in Germany, England and Spain. His three major works to date are: "A History of Ethnic Minorities in Northwest China and the Khan Kingdom of Jagatai," "The Culture of the Silk Road," and "A New History of the Yuan Dynasty."

Liu has written many articles such as "Indirect Influences of Greco-Roman Culture on China's Muslims." Seven of them have been published in English and German.

His treatise "Jews In Yuan Dynasty China" appeared in the academic periodical *Yuan Shi Lun Cong (Collected Essays on the History of the Yuan Dynasty)*. The main theme of Liu's treatise concerns those Jews who already were permanent residents. His dissertation follows. Unless indicated otherwise, the words are Liu's. My own comments are in italics.

Although it lasted only about one hundred years, from 1260 to 1368, the Yuan dynasty had an important impact on Chinese and world history.

The founders of the Yuan were not Han Chinese, but Mongols, tough hardy horsemen from the northeast who gradually conquered the declining, corrupt Song regime. At the same time, they extended their conquests across central Asia into Europe from Korea to the Danube. They learned quickly how to rule this vast empire. They internationalized, making use of the talents of people from many different lands, not only within mainland

China, but in all of their holdings abroad, as well. It worked fairly efficiently for over a century. But the territory was too vast, the governing too complicated. Finally the empire collapsed, and was succeeded by the Ming dynasty in 1368, putting the country back in Han Chinese hands.

At its height the Yuan dynasty was the hub of a far flung network of cultural, economic, scientific and religious international exchange.

Mongol rule made for a certain degree of security for travel in a vast area, which had never before been brought together under one rule. China's foreign commerce flourished accordingly, reaching dimensions never previously attained. Merchants from many countries frequented the chief marts. Arabs, Persians, and representatives of Central Asian nationalities entered in large numbers.

Ibn Batuta, an Arab traveler from North Africa, left a record giving a vivid picture of the extensive colonies of foreign merchants in China's leading commercial centers in the 14th century. Traffic also moved in the other direction. Chinese junks called at Java, India and Ceylon. Chinese engineers were utilized on the irrigation of the Tigris-Euphrates Valley. There were Chinese colonies in Moscow, Novgorod, and Tabriz. The Yuan emperors had commercial agreements with the princes of at least two of the states of South India.

Foreign visitors were very impressed with Chinese affluence under the Yuan. A European traveler in the fourteenth century, for instance, remarks that China contained "two hundred cities all greater than Venice."

Foreign trade was China's earliest known friendly contact with the peoples of Western Europe. Their kingdoms were smaller in area and population than those of the major powers of those days, and their trade was of relatively minor significance. Still it was welcomed, and new routes were opened on land and by sea. Along these came Jewish merchants, some of whom were known as Radanites.

In general, the Jews were well treated by the Mongols. Kublai, reigning as the Grand Khan from 1260 to his death in 1294, was religiously tolerant. He held to some of the primitive shamanistic practices of his fathers, and seems to have been inclined toward Buddhism of the Tibetan type. Officially, however, he gave support, financial and otherwise, to several faiths. He exempted Taoist and Buddhist monks, Nestorian priests, and Muslim teachers from taxation, on condition that they offer prayers in his behalf. Jews in Mongol China were relatively few in number but, as we shall see, were also given favorable treatment.

[For much of the foregoing I am indebted to Kenneth Scott Latourette for his superb The Chinese, Their History and Culture (Macmillan, 1946, New York)]

I. WRITTEN EVIDENCE OF A JEWISH PRESENCE PRIOR TO YUAN

Liu Yingsheng starts by saying that quite early in antiquity, Jews were among the merchants who came along the Old Silk Road and settled in China. He then continues more specifically:

> Traffic with the West during the Tang dynasty (618–907) was unprecedentedly heavy. Nestorianism and Manicheanism arrived one after the other. Although there are no records in Chinese specifically mentioning the presence of Jews during the Tang dynasty, there is no doubt they were here. Among the documents Western "adventurers" purloined from our country at the turn of the century, several related to Jews.
>
> The letter discovered by Aurel Stein in 1901 near Dandan-Uiliq outside of Hotian, written in Persian but in Hebrew script, has been dated by experts as 718. What is more, the prayer in Hebrew written on paper found in Dunhuang by Pelliot, was probably composed between the 6th and 9th centuries. Clearly, there were Jews in China in Tang.

They may have come even earlier. See Pan Guangdan, p. 82, who says Jewish traders probably came with caravans buying silk for the Roman markets starting in the Eastern Han dynasty (25–220). Pan thought the caravans traveled overland from Antioch, across Central Asia, to Kashgar (today Kashi in Xinjiang province, which technically, at that time was not yet a part of China). Some Jews may have settled permanently and set up trading posts.

These should be distinguished from the Jewish merchants known as "Radanites," who began trading with China much later, during the Tang dynasty (618–907). See Gong Fangzhen's article, page 202. It seems likely that those taking the land route only went as far as Khazaria, where Jewish converts in that country trans-shipped into China proper. Other Radanites, who came by sea, did trade directly with Chinese cities.

> That the Jews existed in other lands was known in China very early. A Nestorian tablet, erected in Chang An (Xian) in 781, makes the first mention in Chinese documents of the "Israelites."

Nestorianism was an early Christian religion in Mesopotamia welcomed into China and its insemination encouraged by Tang emperor Tai Zong.

The largest concentration of Jews was in Kaifeng. By not long after the "Opium War" (1839–1842), they had vanished. Fortunately the Jewish communities in Kaifeng erected four memorial tablets, dated 1489, 1512, 1663, and 1679, respectively. Invaluable primary sources for research on the entry of Judaism into China, they are useful material for academic theses by Chinese and foreign scholars.

The 1489 tablet says the Jews "came from Tianzhu (India)", and presented entry tribute of "Western cloth" to the imperial court after which the emperor decreed: "You have come to our Central Plain. Preserve your ancestral customs and settle in Bianliang (Kaifeng)."

See Yin Gang, page XX, who questions the dynasty in which the emperor is alleged to have made this statement.

According to the 1512 tablet: "as to the religion of the Israelites, its first ancestor was Adam, and it originated in Tianzhu, Xiyu (India, in the Western Regions)."

The 1663 tablet says the religion "came from Tianzhu." Professor Chen Yuan, in "A Study of the Israelite Religion In Kaifeng", points out that in the rubbings made from the two earlier tablets, the word "Tianzhu" is missing, as if the person who made the reproductions considered it an error and deliberately removed it. An examination of the rubbing of the 1512 tablet made in Kaifeng by Italian missionary Gozano Giampaopi in the early 18th century shows that the word "Tianzhu" was still there.

According to Chen Yuan, not only was "Tianzhu" obliterated after the 18th century, but of the seventeen Jewish family names originally inscribed on the 1512 tablet, all but three were removed. "This was because of the Muslim uprisings in the Tong Zhi period (1862–1875) and the Boxer Rebellion (1900)," Chen explains. "The descendants of the Israelites hoped in this way to avoid trouble."

They didn't want to be confused with the Muslims, who also came from "Tianzhu, and were also "Hui Hui," and "people with colored eyes." Actually, the Jews were never troubled as a race or religion by the Chinese authorities, or by the local populace.

Professor Pan Guangdan was of the opinion that the ancestors of the earliest Kaifeng Jews, after leaving their original homes in the Middle East, probably went to the Bombay area in India, remained there for some 1100 years, and then journeyed east by sea to China.

Articles by professors Chen Yuan and Pan Guangdan, both in this book, provide more detailed expositions regarding the dates of Jewish arrivals in

China and the routes they followed. Joining in the search, Liu seizes on a particular word which he feels offers a significant clue.

Very few of the scholars studying the origin of the Kaifeng Jews have paid much attention to the statement in the 1489 statement that they brought "Western cloth." The word "Western" was seen for the first time in Chinese documents in the "Western Hills Gazette," published during the Five Dynasties (907–960). It said that in Quanzhou (then a major seaport in Fujian on the southeast coast of China), a member of the Pu family named Pu Youlang was "engaged in transshipping Western goods." Again, in the Song dynasty (960–1127) the Gazette said the same thing about Pu Jiayou, another member of the same family. Clearly the geographical concept of "Western" was already well established by the Song dynasty.

In Song and Yuan (1279–1368) the term "Western" had wide application. Although it was the same word as the "Western" in the Five dynasties, its meaning was very different. In Yuan it was pinpointed as Malabar on the southwest coast of India. Malabar was a region which produced woven cloth. The "Western cloth" which the Jews proffered as "entry tribute" to the Northern Song court must have been the same. And in all probability they came from the largest city in the Malabar area—Bombay.

See Yin Gang in this volume: " The Jews of Kaifeng, Their Origins, Routes, and Assimilation" in the section: "Northern Song: The Year They Settled in China." Yin suggests the Jewish arrivals may have brought the cloth from Central Asia, where colored cloth was then being manufactured.

II. JEWISH "HUI HUI" IN THE YUAN DYNASTY

Entries about Jews in Chinese records increased in the Yuan Dynasty. The Yuans were Mongols who had defeated and succeeded the Han Chinese of the Song dynasty, but they kept their records in Chinese. Their pronunciation of the Hebrew word "Yahudi" was erratic, and they inscribed it in various garbles such as "Shuhu," or "Zhuwu," or called the Jews "Shuhu Hui Hui." The term Hui Hui in Yuan, and the following Ming dynasty, was at first used for the Muslims, but then was expanded to include all races [and religions] from the "Western Regions," or the Middle East—those the Mongols called "people with colored eyes."

For example, members of the Nestorian Church, an Eastern orthodox Christian faith, were dubbed Green-Blue Hui Hui (*because of the color of their eyes*), gypsies were Luoli (*Romany?*) Hui Hui. In a

Yuan volume entitled "Hui Hui Pharmacopoeia", even the ancient Greeks and Romans were listed as "Hui Hui!"

Hui Hui simply meant people from the so-called Western Regions. Because the Jews had many customs identical with those of the Muslims, their appellation in the Yuan dynasty of "Jewish Hui Hui" was inevitable.

In Yuan Shi (Yuan History) we have this entry, dated December 1279: "When Hui Hui were offered food, they refused to eat sheep unless they had slaughtered it personally. This was very troublesome. The Emperor said: 'They are our subjects. How dare they eat differently from the way we ourselves eat in our court?' He forbade it."

The Mongols slaughtered sheep by eviscerating them. The Hui Hui—including the Muslims and the Jews—cut their throats. From their point of view, the Mongol method was unsanitary. A special regulation required the host of any inn at which Hui Hui or Jewish merchant travelers stopped, to provide them with food. But the Hui Hui rejected mutton which the hosts offered, and demanded to do their own slaughtering. This caused a great deal of difficulty, and the hosts complained.

Word reached the emperor, Kublai Khan, and he issued a decree prohibiting the Hui Hui from slaughtering sheep. The injunction did not mention Jews specifically.

Rashid al-Din (13–14th century), a historian in the Persian court, in his "Historical Notes," tells this story: "A band of Hui Hui merchants, calling at the court of the Mongol Khan, presented gifts of white-footed, red-throat osprey and white falcons. The Khan gave them a banquet, but they did not eat. 'Why don't you eat?' the Khan asked. They replied: 'This food is not clean.'

"The Khan was furious. He decreed: 'From now on Hui Hui and the People of the Book are forbidden to slaughter sheep by slitting their throats. Sheep must be disemboweled in the Mongol fashion. Whoever slaughters a sheep by cutting its throat shall be executed in the same manner. His wife and children shall be confiscated and given to the man who has exposed him.'"

This obviously is the same story as the one set forth in the Yuan History, but in more detail. Rashid al-Din, writing in Persian, uses the term "ahl-ikitab," that is, "Book People."It is rendered as "People of the Book" in English and Russian translations. In Persian, "Book" here means "Holy Scriptures," and refers to the Bibles of both the Christians and the Jews.

The Jews did indeed attach great importance to their Bibles. The Kaifeng Jews called the tablet erected in 1512 "A Record of the Synagogue Which Respects the Scriptures of the Way." "The Way" is a

Sinified term for the Five Books of Moses, or the Torah. The tablet says of the Scriptures: "We have four Torah scrolls, each containing fifty-three sections. Meticulous in principle and excellent in method, they are as veneration-worthy as Heaven." It says: "The Founder of the Religion was Abraham and Transmitter of the Torah was Moses," and that "after the Jews settled in Kaifeng they built their synagogue with the purpose of worshipping the Scriptures of the Way."

Rashid al-Din continues in his "Historical Notes" to say that Anxue, a prelate in the Nestorian church in Chang'an, seized upon Kublai's edict against non-Mongolian methods of slaughtering to attack the Hui Hui. Since the Hui Hui named in the decree would ordinarily include the Christians of all sects in China, why would a Nestorian Christian slander other Christians?

Fortunately, we also have available the Yuan Dian Zhang (Yuan Dynasty Regulations). The pertinent section is entitled: "The Hui Hui are prohibited from slaughtering sheep by slitting their throats." While the content is essentially the same as that in the Yuan History and in the Persian Historical Notes, here the section of the Regulations specifically describes the Hui Hui as "Muslims" and "Jews." Since it does not include Christians, the Nestorian prelate felt free to use Kublai Khan's decree in an attack on the Muslims.

III. JEWS IN HANGZHOU DURING THE YUAN DYNASTY

Chinese and foreign histories make only a few scattered references to Jews in the Yuan dynasty. Yang Yu, in his "Shan Ju Xin Hua" ("New Words Written In a House on a Hill"), dated 1360, says: "The officials in the Hangzhou Sugar Bureau are all rich Jewish and Muslim merchants." They had been put in charge because they probably knew about the manufacture of sugar.

The method of making white sugar had been learned from abroad in late Song or early Yuan. It earned a significant part of the local government's income, Marco Polo said in his description of Quinsai (Hangzhou). Sugar cane was planted in and around Hangzhou, and was processed locally. Since the Jews heading the Sugar Bureau were mainly merchants from the Western Regions who knew the technique, the Mongols trusted them. Their white sugar was of much higher quality than the locally produced native sugar.

Moroccan traveler Ibn Batuta who visited Hangzhou in the 14th century wrote that the city had many Jews, and that its Second District had an entry called "The Gate of the Jews."

These foreign descriptions confirm the Chinese own writings on the presence of Jewish merchants in Hangzhou.

China's white sugar, in addition to satisfying the domestic market, was also exported. Wealthy Indians relished the Chinese product to such an extent that they stopped eating local sugar. The word for white sugar in India became "cini," from the Indian pronunciation of "China." It no doubt included the sugar manufactured by the Jewish merchants of Hangzhou.

Italian Jesuit missionary Matteo Ricci arrived in Beijing in 1601. In the latter half of June 1605, a Chinese Jew named Ai Tian also came to Beijing and called on Ricci. According to the missionary, Ai Tian, in addition to telling him about the Jews in Kaifeng, reported that Hangzhou had even more Jewish families, and a Jewish synagogue, as well. These Jews most likely were descendants of the merchants who had run the sugar factories in Hangzhou in the Yuan dynasty, and whose family lines had extended another two or three hundred years.

Ricci, in a long letter home, which he sent from Beijing in July, 1605, describes in interesting detail his meeting with Ai Tian. I take the liberty of inserting extracts from it here:

He came to our house during the octave of St. John the Baptist. We had placed a large and beautiful image of the Madonna with the Infant on one side of the altar and, on the other, St. John the Baptist.

This man did not know the designation of Jew, but called himself an Israelite. When he saw the image he thought it represented the two children, Jacob and Esau, with Rebecca.

He said: "Although I do not worship images, I want to do reverence to my earliest ancestors." And so, he knelt and bowed. He had told me the head of his sect had twelve sons, and so I thought he was a Christian and was talking of the Twelve Apostles.

Ultimately, I discovered he was not a Christian, but was not much opposed to Christianity. He admitted to me that they (the Jews) were not able to uphold their Law because circumcision, the purification, the (non-eating of) pork, and other things impeded their relations with others, especially for those who wanted to become officials.

He also gave us to understand that "factus erat extra synagogam" (he had been excluded from the synagogue) and did not know much. But he told many Old Testament tales, from the Twelve Tribes, to Moses, to the story of Haman and Mordecai.

He said the general belief was that many Moors (Muslims), Christians, and Jews had come with the king Tamerlane when he conquered the whole of Persia and also China 800 years ago.

The Muslims are the majority in China, the Christians and Jews are only a few in number.

see p. 72. Pan Guangdan says the recital is "riddled with errors."

Ricci also kept a diary, and this entry is pertinent to the comment in his letter on the foreign religionists:

> The Chinese call all these foreigners "Hui-Hui." They call the Muslims the "Hui-Hui of the Three Laws" (San Jiao). The Jews they call the "Hui-Hui Who Extract the Sinews" (from the meat they eat). The Christians they call the "Hui-Hui of the Word for Ten" (which in Chinese is written as a cross).

IV. WHAT THE SYNAGOGUES WERE CALLED

Liu notes that the 1483 tablet in Kaifeng alleges; "In the first year of the Long Xing period (1163) of Song emperor Xiao Zong, when Wusida Liewei was the leader of our faithful, Andula commenced the building of our synagogue." He offers the results of his research on the matter:

By 1163 the Song court was no longer in Kaifeng, having fled south more than thirty years before. Kaifeng was under the rule of the Tatars, also known as the Golden Horde. According to their dynastic calendar, 1163 was the third year of their Ta Ding period. Wusida is a Chinese version of the Persian word *ustad*, meaning "master craftsman" or "religious leader." He would have to be someone who knew Hebrew, a Jewish rabbi who could propagate the Holy Scriptures.

The Kaifeng Jews called the rabbi who could read the Scriptures in Hebrew a "manle," that is *mullah*, which is the traditional Persian term for teachers of the Islamic religion. The Persian cultural influences were clearly very strong.

The Jewish religious leader in charge of rebuilding the synagogue in 1163 was described as the andula. This is a transliteration of the Arabic phrase *Abd al-Allah*, meaning "Servant of Allah."

All of these terms demonstrate the close relationship between the Kaifeng Jews and the Muslims who had migrated to China.

The rebuilt synagogue was used for more than one hundred years.

According to the 1489 tablet, what was described as the "Ancient Temple Synagogue of Purity and Truth" was again rebuilt in 1279, " southeast of the Local Products Market," on a plot "four by 35 zhang" (one zhang equals about ten feet). In the mid-17th century, an author whose name has been lost, wrote a piece he called "As In A Dream." A scholar named Chang Maolai annotated it in 1852.

He quotes "As In A Dream," referring to the section on the Kaifeng synagogue: "If you proceed in a direct line east from the Local Products Market along the Li Family lane, you come to the Ancient Temple Synagogue of Purity and Truth."

To this, Chang adds the comment: "The lane outside the southern wall of the temple compound of the Sinew-Plucking Religion no longer goes through to the Local Products Market." Regarding the synagogue, he adds the further note: "It had stood south of the Fire-Worshippers Temple near Cao (Trough) Gate (of the city wall), but today it is in ruins." "Fire-Worshippers" was the colloquial term for believers in Zoroastrianism, a Persian cult originally, because fire was deemed the good light spirit in the cosmic conflict between light and darkness.

We can see that the Kaifeng's Jewish synagogue at the end of Ming and the beginning of Qing was popularly known as the "Temple of the Sinew-Plucking Religion."

Although we don't know what the synagogue was called at the time of the first rebuilding in 1163 during the Yuan dynasty, we do know it was called the "Ancient Temple Synagogue of Purity and Truth" when it was again rebuilt in 1279, still under Yuan rule. The Ming (1368–1644) dynasty tablet in 1512, when referring to the 1279 structure, drops the "Ancient Temple" from the title and simply calls it the "Qing Zhen Si" ("Synagogue of Purity and Truth"). The Jews appeared to have been strongly influenced by the Muslims, who used the Chinese phrase "Qing Zhen Si" to mean "mosque." But were they?

There is some dispute among historians as to which of the two—the Jews or the Muslims—were the first to use the term for their houses of worship. Only a few historical records exist of any Hui Hui mosque, either during Yuan or before, being called a "Qing Zhen Si." Quanzhou, in Fujian Province, did have one built in 1131, after the Song dynasty had fled south, abandoning Kaifeng to the Jin conquerors, called the Golden Tartars.

The Jewish memorial tablet erected in Kaifeng in 1489 commemorated the rebuilding of the first synagogue to be called, in Chinese, a "Qing Zhen Si." Its construction, the tablet said, had commenced in 1163. This was thirty years after the erection of the Quanzhou "Qing Zhen Si." Surely, Muslims in other parts of China would have been aware of the famous mosque. Perhaps Kaifeng Jews were the first to use the term in Kaifeng. In any event, it seems to me an unimportant quibble.

We know very little about the relations between the Muslims and the Jews during the Yuan dynasty. From the historical records cited above, it is obvious the Mongol rulers treated the Muslim Hui Hui and the Jewish Hui Hui more or less the same.

But although the Han Chinese and the Mongols hadn't made much distinction between the Muslims and the Jews, by the middle of the

Qing dynasty (1644–1911) the Chinese Muslims were very much aware of the difference. They considered the Jews an alien faith.

They distinguished also between the Jewish and Christian religions. An article in volume 7 of "Tian Fang Zheng Xue" ("Arabian Studies") notes, "There are two heretical religions—the Jewish and the Christian. The Jewish religion was transmitted by Moses, the Christian religion was transmitted by Jesus."

Muslim believers acknowledge Moses and Jesus as forebears of the Islamic religion. Their respect for them is beyond doubt. When the Muslims say the Jews and the Christians propagate the teachings of the two sages, they know exactly what these teachings were, and the difference between them.

We know that in the Yuan dynasty many Muslim mosques were called "Li Bai Si" ("Temples of Worship"), and Jewish synagogues were called "Qing Zhen Si" ("Temples of Purity and Truth"). These were their official public names.

What did the Muslims privately call the Jewish synagogues? There are no records in Yuan. But (says Liu Yingsheng), I made an unexpected discovery in a Muslim work entitled "Tian Fang Dian Li" ("Arabian Regulations"), written by Liu Zhi (1660–1730), a Nanjing scholar who specialized in the Hui ethnic minorities.

Chapter 14 issues an injunction with regard to Muslim communities. "All of the non-Muslim communities have their distinctive trappings," it says. "We shall not permit in our midst European cathedrals, 'Zhuhu yuan,' Buddhist temples, or Taoist monasteries to dazzle and confuse our people."

Liu Zhi explains: "'Zhuhu yuan' ('Jewish compounds') or 'Zhuhude Si' ('Yahudi temples') refers to the synagogues of the Sinew-Plucking Religion."

It is obvious that the Muslims wanted to keep a distance between Judaism and the Muslim faith "lest their people be dazzled and confused." If that is how they felt about the Jews in the Ming and Qing periods, it is likely in the Yuan dynasty their attitude was the same.

Gong Fangzhen

JEWISH MERCHANTS ON THE SILK ROAD

Gong Fangzhen was born in Shanghai in 1923. He is a member of the Religious Research Division of the Shanghai Academy of Social Sciences, a member of the board of directors of the Institute of the History of Sino-Foreign Relations, and an academic advisor to the Shanghai Institute of Religions. Gong is a specialist in the history of Sino-Western communications, Judaica, Iranian studies, and contemporary Western religions. He has attended academic conferences in America, Japan, and Iran.

His major works include: "Byzantine Wisdom," "Man, Society, and Religion," and "A History of Zoroastrianism." The Commercial Press, Shanghai, scheduled the release of his latest book, provisionally entitled *Jews and the East*, early in 2000.

Introduced below is an unusual treatise by Gong Fangzhen called "Jewish Merchants on the Silk Road." It appeared in *Studies in the 90s on the Chinese Jews*, a compilation published in Shanghai in 1992 by Sanlian Books. He followed this with another piece called "An Appraisal of Studies on the Jews in Ancient China," also carried in the 1992 collection. From the "Appraisal" I quote, in addition, a few pertinent passages.

The words are Gong's unless otherwise indicated. My own notes and comments are in italics.

I. WHEN THE JEWS FIRST CAME TO CHINA

Gong Fangzhen briefly reviews the disputes among scholars regarding the time of the first Jewish arrivals in China.

The views of Chinese and foreign scholars differ widely. A few favor pre-Zhou. Others claim Zhou (1066–256 B.C.), or Han (221

B.C.–25 A.D.), or Tang (618–907). Some are only guessing, basing their views on what others have said, and lacking any evidence. Several misinterpret records or documents. The only worthwhile proofs I have seen so far of the first arrival of the Jews in China are two documents, one discovered near Hotian, in Xinjiang, the other in Dunhuang, in Gansu.

In 1901 Aurel Stein found a letter in Dandan Uiliq, near Hotian. It was written on paper, in Persian, but using the Hebrew alphabet. Parts of it were missing. It contained 37 lines, and was 16 inches long, and 4 to 8 inches wide. The letter, obviously written by a Persian Jew, was addressed to a business associate in Tabriz, in Tabaristan, a part of Persia. It says the writer was stuck with some inferior sheep he had recently purchased, and begs his associate to help him dispose of them. Scientific tests have dated the document around 718A.D., during the Tang dynasty. This indicates there were already dealings at the start of the eighth century with Jewish merchants in Tabaristan.

The region is south and west of the Caspian Sea. To get to China the Jewish merchants either had to sail north on the Caspian into Khazaria, a country whose people were converts to Judaism, or sail east into Turkestan. Both routes continued overland. As the earliest document in Persian written in Hebrew script found in China, it is of particular value to researchers in the Iranian language. The letter was never sent. The Tang dynasty and the Kingdom of Turfan were involved in territorial disputes, and fighting constantly disrupted travel and communications.

The document discovered in Dunhuang is a *selihah*, or penitential prayer written on paper in Hebrew. I have seen it. It has seventeen lines, but probably was longer. It was taken from the Psalms in the Old Testament. Michael Pollak, in his "Mandarins, Jews, and Missionaries," dates it as the 8th or 9th century, but notes that Rabbi Marvin Tokayer believes it is more likely the 6th.

From these two documents we can reasonably speculate that Jews arrived in China between the 6th and the 8th centuries, at the latest.

See Yin Gang, page XX, regarding Jews in the Persian emirites of Bukhara and Samarkand in Transoxiana where passes through the Pamirs lead into present day China. Some of them may have migrated, with their families, to Dandan-Uiliq and Dunhuang. They evidently retained commercial ties with Persia. Others, during the Tang and Song dynasties, probably moved into what is now Ningxia province, in northwest China.

Among those who attempted to prove a pre-Tang arrival was French Sinologist Georges Prevost. In 1926 Prevost published a paper claiming that three fragments discovered in Loyang are inscribed in Palmyrian Hebrew. Palmyrian text using Hebrew script was a popular form of writing among Palmyrian Jews in the first to third centuries. According to Prevost, since this corresponds with the dates of the Eastern Han dynasty (25–220), it confirms the contention in the Kaifeng 1512 monument that "in Han times, the Religion entered China."

That does seem to make a strong case. But witness the rebuttal by an English sinologist. John Brough wrote an article entitled "A Kharoshti Inscription From China" in 1961which appeared in the Bulletin of the School of Oriental and African Studies. Brough says the fragments are parts of the rim of a well, and that the inscription is Kharoshti, not Hebrew. Brough thinks it may have been written by some Buddhist monk from northern India. Inscribing well rims with pious sentiments was common among monks in northern India at that time. Kharoshti dialect prevailed in northwest India from the third century B.C. to the fourth or fifth century A.D.

Many Kharoshti documents have been found in neighboring Xinjiang. Its script is derived from Aramaic and, like Hebrew, is written from right to left. Although the Hebrew alphabet is also derived from Aramaic, the language itself is Semitic *(as distinguished from Kharoshti, which is an Indo-European language).*

Xia Nai, Director of the Institute of Archeology of the Academia Sinica, wrote to Sidney Shapiro in April 1983, stating he believed Brough was correct, and that Professor Ji Xianlin concurred in this opinion. Today, few people place any credence in Prevost's theory.

cf . pp 57- 59 this volume, Pan Guangdan

II. ROUTES JEWISH MERCHANTS TOOK TO CHINA IN ANCIENT TIMES.

Gong says that according to Hebrew records, two Jewish merchants in Tyre began trading in silk in the 3rd century. They bought Chinese silk in central Persia. After weaving and dyeing it they sold their products in other cities along the Mediterranean. They certainly knew that China was a silk producing country, and that if they could buy in China directly they could earn much higher profits. In later years they found various routes to China, by land and by sea.

A detailed account of these routes was set down in the 9th century by Arab scholar Ibn Khurdadhbe (820 - 913) in his book "Kitabal

Masalik Wa-l-mamalik." He wrote it in 846-847, and subsequently amended it in 885-886. The book includes a chapter entitled "Jewish Merchants Known as Radhaniya." At that time he was the Postmaster of a province (which today is Media) in Iran under the Abbasid dynasty. He based his material on government documents and what earlier officials had recorded. He also had supervisory control over newspapers and gazettes, Gong says. His sources were therefore reliable in general.

The first translation of the book was by Charles Barbier de Maynard. It appeared in the Journal Asiatique *in Paris in 1865. Gong presents it as follows:*

These merchants speak Persian, Roman, Greek, Arabic, French, and Slavic. They travel from west to east and from east to west, partly by land and partly by sea. From the West they carry eunuchs, female slaves, children, silk, furs and swords. They board ships in Firanja (France) and cross the Western Sea (the Mediterranean) to Farama (an Egyptian city also on the Mediterranean). There they load their merchandise on camels and proceed by land to Kolzoum (Suez). It takes them five days to cover twenty farsakh (about 120 kilometers). From Kolzoum they cross the Eastern Sea (the Red Sea) to El-Djar (a port in Medina), and Djeddah, and from there on to Sind (*Karachi?*), India and China.

On their return journey they carry from the Eastern countries musk, aloes, camphor, cinnamon, and other products. They go first to Kolzoum, and then to Farama on the Western Sea, where they load their cargo on ships. Some sail to Istanbul (Constantinople) to sell to the Romans. Others bring their goods directly to the palace of the King of the Franks and display them there.

Some prefer to sail on the Western Sea to Antioch, then travel three days overland to Baghdad on the banks of the Euphrates, then go along the Tigris to Oballah (a port in southern Mesopotamia), and from there sail to Oman, Sind, India and China.

There are also land routes. Merchants leaving from Andalus (Spain) or France travel to Sous Al-Aksa (Morocco), and then to Tangiers. From there they sail to Kairowan (a city in Tunis) and then to the capital of Egypt. They traverse Ramla (a city in western Palestine), Damascus, al-Kufa, Baghdad, Basrah, Ahwaz (a city in western Iran), Firs, Kirman, Sind, and India, into China.

Sometimes they follow another land route, skirting the Byzantine, and crossing the Slavic territories into the capital of the Khazars. They sail over the Caspian and proceed to Balkh. From there they cross the Oxus (Amu Darya), continue on to the land of the Uygur people, and from there enter China.

To sum up, Jewish merchants traveled four routes to China, two by sea and two by land. One sea route came down the Red Sea. This was the most ancient. The other sea route followed the Persian Gulf. The first land route went from Kirman, then via Sind and India. The other land route went thru Khazaria and the Oxus River region (Transoxiana) into China's northwest.

Cf. below, regarding the trans-shipment at Khazaria of Radanite Jewish cargo.

Although Ibn Khurdadhbe is not very detailed regarding the sea route east from India, he is quite specific about the final stage:

> The main seaport in Tonkin is called al-Wakin (known as Lukin in Tang times, or Haiphong today). It is about 600 kilometers from China, which has excellent iron, ceramics and rice. The trip by sea to Khanfu (Canton) takes four days. Going by land takes 20. The area has many kinds of fruit and vegetables, as well as wheat, barley, rice and sugar cane. A journey by sea of another eight days brings you to Quanzhou. It has the same produce as Khanfu. Another four days' sail and you reach Hangzhou. Its produce is also the same.

From the foregoing, we can see there were three main ports at that time—Guangzhou, Quanzhou, and Hangzhou. Records show that Jews lived in all of them. Arab travelers Abu Zaid in the ninth century, and Masuda in the tenth, both talk of a massacre in Guangzhou (Canton) of foreign religionists, including many Jews, by Huang Chao's mutinous troops.

c.f. Pan Guangdan, this volume, page 61, claiming that the massacre took place in the Ganpu-Hangzhou area, not in Guangzhou.

Gong Fangzhen notes numerous evidences of the presence of Jews in China in the Middle Ages, and the routes they followed. He points out that the 1512 memorial stone in Kaifeng records: "An, Li and Gao of Kaifeng, and Jin Pu of Weiyang (Yangzhou), together contributed a scroll of the Torah and constructed a second gateway for the temple." He continues with further proof of the existence of Jews in various parts of China:

> In 1326, Andrew of Perugia, who served as the Catholic bishop of Quanzhou, complained in a letter to Rome that he was unable to convert any Jews or Saracens to Christianity.

Moroccan Ibn Batuta noted in the tenth century that a walled district inside the city of Hangzhou had a "Gate of the Jews," and that there were Jews living inside the district.

Other material attests to the arrival of Jewish merchants by land. In the tenth century, Arab traveler Abu Dulaf Misar, known simply as Misar, visited Central Asia, China and India. He says in the city of Turfan (in present day Xinjiang) he saw Muslims, Jews, Christians, Zoroastrians and Indians.

Both the 1489 and 1512 Kaifeng tablets state that Jin Xuan, Jin Ying. and Jin Run were all from Ningxia. They probably were descendants of Jews who migrated overland from Kushana (in Northwest India). The king and many of the inhabitants were believers in Judaism.

Of the four routes listed by Ibn Khurdadhbe, three started from Spain or France, and one from the Byzantine. That is not to say these were the only places from which Jewish merchants traveled to China. Some set out from various points along these routes and returned to the same places.

Besides, we've only been discussing west-east traffic. Some Jewish merchants went from Palestine to Apulis in southern Italy, then north via Lucca and the Alps into France. Another route went from the Byzantine north up the Danube into Germany. Still another route followed the Volga into eastern and northern Europe.

Gong says two questions need clarification regarding these long commercial treks across Europe and Asia. First, why did most merchants leave from Spain and France? Second, what method did they use to maintain this particular route? Gong Fangzhen offers his interpretation:

Jewish merchants setting out from Spain or France enjoyed two advantages. First, their relations with the rulers of those countries were good. The Abbasid caliphate which the Arab Muslims had established in Spain maintained a friendly attitude toward the Jews. In fact they appointed Jewish controllers in three cities—Cordoba, Grenada, and Toledo. The 8th to the 12th centuries were a golden age for the Spanish Jews. They could engage in trade and mercantile shipping relatively easily.

In Provence in southern France, Jews proudly bore the appellation "the Jewish Princes." They were enabled in this salubrious atmosphere to make full use of their commercial connections in the ports girdling the Mediterranean.

The Mediterranean was originally part of the Roman world. When the Arabs rose up in the 7th century and forced a division into realms under the crescent flag and the sign of the cross, the only ones who could safely sail the Mediterranean were the Jews, who maintained a neutral stand between the two powerful hostile forces. They therefore were able to control the movement of merchandise east and west across the body of water. This was their second advantage.

(It was too good to last. After the 11th century, their monopoly was gone. In 1215 France issued a decree ordering all Jews to wear distinctive identification on their clothes, and finally banished them completely.)

Another reason why the Jewish merchants preferred to depart from Spain was an important item in their commerce—eunuchs. At that time the Slavs, the Venetians, the Arabs, and the Jews were all engaged in the slave trade. Black slaves were from Somalia or Zanzibar, and had been bought or captured by the Arab traders. There was a market for them in Tang dynasty China. White slaves, who were mainly Slavs, Greeks and Khazars, were generally handled by the Jewish merchants. They had no castration facility of their own, and would bring the slaves to one run by Spaniards in Spain. After the operations were performed, the merchants sold the slaves as eunuchs.

Arab geographer al-Muqaddasi noted in a tenth century report: "Outside Khorazm (in present day Uzbekistan) I saw Slavs who Jews had bought for resale. Later, they were taken to be castrated in Spain" (*see Luce Boulnois "The Silk Road" p. 197*).

As translator and editor permit me to interject: The existence of slaves was unemotionally accepted in Jewish, Christian, and Muslim societies from their earliest days. According to Leviticus 25 in the Old Testament, the Lord said to Moses on Mount Sinai: "You may acquire male and female slaves from the nations around you." The only restriction was that Jews were not allowed to enslave other Jews. According to the Masoretic text the Babylon scribes compiled, the Lord is alleged to have said: "As for your Israelite brothers, no one shall rule ruthlessly over the other."

Even if this actually was a Divine tenet, it was no endorsement of international commercial trade in human flesh, nor of "improving" the product by castration. Of course these slave traders were not typical of all Jewish merchants, or even of all Radanites. But they were guilty of a despicable practice, and we duly report it.

Gong observes that Jewish merchants had no political power, no strong military backing. How were they able to sustain that long trade route between east and west? Jewish scholar S.D. Gotein offers an explanation. Gong quotes him:

There were many small station-holders on the road between Spain and India, some of whom were no better than brigands or pirates. Even in a well-ordered country a merchant had no recourse to the authorities if he was extorted or robbed. Also, if a foreign merchant died on the way, his goods would simply be confiscated by the local rulers.

To protect themselves from such eventualities, the Jewish traders engaged "representatives" at every major port of call. These representatives would show the cargo to the highest local authority, who was always on excellent terms with the scoundrels roving the deserts and the seas. If anything happened to the ship, or if the merchant himself died, compensation would be paid to the representative.

The representatives had a number of other functions. They kept warehouses where goods could be stored. They served as bankers from whom the merchants could borrow money, or with whom they could make deposits. They forwarded and delivered the merchants' mail. Usually they were themselves merchants of the highest integrity (see S.D. Goitein, "Jews and Arabs: Their Contacts Through the Ages" pps 118-119, 1955).

Leaders of Jewish communities often served as representatives, known as "nagids." Jews were scattered all over the world. In some countries they were isolated in ghettoes. Even where they were not, they tended to congregate in communities. During the Fatima dynasty in Egypt in the tenth century, Al-Muiz, the ruling Arab monarch, permitted the Jews to administer their own affairs. The leader of the community was called the "nagid," which is how the name originated. There were "nagids" in Jewish communities in Spain, North Africa, Palestine, and Yemen.

III. WHO WERE THE RADANITES?

Ibn Khurdadhbe called them Radhaniya, says Gong. But who were they, and where was Radhan (or Radan)? In the past century there have been nearly a dozen different schools of thought regarding this important question.

Gong Fangzheng analyzes them in detail, finding only a few worth considering. He concludes:

The theories are mutually contradictory. I can only speculate that the Radanites originally were Jewish merchants from the district of Radan in Persia, who plied the trade routes between east and west. The application of the term was subsequently widened to include Jewish merchants in the west, and in north Africa. As to the exact location of Radan, we can only say it was east of Baghdad.

Statements of ancient Arab geographers were frequently vague and confused. And so, we needn't be surprised when we see al-Bakri, 11th century Arab traveler, claiming that Radan was a village within the district of Baghdad.

Even Ibn Khurdadhbe was no exception. He described the route from western Europe to China accurately enough, but he wasn't terribly clear on where China was. He divided the world into four areas, which he called Europe, Libya, Ethiopia, and Scythia, and placed Sind, India, and China all within the realm of Ethiopia.

He was correct, however, in saying that the ruler of China was known as the "Son of Heaven."

IV. KHAZARIA, IMPORTANT TRANSFER POST ON THE SILK ROAD

In ancient times the main land route of the Jewish merchants to China was through the kingdom of the Khazars, Gong claims. The Khazars were descendants of a Turkic people. They spoke a Turkic dialect different from the main stream. Russian scholars say it was similar to what Chuvash people speak in the former Soviet Union today, a very early form of Turkic. A Russian historic album describes the Chuvash as a "White Ugri" people, or "Saragur," or "Ogur."

Gong cautions in his "An Appraisal of Studies on the Jews in Ancient China," not to confuse "Ogur" with "Ugyur," one of China's largest ethnic Turkic nationalities today. He says "Ogur" was one of China's many Turkic tribes, and were not necessarily the same as the Ugyurs. Gong continues:

East Roman historian Priscus also refers to the "Saragur," or "Ogur." He says they originally lived in the east, but were forced to move west by another race *(the Xiong Nu, or "Huns")*, finally settling in the Volga valley, and north of the Black Sea. This is precisely where the Khazars were found in the fifth century. Priscus in 448 was appointed emissary to the court of Attila (the Hun), to whom the Khazars were then subservient, and went out with his army on military campaigns. Priscus' reports are therefore reliable.

By the 7th century the Khazars already had a strong country. Their king, who was called a khan, sent 40,000 troops to help the Byzantine Christian emperor fight against the Persians. A word here about the Byzantine Empire, also called East Rome. With the final disintegration of the old Roman Empire in the 4th century, the capital was moved from Rome to Byzantium, a vital port on the mouth of the narrow Bosphorus Straits separating Europe from Asia, where the Black Sea pours into the Mediterranean. The Roman Empire was divided into an "Eastern Empire" and a "Western Empire," with a ruler appointed to each. After a ferocious struggle for power, Constantine emerged as the victor in the Eastern Empire, and the old city of Byzantium was named Constantinople. Constantine converted to Christianity, and the Eastern Empire, now also known as East Rome, or the Byzantine, became its bastion.

Arab traveler Ibn Fadlan visited Khazaria in the 9th century. He reported that the king and his intimates were observers of the Jewish faith, but that the rest of the Khazars were either Christians, Muslims, or members of other religions.

Masuda says the king and all of the Khazars were Jews, except for some Muslims in the army, and people of other faiths among the Slavs. But regardless of the proportion of believers, because the king himself was a convert to Judaism, Jewish merchant travelers were afforded protection. Fadlan said when the king heard that Muslims had destroyed a Jewish temple, he swore he would seize the Muslim mosque in the capital city Atil and raze it to the ground.

In his "Appraisal" Gong Fangzhen reports a recent find in the library of Cambridge University of several letters by 10th century Khazarian Jews written in Hebrew. They no longer refer to the ruler as the "khan," but use a Jewish name instead. This proves the Khazars had been completely Judified, he maintains. There's no reason to doubt their faith in Judaism. Gong continues:

When had the Khazars become Jews? In a 10th century letter to Spanish Jew Hasdai ibn Shaprut, Gong alleges, Joseph, khan of the Khazars, gave the answer.

Shaprut (915 to 970 or 990) was a Jewish physician who was also a prominent statesman in Spain. He had heard there was a Jewish country in the Far East, and that the rulers were also Jews. He was eager to make contact.

At that time a Slavic emissary arrived in Cordoba. In his entourage were two Jews—Mar Saul and Mar Joseph who lived in Khazaria. They confirmed that Khazaria was a Jewish kingdom. Shaprut entrusted them with a letter to the khan, or king. In it he described the location of Spain in Europe, and begged the king to write back and tell him about Khazaria.

Mar Joseph brought a reply from King Joseph around 960. It said that a few decades earlier, Bulan, the khan, dreamed he met a god who promised to give him power and glory. Thus encouraged, Bulan did indeed grow to be very powerful. The emperor of the Byzantine and the caliph of the Arabs sent representatives, one to urge him to embrace Christianity, the other to become a Muslim. Bulan also invited an Israeli religious scholar. After discussions with the three, Bulan decided on Judaism. Abba Eban in his *My People* fixes the date of Bulan's acceptance of the faith of Moses as 740.

The capital of the Kingdom of the Khazars was Atil. It straddled both sides of the lower reaches of the Volga where it flows into the Caspian Sea. On the west bank was the palace of the khan. The east bank was occupied by merchants from various foreign lands. Khazaria was not only an important hub for merchandise flowing east and west, it was also an artery for goods going north and south. Cargo moving north up the Volga could sail all the way to the Baltic.

Since the end of the 19th century, thousands of silver Arab coins have been discovered in cities along the upper reaches of the Volga, dating from the 8th to the 11th centuries. The merchants then were Khazars, Arabs, Bulgars, Slavs, and Jews. Slavs came south down the Volga to Atil, where they traded slaves and furs and honey for silver coins.

The khan of the Khazars needed silver coins to pay his Muslim troops. From the end of the 8th to the beginning of the 9th century, Arab silver coins were minted in north Africa for the newly emerging Arab empire. In the 10th century the minting was done in the Oxus region for the use of the Samanid dynasty. This proves that prior to the 9th century, the merchants in Khazaria came mainly from the Near East, whereas in the 10th century most came from around the Oxus.

The large quantities of Arab coins doesn't mean that Chinese trade in that area was small. The Chinese did business primarily on a barter basis. In the Tang dynasty it was forbidden to take coins out of the country. A 713 regulation stated: "The use of coins in trade with foreign merchants is prohibited." In 780 another imperial decree read: "It is not allowed to trade in silver, copper, iron, or slaves with foreigners."

Ibn Khurdadhbe says some of the coins came through Khazaria from Constantinople. In 1953 a gold coin was found in a Sui dynasty (589–618) tomb outside Xianyang. It bore the imprint of Justin II, who reigned as East Roman emperor from 565 to 578 in Constantinople—strong evidence of a northern route to the Byzantine.

"Jiu Tang Shu" ("Old Tang Record"), a Tang dynasty (618 to 907) history, Gong notes, states that Emperor Yang (605 -617) of the previous Sui dynasty: "tried several times to send a mission to Byzantine, but never succeeded." However that does not mean there was no trade between China and Byzantine. Commercial representatives from

Byzantine called at the Tang court in 643, 667, 701, and 719.

In "Sui Shu," the Sui dynasty history compiled in Tang, the tribes which populated the area northwest of the Caspian Sea are set forth in detail, Gong adds. Nearly all correspond exactly with Western historical records of tribes then in the Volga River valley. This information must have been supplied by Khazar merchants who came to Tang dynasty China.

Tang documents recently discovered in Turfan, apparently receipts for merchandise, refer to two men—"Zhuhu Ni" and "Zhuhu Cui." Later Yuan dynasty records frequently used terms like "Zhu" as transliterations of the word "Jew." These men were probably Jews from Khazaria.

Gong repeats the report of Arab poet Misar in the 10th century of having seen Muslims, Jews, Christians, Zoroastrians, and Indians in a city in Turfan, then an independent kingdom, now a part of Xinjiang Province, China. Gong wonders whether any of the Radanites could have gone into China together with the Khazars to do business.

He also notes some comments in Joseph Needham's famous "Science and Technology In China", in which Needham speculates that since the Zhazars understood Chinese, and their palace ceremonials were the same as those practiced in the China court, it was possible that the first Jewish community in Kaifeng was established by Radanites.

My own feeling is that it is clear from the foregoing that the Khazar Jewish merchants, not the Radanites, handled the direct overland trade with China, during the Tang dynasty and thereafter. The "Zhugu Ni" and "Zhuhu Cui" ("Jew Ni" and "Jew Cui") referred to in the Tang documents discovered in Turfan were Jewish Khazar merchants seen in Turfan in the 10th century. The fact that many of the Khazars could speak Chinese, and the ceremonies in the royal court in Khazaria were similar to those of the imperial Chinese court, also indicate that Khazar merchants traveled widely and deeply into China.

We have no evidence that these were Radanite Jews rather than Jewish Khazars. The Radanites were Middle-Easterners and Europeans, strangers in a strange land. The Khazars were Asiatics, familiar with the physical terrain and attuned to the customs and habits of the numerous ethnic nationalities encountered in Central Asia en route to China, and to the culture of the powerful Chinese empire.

Obviously, it made better business sense for the Radanites to conduct their overland trade with China through the Khazars rather than spending many arduous weeks traveling across the vast territory of Central Asia.

They could sell their goods in Khazaria and, in the same place, buy what the Khazars would bring back from China at their request.

I believe that is what happened. It was an attractive arrangement for the Radanites, since they could feel assured of good will and fairly honest dealings from the Khazars, who were Jews like themselves. They paid in gold and silver Arab coins.

While there was no need for the Radanites to travel personally across Central Asia, they did apparently make the easier journey by sea. For this, the reports of Ibn Khurdadhbe seem reliable.

I do not agree with Joseph Needham's speculation that the first Jewish community in Kaifeng was probably established by Radanites. The Jews who came to Kaifeng brought their wives and children (from Bukhara and Samarkand in Transoxiana? See Yin Gang, this volume). They came to settle permanently. The Radanites were transient merchants. They bought or sold commercial commodities, and returned to their native lands.

Yin Gang

THE JEWS OF KAIFENG: THEIR ORIGINS, ROUTES, AND ASSIMILATION

Yin Gang was born in Beijing in 1951. He graduated from the Beijing Insti-
tute of Education in 1981 and served as an editor of the magazine *Nexus*.
From 1995 to 1996 he was a visiting scholar at Hebrew University in
Jerusalem. A Fellow in the West Asia and Africa Institute of the Chinese
Academy of Social Sciences, he specializes in Arab-Israeli relations, and
Sino-Israeli relations. Published works include: *In Search of Chinese Jews*,
Jerusalem And Arab-Jewish Conflict, and *A History of the Peace Negotia-
tions In the Middle East: 1913 –1995*.

In the comprehensive treatise presented here, Yin Gang explores the history of the Chinese Jews from the beginnings of their travels to China up to
the end of the 19th century. He combines careful research with challenges to
several of the long-accepted premises of both Chinese and Western scholars.

I have been fairly literal in my translation. In a few places I insert my own
comments in italics.

I. THE PERSIAN JEWS

*The 700 years which passed after the Persian Jews built a synagogue in
Kaifeng in 1163 and established a Jewish community embraced four dynasties. These were the Jin (1115 - 1234), Yuan (1279 - 1368), Ming (1368 -
1644), and Qing (1644 - 1911), created by Nuzhen (Golden Tartars), Mongol, Han, and Manchu nationalities, respectively. Language, culture, religious observances, social customs, and governmental policies toward ethnic minorities changed, and with them the status and livelihood of the Kaifeng
Jews.*

*Their history before entering China was even more complicated. Yin Gang
discusses the stages of their assimilation, starting with their origins. He
alleges the majority of Chinese scholars believe the Kaifeng Jews originated
in Persia and traveled to China via various routes by land and by sea. They*

base this on the considerable Persian traces found in Jewish documents and stone tablets, and what the Jews told investigating Catholic missionaries. Specifically, Yin contends:

With the deepening of research on the Kaifeng Jews and related historical materials, I am able with more assurance to determine their origins and the dates of their entry into China.

Clearly, the Jews of Kaifeng were descendants of the "Babylonian Exiles". When they were freed by the Persian conquest of Babylon in 538 BC, instead of returning to Jerusalem, most of them remained in areas of Babylon and other parts of the Persian empire. Later, they moved eastward into central Asia. I offer the following evidence:

1. Catholic missionary Antonius Goubil in 1723, after talking with Kaifeng Jews, concluded: "They know nothing of the history of the Maccabees." Nor did they observe Hanukkah, a holiday celebrating the victory of the Maccabean revolt against the Seleucid dynasty in 165 B.C.

2. Jean Paul Gozani, a Catholic priest who visited Kaifeng, in a letter written in August, 1712, said of the Kaifeng Jews: "They are very familiar with the story of Esther, as well as the tribulations of Haman and the punishment he suffered." Gozani said they called the Jewess who saved all the Jews in Persia in 470 B.C. "Mama Esther." The Book of Esther was written in Persian prior to 250 B.C. The great affection the Kaifeng Jews held for Esther shows that their ancestors were still living in Persia at that time.

3. The Jews of Kaifeng knew the Talmud *(commentaries on the Old Testament, and commentaries on the commentaries),* and had several hand-written copies. Composed at the end of the 5th century A.D., the Talmud was edited by over 100 scholars in the Babylonian Jewish community, and was transmitted worldwide in manuscript form during the next several centuries. Only in 1482 did it finally appear in print, in Hebrew, produced by scholars who had returned to Jerusalem. The printing was done in Spain. But the Babylonian manuscript version remained the most popular because it was the most complete. The manuscript Talmud of the Kaifeng Jews made no mention of the revolt of the Maccabees in 165 B.C., another proof that the ancestors of the Kaifeng Jews did not return to Jerusalem from Babylon after liberation by the Persians, but continued to reside for a long time in the border regions of the Persian empire.

4. The Torah *(the "Five Books of Moses," or the "Old Testament" Bible)* of the Kaifeng Jews was divided into 53 chapters, to be read aloud in the synagogue, one each week, completing the entire volume within one year. This practice, which began around the third century,

had a "Jerusalem style" and a "Babylonian style." In the first, the Torah was divided into 175 weekly sections, its recitation to be finished in three years. The latter was divided into 54 sections to be recited in full within a single year.

The Kaifeng Jews, who used the "Babylonian style," improved on it by combining the 52nd and 53rd chapters into one, in the Persian manner. Not until the 13th century did Jews in other parts of the world replace the "Jerusalem style," which they had been using, with the "Babylonian style."

This is further evidence that the ancestors of the Kaifeng Jews remained in the Persian empire and did not return to Jerusalem after being liberated in Babylon.

5. The Scriptures of the Kaifeng Jews were written in Hebrew, but it was a Persian-type Hebrew. The 22 letters of the Hebrew alphabet are all consonants. Vowel sounds may be indicated by diacritical marks written beneath them. However none of these can represent certain sounds in the Persian pronunciation of Hebrew. For that purpose five letters were chosen with diacritical marks written above them, creating a total of 27 letters, to satisfy the needs of the majority of the congregation, who obviously were of Persian origin.

6. In 1619, Italian priest Nicolaus Longobardi visited Kaifeng and called at the Jewish community center. "I spoke a few sentences in Persian, to the great delight of everyone. They assumed their guest was a member of the same race as they," he wrote. There are numerous similar reports. Until the 18th century many Kaifeng Jews could still speak Persian.

7. Of all the missionaries who investigated the Jewish community in Kaifeng at the beginning of the 18th century, French priest Jean Domenge undoubtedly made the most valuable contribution. In order to be able to read their bible, he spent three years studying Hebrew. In addition, he drew sketches of the interior and exterior of the synagogue, providing the only pictorial evidence of its construction and furnishings. He also discovered and copied in 1721 the Judaeo-Persian colophon (*introduction written in Persian but using Hebrew script*) by a scribe of Genesis.

8. Some of these introductions contained dates calculated according to the Seleucid calendar created in 312 B.C. The Kaifeng Jews had no knowledge of Jesus, and consequently no concept of B.C. and A.D. Their ancestors had been using the Seleucid calendar in Persia, and they continued using it in Kaifeng, not knowing that the Seleucid dynasty had been destroyed by the Romans in 64 B.C.

9. After the Arabs defeated Persia in the 7th century, many Persians adopted Islam. They pronounced the Arab word for leader of a

non-Arabic mosque as "mullah." The Persian ancestors of the Kaifeng Jews brought the term to China, where they rendered it in Chinese as "man la" on many of their stone stelae to indicate "scholar" or "teacher," instead of the Hebrew term "rabbi."

This shows that the Persian Jews could not have come to China until they became acquainted with Islam, with its mosques and mullahs, after the Arab conquest of Persia.

II. FROM BUKHARA TO KAIFENG

Bukhara, says Yin Gang, a Persian emirate in the region of Transoxiana in central Asia, was listed in Chinese histories as the kingdom of An. {Transoxiana was a fertile plain between two rivers, Syr Darya (the Jaxartes) and Amu Darya (the Oxus), both of which empty into Lake Aral, and embraced a number of small Turkic kingdoms.} From the middle of the 7th century to the beginning of the 8th, Transoxiana appeared on Tang dynasty maps. The city of Bukhara and the city of Samarkand, then in the neighboring kingdom of Kang, became major commercial hubs on the busy east-west highway. Yin continues:

Many Jews and Persians lived in these cities, and many so-called "Persians"—actually central Asian ethnic nationalities—lived in China. Not a few held important positions during the Tang dynasty in local government bureaus and in the imperial army. Jews, who moved about even more widely than the Persians, were surely among the office holders. For example, a Tang record shows that a certain "A Luo Han" (Abraham) was given the rank of general and ordered to the "Western Regions" to "preserve peace among the barbarians." Most probably he was a Jew.

Between 705 and 715 the Arabs invaded the Transoxiana region, and destroyed the temples and documents of the Buddhist, Manichean, and other religious faiths. Combining guile and force, they promoted the religion of Islam. Those who refused to convert had to pay a heavy toll tax. Many fled to China.

In the second month of 720, Masapoti, the king of An, and Wulejia, the king of Kang, dispatched envoys bearing expensive gifts to Xuanzhong, emperor of Tang, pleading that he send an army to rescue them. But the monarach lacked the courage to confront the rising Arab power. The region of Transoxiana fell under Arab rule, and vanished from Tang dynasty maps.

Why didn't the Persian Jews in the region migrate to China at that time? For one thing, Arab control of Transoxiana was not completely secure. The conquerors were unable financially to simultaneously reward their own religionists and support political expansion. Resistance by the local ethnic races was inevitable. Revolt followed revolt. Many who had been forced to convert to Islam returned to their original religions. Arabs opposing the Sunni Arab caliphate in Bagdhad, as well as Shiite Persian Muslims, came to Transoxiana in batches, seeking refuge.

China, meanwhile, was in a state of continuous upheaval. One hundred twenty-six mutinies occurred between 755 and 873. The east-west trade routes were cut. Tang emperor Wu Zong, under both political and economic pressure, in 845 issued a severe decree forbidding the entry of all foreign religions. For the succeeding 100 years, China was not an ideal haven for Jews and Persians, and few of the ancestors of the Kaifeng Jews came.

In 874, Persians who escaped from Arab rule established the Samanid kingdom in the former Bukhara emirate, and placed its capital in Samarkand. A Persian cultural renaissance blossomed in Transoxiana and lasted a whole century. The Jews, who had always been on friendly terms with the Persians, had no reason to emigrate. It was in this period that the more moderate Shiite Muslims established dominance over the Islam religion.

At the end of the 10th century, the Samanid kingdom was attacked and destroyed by a Turkic kingdom, which had broken away from Tang rule, and a new Turkic kingdom in the Afghanistan region. Since both of these kingdoms were adherents of the Sunni Muslim sect, their victory had a religious as well as a political significance. The land of the Samanid nobles was confiscated, and the people were enslaved. Large numbers of them fled.

By then China had ended the turbulence of the Five Dynasties period (907—960) and created a unified Song dynasty (960–1127). Kaifeng, in the Yellow River area, became the capital, replacing the old capital of Chang An as China's political center. While continuing to maintain the prosperity of the "silk road by sea," Song restored the land routes, thereby providing facilities for the merchants of Transoxiana and various refugees from Central Asia to enter China.

After the Sunni sect came to power in Transoxiana, commercial traffic with the Song dynasty grew rapidly. Merchants, refugees, and emissaries bearing gifts from the small kingdoms came in such numbers that the Song court was unable to cope. Emperor Shen Zong (1068–1085) issued an edict that only envoys with official documents and gifts from their kingdom would be allowed into the Song capital.

Numerous Muslim stelae and documents record a significant event. One states that during Shen Zong's reign, Sufeyir, king of Aspuhala, himself of Arab descent, fled from Bukhara to China with family members and an entourage of hundreds, seeking refuge. Shen Zong refused to allow them to live in Kaifeng, and ordered them to settle in the Huai River area.

A family history of a Muslim scholar places the event much earlier, namely during the Jian Long period (960–963) of Emperor Tai Zu (960–976), and describes Sufeyir as a "High religious leader from Bukhara."

Despite the discrepancy in dates and identity, we know that an important personage from Bukhara, fleeing Sunni persecution, was refused residence in Kaifeng in early Song, and compelled to live away from the capital.

Jews from Bukhara no doubt received the same treatment, and were required to settle outside Kaifeng. This would account for there being no records of any Jewish synagogue in Kaifeng during Northern Song (960–1127).

If we are to believe the claims of the Kaifeng Jews that their ancestors presented "an entry gift of Western cloth" to an emperor of Song, it would have to have been very early, probably during the Zhen Zong dynasty (998–1022). Their allegation that he welcomed them, saying: "You have come to our Central Plain. Preserve your ancestral customs and remain in Bian Liang (Kaifeng)" was not true. These words could not have come from the mouth of a Song emperor.

Foreign refuge seekers were not allowed residence in Kaifeng, though they were permitted to do business and conduct trade. Were they indeed received by an emperor of Song?

The Kaifeng Jews were deliberately creating a false impression. Their reasons will be discussed below.

III. CHINESE JEWS OF DIFFERENT ORIGINS

In addition to those Jews who migrated to China overland, others arrived by sea. Subsequent to the late Tang dynasty, east-west traffic was mainly maritime, Yin says. Large numbers of Persian, Arab, and Jewish merchants settled in major cites on or near the coast such as Guangzhou (Canton), Quanzhou, Hangzhou, and Yangzhou. Jewish community centers were built in places like Hangzhou during the Yuan (1279–1368) dynasty.

But these Jews didn't come from the same places, at the same time, or along the same routes as the Kaifeng Jews. That must be recognized in order to understand why the Kaifeng Jews did not follow the Northern Song dynasty court to the new capital in Hangzhou. Yin Gang explains:

They had already been living, while not in the city of Kaifeng proper, at least in the nearby Huai River area, for well over a century.

Hangzhou was an unknown entity, a long distance away. Moreover, there was, as yet, no Jewish community in Hangzhou.

Jews, coming by sea, did not settle in Hangzhou until well after the establishment of the Southern Song in 1127. Links between the Hangzhou and Kaifeng were cut. They were not re-established until 150 years later when the Mongols re-formed a unified China in 1279.

Hangzhou flourished during Yuan. We have reports of "rich Jewish and Muslim merchants controlling the Sugar Bureau," of a Jewish district within Hangzhou, of a "Gate of the Jews" in the district wall. Catholic missionary Matteo Ricci relates that in Kaifeng Jew Ai Tian, visiting him in Beijing in 1605, told him there were many more Jews in Hangzhou than in Kaifeng, that Hangzhou had a Jewish synagogue. Yet none of the 18th century Catholic missionaries say anything about a Jewish community in Hangzhou, nor is there any reference in the Kaifeng memorial tablets to dealings with the Hangzhou Jews. Clearly, there was a wide gap between the two communities.

The relationship with Ningbo and Yangzhou was different. According to the 1489 memorial tablet, after the 1461 flood, the Jews of Ningbo sent several sets of "Scriptures" to the Kaifeng Jews who placed them in the rebuilt synagogue. This was not so much a sign of the close relations between the two communities, as of the fact that the Ningbo Jews wanted the Scriptures to be given a safe haven, since their own community was deteriorating. There are no further records of any activity by the Ningbo Jewish community.

The Yangzhou Jewish community vanished from the records somewhat later. The 1512 Kaifeng memorial tablet states that Kaifeng and Yangzhou Jews "contributed a scroll of the Scriptures and constructed a second gateway to the temple." But the 1663 tablet does not mention the Yangzhou Jews, nor is there any further reference to them in other documents.

Those with the closest relationship to the Kaifeng Jews were the Jews of Ningxia. The 1489 tablet notes that after a severe flood, Ningxia Jews presented an altar, a bronze censer, vases and candlesticks, and spent a large sum of money to buy a synagogue site. Another Ningxia Jew paid for the kiosk which housed the tablet. In a sense, we might say the new synagogue was built by the joint contributions of the Jews of Kaifeng and the Jews of Ningxia. In the 17th century, the whole Jin clan moved from Ningxia to Kaifeng and settled there permanently. In 1989, their descendants erected a stone tablet at their family cemetery in the suburbs of Kaifeng describing their ancestors' move.

The forebears of the Kaifeng Jews and those of their southern brethren came from different parts of the world, traveled by different routes, and had different characteristics. The first clung more tenaciously to their religious traditions and culture, and did not easily adapt to their new environment. The southerners were essentially merchants, not so resistant to change. And so, the Kaifeng Jewish community lasted much longer.

IV. FROM PERSIAN JEW TO CHINESE JEW

Yin maintains the transition began with the settlement of the ancestors of the Kaifeng Jews in China during the Song dynasty, continued through the era of Jin dynasty control of the Central Plain region north of the Huai River (1126-1232), and concluded with Yuan dynasty dominance over that same region (1233-1358). He says:

> Except for a statement in the 1489 memorial tablet that the Kaifeng Jews built a synagogue in 1127, which was during Jin dynasty rule, the memorial tablets tell nothing of the activities of the Kaifeng Jews in either the Song, Jin, or Yuan dynasties.
>
> In other words, they left no record for their descendants of their history during more than three hundred years.
>
> Nevertheless, based on a great deal of Chinese historical material, plus the reports of a few Arab travelers, together with what the tablet tells us about the building of the synagogue during Jin, plus the political and economic conditions of the Kaifeng Jewish community at the start of the Ming dynasty, we can piece together a general picture of what happened to them in that three century period.

Yin provides a time-frame breakdown:

1. Northern Song: The Year They Settled In China

> According to Chinese tradition, if a Song emperor had welcomed the Jews, they would have been granted land to live on and as a place to work. I have found no such record. But the verbal statements of the Kaifeng Jews, and what we know of the economic conditions in Northern Song, give us clues regarding dates.
>
> The Kaifeng Jews say their entry gift to the Song emperor was not ordinary cloth, but "cloth of five colors." When I visited Kaifeng in 1992, I learned that farmers in the suburbs of the city had been planting brown cotton right up until the 1940s. In Uzbekistan and China's Xinjiang province, agronomists recently have re-created colored cotton, adding credence to the Kaifeng Jews' story that they brought in colored cloth from the outside.
>
> Transoxiana was one of the earliest cotton planters in the world,

and the dyeing of cotton and trading in cotton goods were major occupations of Jews in Central Asia. We cannot exclude the possibility that Jews were engaged in these activities at the time of their initial entry into China, and that they introduced the planting of cotton to the Central Plain.

In other words, the theory that the Kaifeng Jews must have come from, or via, India, with their tribute gift of cotton cloth because "only" India was producing cotton during the Song dynasty, is without foundation. Transoxiana in Central Asia was long a producer of cotton, and dyed cotton cloth, and even colored cotton. Jews coming to China from that region could well have brought such commodities.

Northern Song instituted a "New Deal" which provided ideal conditions for Jewish expansion in China. The program was the brainchild of China's most famous reformer—Wang Anshi, (1021–1086). In essence it called for using government funds to stimulate the production and circulation of commercial commodities, with the government serving as a bank extending credit. The Jews, who had extensive experience in handicraft production and commerce, undoubtedly were able to benefit.

The economy of Northern Song flourished. Kaifeng became the most prosperous capital in the world. The role of the Jews in Kaifeng's commerce was almost inevitable. The Jewish community expanded. By the time the Nuzhen (Golden Tartars) swept down from the north and established the Jin dynasty (1115—1234), replacing Northern Song as the rulers of Kaifeng, the Jews were strong enough to build a synagogue.

Song was a period of adaptation. Han Chinese, indispensable for daily life and for business, became the Jews' new language. Following the custom of the Tang dynasty, Song permitted foreigners to sit for the civil service examinations. The type of questions were the same. When the results were announced there were always two or three "strange-sounding names" included among the successful candidates.

There is little indication the Jews hoped to learn Chinese culture and advance via the examination system at that time. China, for them, was only a place of refuge. This is evident from the fact that they did not follow the Song court when it fled south. But Jews in Kaifeng and other commercial cities in Huai River region during Song did at least begin the transition from being Persian to becoming Chinese.

2. The Jin Dynasty: Searching For Survival Amid Turbulence and Change

In 1126, after two attacks by the Jin Golden Tartars, the Song emperor abandoned his capital and retreated south across the Yangtze to Hangzhou, says Yin. At the end of the year, Jin soldiers occupied Kaifeng, where they massacred and looted at will. A series of battles followed between the forces of Song and Jin for control of the Central Plain. I n 1153 Kaifeng became Jin's "Southern Capital," and the official residence of the Jin emperor. Yin continues:

Thirty-six years after the emperor of Northern Song abandoned Kaifeng in 1127, the Jews of Kaifeng in 1163 built their first synagogue. For them it was a particularly auspicious time, because they enjoyed several favorable conditions:

1) The construction of Jin's "Southern Capital," as Kaifeng had become known, was virtually complete, and the war-ravaged city was partially restored.

2) The see-saw battles between Jin and Song had come to a temporary halt, and a relatively stable peace had been established.

3) Many buildings had been left empty when the Song court fled south. While the Jewish memorial tablets do not say where they erected their first synagogue (during the Jin dynasty), we note that the Ming dynasty synagogues (whose location we do know) were all built in what had been the most prosperous section of the city in Northern Song. The posh Song restaurants and fancy amusement houses had been looted and smashed by the marauding Jin soldiers, and their abandoned ruins could be bought and built upon cheaply.

The Jews did not retreat south with the Northern Song government. They continued to live peacefully all through the frequent battles and turmoil of the early years of Jin rule. What's more, they found the opportunity to erect a synagogue, displaying a remarkable degree of adaptability.

Han culture rapidly conquered the Jin dynasty which the Nuzhen victors had created. By the middle of their reign, even the son of the emperor could scarcely speak or write his native tongue. Han Chinese was the language used throughout the Central Plain. The Sinification of the Kaifeng Jews continued unabated.

The construction of the Kaifeng synagogue signified the establishment of the Jewish community. Although we have no documentary evidence of how the Jews lived under Nuzhen rule, building of the synagogue proved they had successfully adapted.

The Nuzhen had no formal religion. They were still in a stage of primitive shamanism. Apparently they had no religious prejudices. When their soldiers entered Kaifeng they slaughtered officials of the Song court and ordinary citizens alike. The only exceptions were religious leaders and clergy, and houses of worship. They permitted their existence for economic reasons: Monks and priests had to pay high fees for "du tie" (religious identification certificates), bringing revenue into the government treasury. The religious policy of the Jin dynasty was of undoubted benefit to the Jews, just as the Jews' skills in manufacture and their commercial know-how were very welcome to the Nuzhen.

However, life for the Jews did not run completely smooth. The Yellow River changed its course in 1194, and flowed close to the northern side of Kaifeng, posing a constant menace. Not long after, the Central Plain became the locale of the decisive battle between the Jin dynasty and the Yuan (Mongols). In 1232 the Yuan emperor inveigled the emperor of the Southern Song into an alliance against the Jin, promising, on victory, to return all of Henan province to Song, including Kaifeng.

The Southern Song army attacked vigorously, causing thousands of refugees to pour into Kaifeng, stretching the city's population from a few hundred thousand to over two million. In mid-summer that year the Mongols tightly besieged the city. Nothing and no one could get in or out. Half the population perished from starvation or plague. There were tragic cases of cannibalism. The Kaifeng Jewish community suffered heavy losses.

For 105 years, from 1127 to 1232, the Jews of Kaifeng lived under Nuzhen rule. In that period they built a synagogue, and made Kaifeng a center of the Jews in China. Increasingly steeped in Han culture, which never lost its dominant position, they completed their transformation from "Persian Jews" to "Jews of Kaifeng."

3. The Yuan Dynasty: A Jewish Paradise, Han Culture Under the Mongols

Yin Gang feels that Yuan had the most complicated ethnic situation in Chinese history. Large numbers of soldiers and military personnel from a variety of Central Asian nationalities returned to China with the Mongol armies and settled on the Central Plain. Their social position was much higher than that of the local ethnics. It was a time of "foreigners ruling China." The Mongols categorized them according to time of conquest or place of residence. Yin specifies them:

First class: Mongols

Second class: "People with colored eyes" (Central Asians).

Third class: Hans (people the Mongols conquered relatively early in eastern and northern China, including members of the Han, Nuzhen, and Korean races living north of the Huai River, plus the so-called "Zhu yin dai" or "Zhu yi dai" (Jews).

Fourth class: Southerners (those living in the area formerly occupied by the Southern Song).

Political status varied with class, as did punishments for violations of the law. The position of the Jews was confused. From a point of view of race, they should have been "people with colored eyes" (second class). Judging by residence, Kaifeng Jews should have been ranked with the "Hans" living north of the Huai River (third class). While if they lived in south China they should have been considered "southerners" (fourth class).

As to "Zhu yin dai" and "Zhu yi dai," historians to this day still have failed to recognize them as part of the third class. The sounds are very similar, and in all probability are the Han pronunciation of "Judah," namely, Jews who were already living in China before the Mongol conquest.

Except for the statement in the 1489 tablet that they rebuilt the synagogue in 1279, the Kaifeng Jews have left us no other record of their life during Yuan. Official Yuan dynasty documents regarding the Jews are erratic. Sometimes their name was mispronounced "Shu hu," sometimes "Zhu hu," or they simply were listed among the Muslims as "Shu wu Hui Hui" (Jewish Hui Hui). "Zhu yin dai" or "Zhu yi dai" (Judah) is another Yuan appellation for Jews. How, exactly, the Mongols considered them is not clear.

Politically, the Mongols relied mainly on the "colored eyes" peoples—central Asians who had accompanied them in their conquest of China, and were thus considered to have "solid roots." When there weren't enough Mongols to fill all the official positions, they drew on the ranks of central Asians who had distinguished themselves in battle, or their descendants. These held government positions on every level. Their function was to help the Mongols enforce their rule over the Hans.

Han Chinese remained the official language during Yuan, but the Mongol and ethnic officials had great difficulty with it. Most could not even sign their names, and used beautiful wooden, ivory or jade seals to affix their signatures. The Mongols were forced to employ many Hans as officials.

The Kaifeng Jews had been in China a long time. They had better linguistic ability than the average "colored eyes" citizen. They, too, therefore, were natural choices for government jobs. The Hans, and the southern aristocrats and wealthy merchants, were favored by the Mongols for political and economic reasons. The Kaifeng Jews, although they had no "solid roots," were also included in the special clique. In fact, they rated higher than the average Han.

Yuan was also distinguished by its liberal attitude toward religion. Kublai Khan called Moses, Jesus, Sakyamuni, and Muhammud the Great Sages of Judaism, Christianity, Buddhism, and Islam. He respected them and beseeched their help. Kublai issued a decree prohibiting disturbance of their places of worship, or the imposition of taxes on their religious property or land. Religious clergy were exempted from personal taxes and public service duties. These edits were incised on stone tablets which were erected in the courtyard of every large place of worship.

Jewish religious services in Kaifeng and synagogue construction were guaranteed full protection. It was under these circumstances that the Kaifeng Jews were able to rebuild their synagogue in 1279.

The date coincided with the final destruction of the Southern Song dynasty. By then the Mongols had ruled Kaifeng for 46 years, and of course the building had the formal approval of the government's Department of Religious Affairs. One of the units over which the Department exercised supervision was the "Lie Ban," which was the Mongol pronunciation for the Hebrew "Rabban" (*who favored a Talmudic, or liberal, interpretation of the Torah*). No restrictions were imposed on the observance of the religion, and the Jews were able to maintain its purity.

But enjoying religious freedom and a favorable social status did not mean the process of adaptation had halted. Han culture remained dominant under Yuan. The Jews of Kaifeng necessarily followed the same path. Taking part in the civil service examination was an important symbol of their Sinification.

The language of the Yuan civil service tests was Han Chinese (mandarin), their content was the Confucian classics, just as they had always been under the Han dynasties. During Yuan the national examinations were held 16 times, and qualified 1200 "jin shi" (*those who attained the highest levels*). Although these constituted only 4% of the total officialdom, because of their top quality, they were highly regarded, and always were appointed to senior posts in the provincial governments and the central national bureaucracy.

Examination candidates in the four classes were all treated differently. Questions for those in the first two classes were fairly easy. For those in the third and fourth classes they were relatively hard. While the Han and the southerners usually did well, there were many failures among the Mongols and the "people with colored eyes".

We don't know whether any Kaifeng Jews qualified as "jin shi," but we do see several non-Chinese names on the lists of government appointees. Among the provincial government leadership appointments was an "Andula (Abdullah) Homan" (The leader of the Kaifeng Jewish community which rebuilt the synagogue was also named Andula)... The judge presiding over the the earliest national civil service examinations during Yuan was called "Shu hu dai" (Yehudi?)... An expert on Confucian philosophy was named "Sha Ban" (Sheba?). Were these Jews?

Reliance on the central Asian ethnics and the Han Chinese intensified. In 1293 there were 16,425 non-Mongol appointees to central government and provincial posts. By 1328 the number had increased to 26,690, among whom 25% were "people with colored eyes." In view of the Kaifeng Jews' familiarity with social conditions and their grasp of Han Chinese culture, we can make the assumption that, during Yuan, they had begun to participate in political affairs.

The most important influence on their lives was the influx of the Islamic religion into Kaifeng. In 1281, two years after the Jews rebuilt their synagogue, Kublai Khan decreed that his "Hui Hui artillery units" (composed of Mongol and Arab soldiers) scattered in various positions, should congregate in the Kaifeng area and open wasteland for farming. Mosques quickly sprang up all over Kaifeng. The influence of Muslim culture on the Kaifeng Jews was now added to the influence of Chinese Han culture. When the Jewish community disintegrated several hundred years later, many Jews converted to Islam.

Jewish, Persian, and Arab commerce was very lively during Yuan. Because the Mongols were not good businessmen, they created semi-governmental commercial entities and entrusted their money to the Jews for investment. It was similar to the situation confronting the Jews during Northern Song, and again they profited from it.

Yuan China was a land of opportunity for foreigners. But they were, after all, very much in the minority. The advance of Han culture was overwhelming. Neither the Mongols, nor "people with colored eyes," nor the Kaifeng Jews could avoid being swept along.

V. FROM CHINESE JEWS TO COMPLETELY CHINESE

In the five hundred years from the beginning of Ming to the end of Qing, the Kaifeng Jewish community enjoyed unprecedented prosperity and yet endured severe hardship, Yin Gang says. Gradually assimilated by Chinese society, it culminated in total dissolution. He itemizes the stages:

1. The Ming dynasty: Prosperity and Assimilation

The Kaifeng Jews lived under first Nuzhen and then Mongol rule for 240 years. In May 1367, Zhu Yuanzhang became the emperor of Ming. His victorious armies entered Kaifeng, which had surrendered without a struggle. Zhu Yuanzhang named the city the "Northern Capital" of the Ming dynasty. The Jews welcomed the restoration of Han Chinese sovereignty.

Zhu remained in the city for three months. Delegations of the Jewish and Muslim communities vowed their loyalty, and he neglected no opportunity to reassure these now docile "barbarian tigers" (meaning the northern "savages" who had opposed him). It was to these Kaifeng Jews, and the Muslims, that this (Ming) emperor said the words: "You have come to our Central Plain. Preserve your ancestral customs and remain in Bian Liang (Kaifeng)."

As we said earlier, they could not have been spoken by an emperor of Song. Kaifeng in Song times had two official names: "Dong Jing" and "Bian Jing." Some writers then referred to the city as "Liang Yuan" or "Da Liang", in honor of the short-lived Liang dynasty which preceded Northern Song. The Yuan dynasty (1279–1368) Mongols combined "Bian Jing" and "Da Liang" into one term to create the name "Bian Liang." How could a Northern Song (960–1127) emperor have used a name before it came into existence?

The words spoken, moreover, were consistent with Zhu Yuanzhang's policy toward non-Han nationalities. The style and several of the phrases were similar to those he used in other proclamations. And further, the alleged Song dynasty sentences in the 1489 tablet are immediately followed by a statement of Zhu Yuanzhang's Ming dynasty policy towards nationalities. They obviously all were part of the same entity, and could only have been spoken by Zhu Yuanzhang.

The Kaifeng Jews put them in the mouth of an emperor of Northern Song to make it appear that he was the one who welcomed them, and that they had been devoted to the Han Chinese ever since. They sought in this way to gloss over their friendly relations with Jin and Yuan, who were enemies of the Han Chinese.

The Jews were not the only ones who sought to conceal a closeness to Jin and Yuan. Muslims in Kaifeng and Hangzhou claimed their mosques were erected in Song, whereas actually they all were built in Yuan. On the main ceiling of the famous "Feng Huang Mosque" in Hangzhou one can still see a pastoral scene of tribal shepherds (typical of Nuzhen and Mongol life).

There is little about the Jews and Muslims during Yuan in Chinese histories, especially material written by themselves. Tablets from Yuan dynasty religious edifices seem to have vanished.

From the Kaifeng tablets it is obvious the Kaifeng Jews were thoroughly familiar with their history. For example, the 1489 tablet gives us the year of the construction of the synagogue three centuries earlier, and the date of its rebuilding subsequently in the Yuan dynasty. It also tells us the name of the leader of the congregation during the first building, and identifies the two men who supervised the first repairs.

This information must have been obtained from earlier inscriptions, probably on Jin and Yuan tablets. These tablets naturally contained other information as well, such as the times the Jews came to China and the routes they followed. Unfortunately, the records were destroyed by the Kaifeng Jews—because they wanted to conceal that epoch of their history.

The Jews of Kaifeng submitted to the restored Han sovereignty quite early. Adjusting quickly to the new environment, they flowed with the mainstream of Chinese society, establishing a close relationship with the ruling strata, some even becoming members of it. During the Ming dynasty, the Kaifeng Jewish community was exceedingly prosperous. Its members were better off than the average Han Chinese.

Of course, they had to pay a price. Emperor Zhu Yuanzhang's policy towards ethnic nationalities was benevolent, but exacting. In 1368 he ordered the revival of Tang dynasty apparel. Mongol dress, speech, family names, even hair styles, were forbidden.

The rule against using "barbarian" names was strictly enforced. Except for Muslim ethnics in Xinjiang, who spoke various Turkic dialects, all Muslims during the Ming dynasty had to adopt Han Chinese names. This was done in two ways. The first, as in the case of An San, was where the emperor bestowed one as a reward for merit. He gave An San the family name of "Zhao," which had been the emperor's name during the Song dynasty, plus the given name of "Cheng," meaning faithful, in praise of his fidelity to the throne. It was a great honor.

The second way was to choose a Chinese surname which had the same, or similar, sound as the first syllable of one's original name. "Muhammud" became "Ma," "Levi" became "Li," "Sheba" or "Shimei" became "Shi," and so on.

This was followed by the promulgation of the "Marriage with Mongols and People With Colored Eyes Law," incorporated in the "Legal Code of the Great Ming." It read as follows:

"All Mongols and people with colored eyes must marry Chinese, if both parties consent. They cannot marry amongst themselves. Violators shall be beaten eighty strokes of the staff and, whether man or woman, shall be designated slaves. But if the Chinese parties do not wish to marry them, they can marry one of their own."

While the law was intended to make it impossible for ethnic people to preserve their racial purity, it frequently didn't work out that way. There had always been intermarriage with Han Chinese, particularly when the immigrating ethnics were not parts of integrated communities. The results of the mixed marriages usually meant the Hans were absorbed by the ethnics. Muslim religious strictures required anyone, whether man or woman, who married a Muslim to convert to Islam. As a result, the Muslim population increased. Large scale intermarriage with Han Chinese during the Ming dynasty created a new category which became known as "Hui Jiao" or "Chinese Islam." Its followers were not assimilated into the Han population.

Jews who married Muslims had to embrace Islam. This is one of the reasons the Jews were assimilated. But it was not the main reason. The Ming rulers did indeed treat their ethnic subjects benevolently. There were not a few Hui Hui officials in the imperial court and army. An San, a Kaifeng Jew, was awarded a rank of Third Grade, because of services he had rendered to the court, and appointed to what today would be the head of security for the province of Zhejiang.

During Ming there were about five hundred Jewish families in Kaifeng. An astonishing number were intimately linked to the ruling elite, or had ties to it through various indirect channels. Some attained civil rank via the examination system.

Jews who distinguished themselves in battle won military promotions. Many became prominent socially. The status of families varied with the positions their leading members held.

Kaifeng Jews engaged in many different occupations: scholar, official, soldier, farmer, artisan, merchant, doctor. Religious activities of the Jewish community proceeded normally. When a flood destroyed the synagogue during Ming, the Kaifeng community was able to rebuild it, and obtain replacements for the damaged Torahs and scriptures from Jewish friends in other cities, while the Kaifeng rabbis copied out thirteen complete new Torah scrolls. Wealthy Jewish merchants, retired officials, and those still in office, gave generously all the financial and political support necessary. These, on the surface, were manifestations of a prosperous Jewish community united in its dedication to a common cause.

Actually, beneath these appearances lurked a severe danger. Jewish intellectuals had become prisoners of Han culture and Confucian thought. Their fascination with the civil service examinations vitiated their interest in the study of Hebrew and Judaism. The worldly atmosphere of Chinese officialdom corroded families serving for generations in the bureaucracy.

It was Ming policy to post officials far from their homes. (Those from Henan province, for example, were usually sent south of the Yangtze.) Officials from the same family could not be appointed to the same government department. Long separation from the influences of their religion caused them to lose faith. Concern for their Jewish community turned into ordinary nostalgia for home.

Kaifeng Jewish intellectuals found a rationalization for their waning interest in Judaism. They expressed it perfectly in the 1489 memorial tablet. It said that Judaism and Confucianism " . . . in mind and deed both respect Heaven's Way, venerate ancestors, are loyal to sovereigns and ministers, and filial to parent. Both call for harmony with wives and children, respect for rank, and for making friends. In short, nothing less than the Five (Confucian) Relationships . . . Our religion and Confucianism differ only in minor details. . . ."

In the minds of Kaifeng Jewish intellectuals, the distinctions between Judaism and Confucianism, between Chinese and Jew, were dimmed.

At the start of the 17th century, after more than two hundred years of control, the Ming dynasty began to decay. Bureaucratic corruption was beyond cure. One peasant uprising followed another. In 1623 the Nuzhen breached the Great Wall and launched a series of attacks, driving to the very outskirts of Beijing. Emperor Chong Zhen hastily summoned crack troops from the northern provinces to bolster the defense. Just at that time a huge peasant uprising under Li Zicheng erupted in the province of Shaanxi. The Ming dynasty was besieged from within and without.

The prosperity of the Kaifeng Jewish community had reached its peak. Although they had been able spend a large sum of money to rebuild their synagogue after the flood at the end of the 16th century, the split between the pragmatists and the traditionalists was already markedly visible and endangering the religion. Matteo Ricci tells how the religious leader urged him to abandon Christianity and accept command of the Kaifeng synagogue (if he would give up eating pork, as well!).

Shortly thereafter, the religious leader died, and was succeeded by his son. This young man's knowledge of Judaism was very limited. Several members of his congregation accepted baptism from Matteo Ricci when the missionary visited Kaifeng, and converted to Christianity.

Reports of other missionaries tell us that by the start of the 17th century the Nanjing Jewish community no longer existed, its last four Jewish families having embraced Islam; that a Kaifeng Jew had been able to buy back in Shaanxi a Torah which an old Jew in Guangzhou (Canton) had sold to a Muslim.

Clearly, by the final years of the Ming dynasty (1368–1644) the "southern Jews" were no more.

Major changes at this time were also factors in bringing to an end the prosperity of the Kaifeng Jewish community. In 1641 the peasant army under Li Zicheng conquered Loyang, the feudal stronghold of

Prince Fu, uncle of Chong Zhen, emperor of the Ming dynasty, and tortured him to death. In order to avoid sharing the same fate, Prince Zhou, sealed up in Kaifeng, poured all of his family wealth into mobilizing the people and military forces in the city for a fight to the death. The Muslim and the Jewish communities organized their own "Hui Hui" battalions and also fought valiantly. Three siege-assaults by Li Zicheng's army were knocked back. In the fierce fighting Li himself was hit in the left eye.

Desperate, both sides breached the Yellow River dykes in an effort to drown their opponents. The whole city was completely submerged. Hundreds of thousands of people perished in the yellow waters. Records say "only ten or twenty percent survived."

The Jewish community fared slightly better. Of some five hundred families about two hundred managed to find boats and get out of Kaifeng. They set up temporary shelters on higher ground on the opposite side of the river.

Kaifeng was the hardest hit city in the battles which raged at the end of Ming and the beginning of Qing, and the Jewish community suffered its severest blows since its inception. It took another 22 years to complete the reconstruction of the synagogue.

2. The Qing Dynasty: From Renewed Affluence To Ultimate Dissolution

Yin Gang concludes with the final denoument of the Kaifeng Jewish community under the Manchus of the Qing dynasty. He says:

Qing was the third non-Han dynasty under which the Jews lived in China. It was established by the Manchus, descendants of the Nuzhen people who had ruled during the Jin dynasty. They were given strong support in their take-over by Ming dynasty Han military officers and wealthy officials, though not by any of the other nationalities. The Manchus treated them all equally. The Hans remained the majority of the population, and Han was still China's prevailing culture. There was no change in the living conditions or the political status of the Muslims and the Jews. All that was required of them was that they wear long queues in the Manchu fashion.

The Manchus were infinitely more receptive to Han culture and the Han political system than the Mongols had been. They seemed to have totally accepted them without demur.

Two years after the demise of the Ming dynasty, the civil service examinations were re-instituted, with no change in either form or content. No special consideration was given to Manchu candidates.

That suited the Jews of Kaifeng perfectly. High Jewish officials under the Ming again qualified as high officials under the Qing, and received appointments to important posts. During the reconstruction of the synagogue they utilized their political positions to protect the interests of the Jewish community.

Twelve years after the devastating flood, in 1653, the Jews began returning to Kaifeng. They had been living on the north side of the river, using a large building they had rented as a temporary place of worship. Work on the reconstruction of the Kaifeng synagogue started in 1663. It was more finely equipped than the old one.

The plaque reading: "Long Live the Emperor of the Great Ming" was replaced by another reading: "Long Live the Emperor of the Great Qing."

This was the ninth construction. In charge was not a member of the rabbinic Li (Levi) family, but a member of the influential Zhao family. Although seven families had joined in the financing, the largest share was contributed by the Zhao's. In 1679 they erected a tablet in the synagogue courtyard praising themselves for their contributions to the Jewish community. To a certain extent the Kaifeng Jewish synagogue became the Zhao family chapel. The effect was to sow discord within the congregation and diminish the interest of the intellectuals in Hebraic studies.

A further weakening of the ties of unity resulted from the change in the system of burials. Formerly the Jewish community had a cemetery of over 20 hectares in the western suburbs of Kaifeng. These were swamped by the big flood of 1641, and consequently abandoned. From then on, each family bought and maintained its own private plot elsewhere.

Jewish intellectuals now found additional "proof" of the identity of Han culture with their own. In the 1663 memorial tablet they noted that China's ancient sages had also believed seven days made one week, and had declared the seventh day a day of rest. Jewish religious scriptures and Confucian classics, the Jewish intellectuals affirmed, while employing different language, "attained the same wisdom."

In 1512 the memorial tablet had been inscribed entirely by Jewish officials, as had most of the religious plaques and scrolls hung in the synagogue. The 1663 tablet and the commemorative plaques were for the most part inscribed by prominent Han personalities, specially invited to do the writing. The concept that "Judaism and Confucianism are the same" inched closer to a full abandonment of Jewish tradition.

The harm to the Jewish community was very apparent. Jesuit missionaries visiting in the early 18th century found that even on the high holidays, attendance in the synagogue never exceeded more than forty or fifty adults, out of a community of some 1,000. On ordinary Sabbaths the synagogue could muster only about ten persons who could understand the prayers. More shocking was the fact that members of the Gao and the Ai families, who had abandoned Judaism, tried to steal some of the scripture scrolls and sell them to the missionaries.

European missionaries made ceaseless efforts to persuade the Kaifeng Jews to convert to Christianity. They had no success. To the Jews of Kaifeng, Christianity was far less appealing then the civil service examination system and Confucian philosophy. The Catholic Church suffered a huge set back in China because it would not permit Chinese converts to pay homage to Confucius.

Moreover, it sided with the forces opposed to the Yong Zheng faction in the struggle for power within the Imperial court. When Yong Zheng acceded to the throne in 1724, he immediately issued an edict prohibiting any Chinese from embracing Christianity, on pain of extreme torture, and ordered all missionaries to leave the country. Three hundred Catholic churches were closed, except for a few in Beijing and Canton. A handful of European missionaries were permitted to remain. Shortly thereafter, the Vatican called them back to Rome.

The restriction against Catholicism lasted for more than 120 years. Only after China's defeat in the Opium War in 1850 were Catholic priests allowed to return to China.

To the Kaifeng Jews the century-long distancing from Western religions seemed to indicate that dealing with "foreigners" was a dangerous business. It did, in effect, cut the Jews off from the outside world. During both Ming and Qing there were government restrictions, in varying degrees, on travel abroad. Chinese could not leave their shores on private matters.

From the 15th to the 19th centuries, the Kaifeng Jews were unable to know anything about the condition of the Jews in the "Western Regions," or in Europe, nor were they aware of the increasingly close contacts between the European Jews and Jerusalem. Although they avoided the oppression endured by European Jews, and the forced acceptance of Christianity, they could not escape the growing threat to their Jewish identity. In the end the combined lure of Han culture and the examination system led them to discarding their faith in Judaism.

In 1841 the Yellow River again breached its banks. It was a fatal blow to the leaderless Jewish community. For eight months the flood waters surrounded the city. "The rich became poor, the poor became destitute." The Jewish synagogue and the Muslim mosques were all wrecked by the flood. Eventually, the Muslims rebuilt their mosques, but the Jewish synagogue never recovered.

Many of the families who had fled did not return to Kaifeng. Only some 200 people remained of the former Jewish community. The Zhao's and the Gao's fought pitched battles for remnants of the synagogue ruins. A few people lost their lives. Two members of the Zhao family were put in prison.

The entire Zhang family converted to Islam. The Li (Levi) family, once the Chief Rabbis of the community, went into business. The Shi's grew very rich, and were probably the leading merchants in Kaifeng. The decline of the Zhao family started with a series of defeats in the courts; after more than four centuries of affluence, it collapsed utterly at the start of the 19th century. Several members changed their family name and decamped for parts unknown.

What followed was a complete betrayal of Judaism in Kaifeng. In 1851 the London Society for Promoting Christianity Among Jews dispatched two Chinese disciples to the city where, for 400 taels of silver they bought from the Zhao family six sets of Torah scrolls. In 1866, when American missionary W.A.P. Martin visited Kaifeng, he was able to buy another two. He found that the former synagogue had vanished. Its site was a watery swamp; most of the earth had been excavated for making bricks and tiles.

In the next few decades the remaining scriptures were all sold to various foreigners. Not a single page was left in China. Fortunately, thanks to the intervention of the people of Kaifeng and the Chinese government, the tablets recording the history of the Jewish community were not shipped abroad. (*The 1663 tablet has disappeared, and remains lost.*)

Yin Gang says a wisp of hope for the revival of the Kaifeng Jewish community seemed to have arisen due to the development of the Zionist movement. "The Society for the Rescue of the Chinese Jews," organized in Shanghai in 1900, tried to help descendants of Kaifeng Jews return to a study of Judaism. A member of the Li family dropped his business in Kaifeng and brought eight young men from four different families to Shanghai to take part in the course.

But the great wave of Russian Jews who had migrated to Europe and America were in urgent need of financial help. The Shanghai Jews were unable to spare any money for the rebuilding of the Kaifeng synagogue, and the dream ended.

Chronological Table of China's Dynasties

ACCORDING TO *XIANDAI HANYU CIDIAN (DICTIONARY OF MODERN CHINESE)*, SHANGWU YIN SHU GUAN (COMMERCIAL PRESS), BEIJING, 1980.*

Xia	2140–1711 B.C.
Shang	1711–1066B.C.
Western Zhou	1066–771 B.C.
Eastern Zhou	770–256 B.C.
Warring States	475–221 B.C.
Qin	221–206 B.C.
Western Han	206 B.C.–25 A.D.
Eastern Han	25–220
Three Kingdoms	220–280
Western Jin	265–317
Eastern Jin	317–420
Southern and Northern Dynasties	420–589
Sui	589–618
Tang	618–907
Five Dynasties	907–960
Northern Song	960–1127
Jin (Golden Tartars)	1115–1234
Southern Song	1127–1279
Yuan	1279–1368
Ming	1368–1644
Qing	1644–1911

*Several of these dynasties started earlier in other parts of China, but did not exercise full control over the country until the dates stated.

Bibliography

CHINESE

Chen Changqi	"Kaifeng Youtairen Lishi de Jige Wenti" ("Some Questions Regarding the History of the Kaifeng Jews") Our extract entitled "Buddhist Monk or Jewish Rabbi?" Zhengzhou, Henan, 1983
Chen Yuan	*Chen Yuan Xueshu Lunwen Ji (The Academic Theses of Chen Yuan)* Zhonghua Shuju, Beijing, 1980
Ci Hai	*The Sea of Terms Encyclopedia,* Cishu Chubanshe (Encyclopedia Press) Shanghai, 1971
Gao Wangzhi	"Guanyu Zhongguo Youtairen de Ruogan Wenti" ("Concerning Chinese Jews") Beijing, 1983
Hong Jun	"Yuan Shi Ge Jiao Ming Kao" ("A Summary of the Various Religious Sects During the Yuan Dynasty"), in *Yuan Shi Yi Wen Zheng Bu (Annotations To the Chinese Translation of the Yuan Annals)* Vol. XXIX, 1897
Jiang Qingxiang and Xiao Guoliang	"Cong Qing Ming Shang He Tu, He Dong Jing Meng Hua Lu, Kan Bei Song Bianjing de Chengshi Jingji" (Glimpses of the Urban Economy in Bianjing, Capital of the Northern Song Dynasty as Seen in the Painting *Riverside Scene at Clear and Bright Festival Time* and the Book *Reminiscences of Dreamland Glories of the Eastern Capital"*) Zhongguo Shehui Kexue *(Social Sciences in China)* Vol. IV. 1981
Li Jixian	"An San Yu An Cheng" ("An San and An Cheng"), Beijing, 1983

Pan Guangdan — *Zhongguo Jing Nei Youtairen de Ruogan Lishi Wenti (Jews In Ancient China—A Historical Survey)*, Beijing Daxue Chubanshe (Beijing University Press), 1983

Wang Yisha — "Kaifeng Youtairen de Hou Yi Ji Tian Jin Jiao Yi Zhi Yi Wu" ("Descendants of the Kaifeng Jews and the Ruins and Relics of the Sinew Plucking Religion"), Kaifeng, 1980

Weng Tu-chien (Dujian) — "*Wotuo* Za Kao" ("A Study of *Wotuo*") in *Yenjing Xue Bao (Yenching Journal of Chinese Studies)* Harvard-Yenching Social Press, 1941

Wu Zelin — "Xu" ("Preface") to Pan Guandan's *Zhongguo Jing Nei Youtairen* (ibid), Beijing, 1983

Xiandai Hanyu Cidian — *A Modern Dictionary of Han Chinese,* Commercial Press, Beijing, 1973

Xu Zhonghe — "*Guanyu Kaifeng de Youtairen*" ("Some Observations on the Jews of Kaifeng") in *Revue Catholique,* April, 1943, Shanghai

Zhang Xinglang — *Zhong Xi Jiaotong Shilia Huibian (A Survey of Historical Material Regarding Contacts Between China and the West),* Vol. III. Zonghua Shuju, Beijing, 1978

Zhu Jiang — "Youtairen Zai Yangzhou de Zongji" ("Jewish Traces in Yangzhou"), Yangzhou, 1983

Zongjiao Chidian — *A Dictionary of Religions,* Cishu Chubanshe (Encyclopedia Press), Shanghai, 1981

WESTERN

Brough, John — "A Kharoshti Inscription From China," in *Bulletin of the School of Oriental and African Studies,* Vol. XXIV, 1961, part 3, pp. 517–530, London

Dimont, Max I. — *Jews, God and History,* New American Library, New York, 1962

Ezra, Edward I. and Sopher, Arthur — *Chinese Jews,* Shanghai, 1926. Reprinted in Kublin, *Jews in Old China,* Paragon, New York, 1971

Fang Chaoying — "Notes on the Chinese Jews of Kaifeng," *Journal of the American Oriental Society,* April–June, 1965. Reprinted in Kublin, *Studies of the Chinese Jews,* Paragon, New York, 1971

Finn, James

"The Jews in China: Their Synagogue, Their Scriptures, Their History," London, 1843. Reprinted in Kublin, *Jews in Old China,* Paragon, New York, 1971

Goodrich, L. C.

A Short History of the Chinese People, Harper, New York, 1943

Kublin, Hyman

Studies of the Chinese Jews: Selections from Journals East and West, and *Jews in Old China: Some Western Views,* both published by Paragon, New York, 1971

Latourette, K. S.

The Chinese; Their History and Culture, Macmillan, New York, 1946

Leslie, Donald D.

The Survival of the Chinese Jews, E. J. Brill, Leiden, 1972

Lowenthal, R.

"The Jews in China: An Annotated Bibliography," in *Chinese Social and Political Science Review,* Peiping, February, 1940

Old Testament

Good News Bible, United Bible Societies, London and New York, 1978

Perlmann, S. M.

The History of the Jews in China, London, 1912, Reprinted in Kublin, *Jews in Old China,* Paragon, New York, 1971

Pollak, Michael

Mandarins, Jews, and Missionaries, The Jewish Publication Society of America, Philadelphia, 1980

Polo, Marco

The Travels of Marco Polo the Venetian, Everyman's Library, London, 1903

Prévost, Georges

"Les Inscriptiones Sémitiques de Loyang," *Impremerie des Lazaristes,* Pekin, 1926

White, W. C.

Chinese Jews, Paragon, New York, 1966

Yule, Henry

Cathay and the Way Thither, London, 1866. Revised by Henri Cordier and reissued in London, 1913–1916.

Index